THE AUDACITY
OF FREEDOM

DENNIS HEDKE

THE AUDACITY
OF FREEDOM

TATE PUBLISHING & *Enterprises*

The Audacity of Freedom
Copyright © 2011 by Dennis Hedke. All rights reserved.

No part of this publication may be reproduced, stored in a retrieval system or transmitted in any way by any means, electronic, mechanical, photocopy, recording or otherwise without the prior permission of the author except as provided by USA copyright law.

All Scripture references are from the New American Standard Bible (NASB Study Bible, Zondervan, 1999)

The opinions expressed by the author are not necessarily those of Tate Publishing, LLC.

Published by Tate Publishing & Enterprises, LLC
127 E. Trade Center Terrace | Mustang, Oklahoma 73064 USA
1.888.361.9473 | www.tatepublishing.com

Tate Publishing is committed to excellence in the publishing industry. The company reflects the philosophy established by the founders, based on Psalm 68:11,
"The Lord gave the word and great was the company of those who published it."

Book design copyright © 2011 by Tate Publishing, LLC. All rights reserved.
Cover design by Shawn Collins
Interior design by Stephanie Woloszyn

Published in the United States of America

ISBN: 978-1-61346-408-3
1. Political Science / Political Ideologies / Conservatism & Liberalism
2. Political Science / Public Policy / General
11.08.04

DEDICATION

This book is dedicated to my mother Ethel, in Memoriam, father Arnold, wife Annette, her parents Milt and Fran, my daughter Reasha, my son Jacob and his wife Kenna. Each in their own way have brought me to this moment and I am grateful beyond words for the impacts each have made in my life.

May Freedom reign.

LIST of PHOTOGRAPHS

Photo 1	3 February 2006 Protests staged in London, demonstration by Muslims angry over the publication in Scandinavian periodicals related to the prophet Muhammad	66, 146
Photo 2	Wind Farm near Palm Springs, California	83, 149
Photo 3	Wind generator fire, rural Minnesota	101, 148
Photo 4	Coal Power Plant	149, 194

LIST of FIGURES

Figure 1	Assigned boundaries of Israel via Biblical definitions	55, 145
Figure 2	Current boundaries of Israel	57, 145
Figure 3	World Muslim Population	65
Figure 4	Electricity Production in the USA	80, 147
Figure 5	Power Density Comparisons of Various Fuels	93, 147
Figure 6	U.S. Energy Consumption-All Sources	97, 150
Figure 7	World Energy Related Carbon dioxide Emissions	110
Figure 8	Monthly Montana Field Production of Crude Oil	130
Figure 9	Monthly North Dakota Field Production of Crude Oil	130
Figure 10	Monthly U.S. Field Production of Crude Oil: 1920-2010	131
Figure 11	Mexico Crude oil Supply 2001-2009	137

Figure 12	Global Temperature Measuring Stations	151, 166
Figure 13	Global HCN Stations 1900-2008	167
Figure 14	11,000 Year Sunspot Reconstruction	169
Figure 15	Solar Activity, Temperature, Hydrocarbon Use 1870-2006	150, 170
Figure 16	MSU and Hadley Monthly Temperatures vs CO_2 2002-2008	151, 178
Figure 17	Global Surface Temperature Anomaly and CO_2 levels, 1940-70	179
Figure 18	Hurricane Windspeed and Number of Violent Hurricanes, 1940-2008	183
Figure 19	Multi-Decadal Temperature Oscillation, 1880-2100	152, 187
Figure 20	IPCC Predicted CO_2 Exponential Growth, 1982-2009	152, 188
Figure 21	IPCC Predicted CO_2 Growth 2009-2100	189
Figure 22	Lieberman, Warner, Boxer Regulation-Mandate Chart	153, 191
Figure 23	CO_2 Molecule	193
Figure 24	400,000 Year Global Temperatures via Ice Cores	153, 197
Figure 25	Southern Hemisphere Sea Ice Anomaly, 1979-2010	201
Figure 26	Arctic Sea Ice Extent, 1980-2009	154, 202
Figure 27	Arctic Temperatures 1901-2004	154, 203
Figure 28	Arctic Temperatures vs CO_2	204
Figure 29	Global Temperatures, 400 BC to 2000 AD	205
Figure 30	1,000 Year Earth Temperature History: Corrected Hockey Stick	155, 206
Figure 31	Atlantic Hurricane Tracks: Globe Cooling vs Globe Warming	156, 207

Figure 32	Great Barrier Reef Calcification Observations	209
Figure 33	20th Century Impact on Emiliana huxleyi	210
Figure 34	Global Sea Level Change 1800-2000	213
Figure 35	Global Sea Level Change 1700-2000	214
Figure 36	Global Sea Level Change 1992-2010	156, 215
Figure 37	Global Sea Level Corrections	157, 217
Figure 38	UN (IPCC) Predicted Sea Level Rise "Savings" Due to Waxman-Markey	219
Figure 39	UN (IPCC) Predicted Temperature "Savings" Due to Waxman-Markey	220
Figure 40	Fed Monetary Policy Headed into Steep Uncharted Territory: Quantitative Easing	228
Figure 41	Medicare and Social Security Deficits through 2040	232
Figure 42	Risks of Growing Entitlement Spending	158, 233

LIST of TABLES

Table 1	U.S. Total Imports of Petroleum	78
Table 2	Fuel sources ranked according to energy density and deliverability	92
Table 3	Elements and Compounds in Earth's Atmosphere	195
Table 4	Greenhouse Gas Components	196

TABLE *of* CONTENTS

FOREWORD 13

PRELIMINARIES & ACKNOWLEDGEMENTS 17

PREFACE 25

INTRODUCTION 27

THE ENEMIES WITHIN VERSUS 39
THE FRIENDS OF FREEDOM

    The Enemies Within 40

    The Friends of Freedom 46

UNITED STATES FOREIGN POLICY 53

    Israel First 53

    Islam 63

    World Muslim Population 2009 65

    Outline of Recommended U.S. Foreign/Defense Policy 69

UNITED STATES ENERGY POLICY 77

    Thirteen Very Costly Myths Surrounding Green Energy 90

    U.S. Energy Policy for the Twenty-First Century— 123
    A Proposed Template

    Ten-Point Plan for Energy Security for the United States of America 125

    Geothermal Energy Considerations 141

GLOBAL ENVIRONMENTAL SURVIVAL— THE NEW GREEN EARTH ... 159

The Scam Artists ... 160

The Most Unreliable Data in the World ... 163

Gate City ... 172

CARBON DIOXIDE (CO_2) ... 193

CO_2 and Ocean Acidification ... 208

CO_2, Temperature and Sea Level ... 212

ECONOMICS: THE FED, FRANK, DODD & OBAMANOMICS ... 223

Fractional Reserve Banking ... 225

Killer Apps ... 232

A NEW AMERICA: EX-OBAMA ... 237

An Alternate Proposal to Restore America ... 238

Parting Thoughts ... 246

THE LAWS OF THE LAND ... 249

BIBLIOGRAPHY ... 253

END NOTES ... 257

FOREWORD

Dennis Hedke's *The Audacity of Freedom* is a timely and welcome "from the heart" wake-up call for those who value freedom and America. Unapologetically, Hedke does not mince words in describing the combination of crises that threaten our country. His irrefutable and precise recitation of compelling facts and refreshingly candid faith and patriotism are infectious. He exhorts us not to stand by and suffer any longer the fools who have been insulting our collective intelligence and bringing us dangerously close to a socialistic irrelevance in the world. His book, in short, is important.

I first became acquainted with Dennis through a mutual acquaintance and was impressed with his scientific expertise, particularly in the field of geophysics. I was at the time and am currently the Speaker of the House of Representatives in Kansas and had been working hard to win support for expansion of the Sunflower Electric coal-fired energy plant near Holcomb, Kansas.

Then Kansas Governor Kathleen Sebelius (now Sec. of Health & Human Services under President Obama) and her hand-picked Secretary of the Kansas Department of Health & Environment Rob Bremby, opposed the plant expansion purportedly due to concerns over carbon emissions. Although the KDHE team of experts had signed off on all aspects of the project, Secretary Bremby refused to approve the permits, backed by Gov. Sebelius, who had her resume in to the Obama camp at an early date. Our mutual acquaintance suggested I reach out to Dennis to discuss strategy and the science of CO_2.

It took Obama appointing Sebelius to his cabinet for us to rid ourselves of a major impediment to progress in developing critical additional base-load energy in the state. Lt. Gov. Parkinson, a former Republican-turned Democrat to run as Sebelius' running mate, became Governor for the remaining year of Sebelius' final term and within 6 days brokered a deal to grant Sunflower authority to expand its coal-fired plant. While the nation now has to deal with Obama-Care and its implementation by Sec. Sebelius, we in Kansas are grateful she is gone.

Remarkably, we have one other reason to give credit to Obama. Yes, that would be his dismal first term, which yielded us the midterm elections of 2010. In Kansas, our Republican House majority of 76 Republicans and 49 Democrats, swelled to 92 Republicans and 33 Democrats after the November elections. The elections, together with additional turnover caused by lawmakers being elected to statewide office and taking jobs in newly-elected Governor Sam Brownback's administration, resulted in 33 freshmen Republicans being sworn in.

The last Republican House member to be sworn in, having been appointed to replace Rep. Aaron Jack, who was appointed Securities Commissioner, was none other than Dennis Hedke. Dennis rounded out one of the most idealistic and impressive classes ever in the history of the Kansas House. The collective experience and talent of this new class is unparalleled, and Dennis is a crown jewel.

His book covers a wide range of issues, which he ties together in impressive fashion. His timely appeal to "stand firm and push back" is as important a message for Americans as any we'll hear. Kansas, a firmly red state, has not been immune to the Washington debacle. We, too, are a microcosm of the national scene. Political, economic and environmental issues abound at the state and national levels and it's time to take our country back. My hope is that Americans, policy makers in statehouses across the country and Congress would read this and take its sincere and compelling content to heart.

Rep. Mike O'Neal
Speaker of the Kansas House

Preliminaries & Acknowledgements

This moment in history has approached at relative light speed. I did not want to be spending nights and weekends working at this task, but the times we live in are just way too "interesting" to sit back and avoid the responsibility I feel to speak up and speak out. We have an administration in Washington, DC, that is attempting to destroy the fundamental fabric of our republic: this is no time for complacency. While the current administration was set back on its feet in November 2010, the fundamental desires it still has for Socialism are anything but dead. I hope this work serves to push it back, way back.

We recently experienced and remain under recovery from one of the most incredible environmental disasters this country has ever seen (the *Deepwater Horizon* and the resulting offshore oil spill), and by the time this book hits the market, we will have all but completely recovered from it faster than most people imagined possible. The question remains: What did we learn from it? Is it time to disable and dismantle our entire energy infrastructure so as to avoid any other possible risks associated with energy exploration and production? We also had a huge chunk of the Peterman Glacier (Northwest Greenland) calve a child iceberg, and head presumably into open waters toward the Arctic Sea. Will sea level rise twenty feet, as some would suggest?

Iran is now up with its first nuclear reactor, no doubt for peaceful energy supply purposes. After all, they are only proximate to some of the most voluminous crude oil reserves on the face of the earth, but they have yet to figure out how to convert hydrocarbons to electricity? As opposed to neutrons. I'm guessing that Iran and Mahmoud Ahmadinejad are going for the "green" solution to their energy needs.

First and foremost, I wish to point out that my goal in putting this out there for whoever wishes to address it is simple: That you may confidently have a discussion with the facts at your immediate disposal. I will only be touching the tip of the iceberg with respect to many crucially important matters related to our fading freedoms, our status in the world, our energy policy, or lack thereof, and other related items, like exploding (not simply expanding) deficits. But, I will attempt to be very succinct and direct, with, "Just the Facts Ma'am," as Joe Friday would have said.

We have millions of poor, sick, hurting, currently dependent (not free) people on the face of the earth. Many of their problems are solvable with relatively minor effort, if the effort is honest, focused, and dedicated to their well-being. Unfortunately, history has shown many improper paths that have led to this moment for those freedom-seeking individuals. They have been held back, deliberately held back, so that the elite "leaders" who have attempted to define how *they* would live could live very well as a result of the shortcomings placed upon them by this ruling class.

The founding of this country came about as a direct result of fighting similar tyranny, and we all know the outcome of the initial battles more than 235 years ago. However, even a great country can be felled by internal forces that act silently, at least for a time. In our case today in America, the strong negative internal forces are becoming emboldened by a few "socialistic" successes, driven by a new leader, who promised "hope and change."

I am a geophysicist, and what I have witnessed scientifically in particularly the last decade has really gotten to me. I was just too naïve, too much wanting to believe that good science always wins out, that fraud would get called out quickly once it was discovered.

I was wrong.

At the present time, science, especially "bad" science, is getting just about all the attention. If I can do anything to change that picture, I will dedicate myself to that task. It won't take long to see if it can happen, and I will not waste your time or mine on a worthless cause. I think we have a 50/50 chance of bringing the truth to the fore, but I cannot and will not attempt to do it alone. No single citizen can stop the tidal wave of socialist policies bearing down on our country. We have never had a greater responsibility to take a stand against the tyranny that is approaching. It is time for Americans to act like Americans.

I think our country is undergoing her first true "Awakening" since its founding moments. No one could have imagined that a blatant takeover of some of our most precious freedoms, our health care system (though that may change materially by the time this goes to press), and our banking system…could occur within the span of less than eighteen months. But, it has. Now, it's time to generate a full accounting on the part of a handsome handful of intransigent individuals who remain in their temporary seats of power. A full accounting it will be. You see, this is *still* the United States of America.

This is not a Socialist State, as some would desire.

This is not a Communist State, as some would desire.

This is not a Muslim country, as some would desire—

This *is* largely, though certainly not exclusively, a Christian nation, founded on Judeo-Christian values, and above all else, a rule of law. Great Britain, from which we extricated ourselves during the American Revolution, has now deemed it appropriate to allow Sharia law to be embedded within its country. They lacked the courage and the will to stand up to the Muslim insurgency that infiltrates virtually every aspect of their "evolving" society.

It is precisely because *We the People* did have the courage and the will in 1776, and we *do* have the will in 2011 to repeat an internal revolution, if that is what it takes, with the goal of taking back most every freedom we have unwittingly squandered over the past hundred or so years.

To put it simply and bluntly, this "thing" we face is a whole lot bigger than just science. But, it is *big*. And, if we want to have anything like the founders envisioned, anything like what I believe the vast majority of Americans want to go forward with, we must engage the real battle like we have not had to engage for more than two hundred years. We need to become engaged, for one example, in the school districts, the state boards of education. The battles there are intense.

You may be virtually unaware of the ongoing battle for our children's minds in the classroom, but it is real, it is insidious, and it MUST be stopped.

> The first goal, to be reached in stages, was an orderly, scientifically managed society, one in which the best people would make the best decisions, unhampered by the democratic tradition. After that, human breeding, the evolutionary destiny of the species, would be in reach. Universal institutionalized formal forced schooling was the prescription.
>
> Gotto[1]

This comes from *The Underground History of American Education*, written by John Taylor Gatto in 2001, who, before retirement in

1991, was voted both New York City and New York State Teacher of the Year. He was referring to the transformation to a whole new realm of public education in America, post-Civil War, away from the earlier established goals set at America's first university, Harvard, circa 1630. That's his opinion as an educator for nearly thirty years, one who observed policy from the inside, on an historical basis. He was certainly not in agreement with the direction in which education headed, and is frankly still headed today, but he captured the essence of what the "new establishment" saw as its First Goal, immediately post Civil War. So, you see, this is not a "new" thing we are dealing with. The real erosion started less than a hundred years into our country's history. It is the Progressive Way, and it is not abating, not in any way, shape, or form.

In my personal opinion, we need to elect anything but Secular Progressives, and make sure that the public knows exactly what that term means. SP's tend to be anti-faith, anti-constitution, anti-free market, and anti-just about everything this great nation was founded upon. They are destroying our legal system, our financial system, and they will endeavor to take control of it all—*if* we let them. Every American student and citizen needs to know *exactly* what the roots of progressivism happen to be: *Marxism*. The Nazis would have you believe that they fought the Marxists, the Communists. In fact, they were and they *are* cut from the same cloth. Redistribute the wealth, drag down the top to meet the bottom, equalize everybody, except for that little, tiny package of elitists at the very top—the Karl Marx's, the Joseph Stalin's, the Mao's, the Gore's, the Soros's, and the Obama's, that tiny little, almost unnoticeable group.

David Horowitz further illustrates the status of education in America today, this time a closer look at one of our universities in Texas:

> *Dana Cloud* is an associate professor of communication studies at the University of Texas, Austin. Professor Cloud "specializes in the analysis of contemporary and popular and political

> culture from feminist, Marxist and Critical Race Theory perspectives," as described in the University of Texas official website. Professor Cloud is a member of the International Socialist Organization, a Leninist vanguard that considers itself a part of the Fourth Communist International. Formed in 1977, the Internationalist Organization describes itself as the largest "revolutionary" socialist group in the United States...
>
> Horowitz [2]

For all intents and purposes, our country has been hijacked. Its schools have been hijacked, therefore science education and the science. That certainly includes economics; just ask Tim Geithner. Social science/social engineering is having a significant impact on medicine. Our courts have been hijacked, oh no, not all of them, just enough to make the Ninth Circuit Court of Appeals become nearly as powerful, in essence, as the U.S. Supreme Court. We are right now one seat away from giving all the courts away, maybe a half-seat, based on some recent rulings. The legislative branch is so out and out Progressively dominated (in both parties) that it will take at least two major election cycles to turn it back to becoming an effective lawmaking body, maybe three. The 2010 election was probably the most important midterm election this country has ever faced.

It was important for at least two reasons:

Firstly, it defined whether this country was ready to expand existing Socialism—it wasn't.

Secondly and directly related to the first, it told Barack Obama we had had enough—enough of him, enough of his policies, and enough of his cronies, all of it.

Beyond that, it sent notice to millions of federal employees. Get ready to clean house; it's time to trim the sails.

I'm not even going to talk about the current "executive" branch of our government, except to sum it up as best I can:

Inexperienced, Incompetent, Inept,
Incorrigible, and In Contempt.

This cannot continue.

Not on our watch, not in the United States of America.

Much of the impetus for this book is based on willful absorption of the work of many talented, gifted, and steadfast individuals who daily do the heavy lifting so that the rest of us can get ready with the notepad and the laptop to record the tidbits. Some of their names will come up later in more detail, but I feel compelled to applaud some of them early on, as my part in this is indeed infinitesimal in comparison to theirs:

Thomas Sowell (*Applied Economics*); Joel C. Rosenberg (*Fiction and Non-Fiction author, focus on Israel*); Thomas E. Woods, (*Meltdown—Capitalism vs Marxism*); Christopher Horner (*Red Hot Lies, The Politically Incorrect Guide to Global Warming and Environmentalism*); Michael Economides (*From Soviet to Putin and Back*); Rush and Glenn (*The Way Things Ought To Be, Arguing With Idiots, Common Sense*); Mark Levin (*Liberty and Tyranny*); Roy Spencer (*The Great Global Warming Blunder*); Robert Bryce (*Gusher of Lies, Power Hungry*); David Horowitz (*The Professors*); Charles G. Koch (*The Science of Success*); Brigitte Gabriel (*Because They Hate*); Robert Spencer (*Jihad Watch*); Nonie Darwish (*Now They Call Me Infidel: Why I Renounced Jihad for America, Israel, and the War on Terror*); W. Cleon Skousen (*The 5000 Year Leap*); Joseph Farah and David Kupelian (*World Net Daily, Publisher and Editor*); Ann McElhinney and Phelim McAleer, (*Not Evil, Just Wrong*).

We all owe a debt of gratitude to these men and women, who are vigilant, who have fought the fight, and who continue to fight the fight, a fight well worth the winning.

I am grateful to a number of anonymous reviewers, including my wife, Annette, each of which selflessly dedicated themselves to providing you a much better document than I could have ever produced without their input and comments.

Preface

I don't want anybody walking into this book with the misconception that it will be apolitical, unbiased, and without controversy.

I am anything but happy with the way current affairs and politics are being handled in my country, and I am willing to expend significant personal political and other capital to change these background conditions, with I hope, the assistance of millions of like-minded Americans.

We will be White, Black, Yellow, Hispanic, Indian, and any other origin you can imagine. We will not be Hispanic Americans, Native Americans, African Americans, Irish Americans, Israeli Americans, Germanic Americans, or any other Americans you can conjure up.

We are Americans. We have been that way since 1776, or slightly before, when the United States of America was officially birthed, and we will be that way until we no longer exist, which I hope is a very long time.

It's time for you so-called "African Americans" to face the fact that you are simply Americans. You are not "African-Americans";

you are black, and you are an American. I am white, with Irish and apparently Polish heritage, but I am simply an American.

Racism be damned.

It's time to decide, again, exactly what it means to be an American.

So, one of the key questions is, 'Does it matter?'

It matters now, more than ever.

American Spirit, American Ingenuity, the American Way.

It is worth defending and preserving.

Whether you have thought much about it or not, those basic tenets are being challenged more and more deeply each and every day. At this moment in time, we are weakened by a global economic recession. The forces working against our freedoms certainly recognize this condition, and they are seizing the opportunity. These forces are both internal and external. Neither is ever easy to recognize, but they are recognizable.

The next question is, "Having recognized these anti-freedom forces, are we actually going to do anything about them, or are we simply going to 'let it ride'?"

We cannot let it (them) ride, and the time to push back—hard —is now. The election of 2010 is history, and indications are that the pendulum has already started to swing in a major way back in the direction of preservation of individual freedoms, as opposed to the suggestion that, according to Newsweek, "We Are All Socialists Now."

In no way are we all Socialists now.

Regardless of the outcome of the elections, I have already arrived at the moment of saying "Good-bye to Socialism" in America, for at least another 235 years. I do recognize that there are significant social programs (Social Security) that would indicate that we are Socialists. However, even that program is not sacrosanct, that is to say that it can be taken out and replaced with something far better for each and every American.

Before we can get there, we have whole lot of work to do. Perhaps this book will lead to some actions that need to be taken very soon.

Introduction

Fraud, deceit, and misrepresentation.

Those would generally not be traits we would desire with respect to the individual occupying the Oval Office. However, I'm afraid that's exactly what we have at the present moment. And, unless *We the People* take the necessary steps to change this picture, it will continue for a long time to come.

We will visit those topics in due detail momentarily, but I want to lay a few things out before we go there. I am a law-abiding, peace-loving citizen, who periodically editorializes, who has spoken to various public groups and on various college and university campuses, and who would rather watch real news than a sitcom. However, I do love a good sitcom, and "24" (certainly not a sitcom) was my favorite show of all time, behind "Mission Impossible" of the '60s. I just recently went to my first Eagles concert, right here in the new Intrust Arena in Wichita, Kans. For my taste, it was by far the best rock concert I've ever been able to witness, and I've seen some good ones.

I like peace, and I did serve briefly in the military, in the Army and Air National Guard in the early to late '70s. I also appreciate a well-managed enterprise. I prefer to be complimentary rather than critical. However, I do not appreciate a government that has lost total touch with reality, one that has instead became exactly what our Founding Fathers so carefully warned us about. We have a government that actually believes they know what is best for all of us. They also believe they can spend *our* money at will, without really asking us how they should spend that capital. We now have a "new" Congress, but it remains to be seen whether they actually have the complete resolve necessary to turn the fraud, the waste, and the mismanagement around. We will find out very soon whether that resolve was campaign rhetoric or a new dimension in American governance.

While they are now somewhat in hiding, they thought they knew best. Just ask Barney Frank, Al Franken, Frank Lautenberg, and frankly, that's all of the 'Franks' I can stand to cite for the moment.

This is out of control, and it will not get back into control until *We the People* stand up and do something about it. I was one of those approximately 1.7 *million* American citizens who showed up in Washington, DC, the morning of September 12, 2009, and marched a while on Pennsylvania Avenue, landing a hundred feet below the podium on the Capitol steps.

We had heard rumors the night before about just how big the crowd was going to be, but truth hit at the subway in Arlington Saturday morning. We went down to board the train and couldn't get on due to the people jammed in like sardines. At 7:30 on a Saturday morning. So we waited for the next train, due to arrive in about six minutes. Twenty minutes passed, no train. Metro workers came down the track from the north, and we were going to be northbound. They said there were no problems with the track and could not communicate with the oncoming train, which was south of our position. Finally, a train approached, with its lights out, and no passengers, and it did not stop. I'm thinking, *Obama intentionally shut down the system so that we would have to walk across the Potomac, significantly delayed, just to make it nice and inconvenient.*

Another few moments passed, and now a Blue Line train, with its lights on, arrives, and we board. It was virtually empty, so here's what I surmised. The train that was supposed to pick us up, the one with the lights out, broke down due to the overload, forcing all passengers off and up out of the system at that station. They probably migrated elsewhere, or got cabs, or who knows what.

All I can tell you is that there were a whole bunch of Tea Party patriots headed to the Capitol, and most of us got there. We heard stories from the podium, which of course the "media" did not report, to the effect that inbound traffic attempting to get into DC was at a virtual standstill for miles and miles, all thoroughfares. Thousands of people did not get to participate on the Mall due to these unexpected delays.

That was the first time I had ever been in a single crowd of that magnitude, but I have a sneaking suspicion that it will not be the last. Words cannot adequately express the disdain I had with respect to so many of the "signs" that kept popping up out of Washington. More new regulations for finance, for energy, for health, for who knows what…all I know, without having any more information, is that it needs to be stopped dead in its tracks and that it will not be good for America.

It will be good for all the Franks—that's it.

August 28, 2010, brought something very fresh and completely unprecedented to Washington, DC. The same mall where we gathered for the 9/12 event the year before was filled with, again, hundreds of thousands of Americans. This time, the tenor was different. There certainly was prayer; there were passionate, patriotic speeches given on the anniversary of Martin Luther King's historic address from the same location. There were complaints that Glenn Beck usurped the sanctity of the moment, and that what was going to take place could not possibly bring honor to the historic figure. But, those complaints were unfounded. Martin Luther King's niece,

Alveda King, delivered a memorable speech that any American should appreciate. At the end of the day, it was simply another one of those sights to behold. This time, my wife and I observed from the TV at home. No surprise, the media that did show up missed the message entirely, and it is sad that they just can't seem to get the facts straight. CBS reported 87,000; estimates from Keith Olbermann and CNN reverted to "jelly beans in a candy jar, too difficult too estimate." But, the real story—that of "Restoring Honor to America"— was completely ignored. I guess it's just too insignificant for them to report on the awards that were given out to people like Rev. C.L. Jackson (Faith Award), Albert Pujols (Hope Award), and John Huntsman (Charity Award). America has some significant distance ahead of her before she gets back to anything like the founders envisioned, but she can get there, and the weekend of 8/28/2010 was a big step in the right direction.

Whatever the number, the throngs of people who took the time to show up and demonstrate that something is seriously out of order says something about the times we are living in today.

The America I grew up in is gone forever.

I get it, and I was happy to move on from the '70s into something else. What I did not anticipate for a moment is where we find ourselves today. How we get out of this place is a really good question. I have thought a lot about it, as I'm sure many of you have as well. For whatever set of reasons, I have felt it incumbent upon me to share my suggestions as to how we can, how we must, react to the current condition we are in. In the pages and chapters ahead you will find policy recommendations related to energy, environment, and our economy. In my mind, those three elements of our society are inseparable, inextricably linked.

Back to fraud, deceit, and misrepresentation.

Al Gore and Barack Obama are masters at it. Therefore, they are certainly among the primary "targets" of this quasi-investigative, political piece of work. Al Gore was first on the scene, and he continues to hold the stage as frequently as possible, but I have a prediction to make—he will be soon taken off the stage, and he may well end up in jail.

Barack Obama is so fresh, isn't he? I mean he can take command of his carefully chosen audience and just run on and on. He's especially good when the teleprompter goes down, very creative. You know, his "57 United States of America," his "…under my plan of 'cap and trade', electricity costs will necessarily skyrocket…" What a genius, heaping on taxes, spreading the wealth, fundamentally transforming this country. If only he could have gotten away with it. Unfortunately for him, that is not going to happen.

He is on the record in tacit support for building the Cordoba House two blocks from Ground Zero. His logic, and he is clearly not alone on this, is "religious freedom," protection of the First Amendment. His speech announcing his blessing to build the mosque also denounced "terrorism." Yet, he ties the hands of our military and our intelligence services as they wage the Global War on Terror that continues to ravage innocent citizens the world over. I will never agree with the strategy that prohibits our military / intelligence officers from extracting the maximum amount of information necessary for the protection of our forces and our citizens from our enemies. Enemies are enemies; there is no further explanation necessary.

As this goes to press, Osama bin Laden has just been taken out by Navy SEALs. Once the story unfolded, it was noted that 'extraordinary interrogations' were certainly involved in the gathering of intelligence from what turned out to be high credibility sources. While you may not personally agree with (nor do I) all elements of the Patriot Act, there remains little doubt that guidance obtained via that legislation provided significant support in the incident that brought some measure of justice to the thousands of lives lost due to one solitary madman. We now move on with the continuing battle to protect against the terroristic encroachment on many freedoms.

President Obama deserves credit for executing the plan that undid Osama bin Laden, but much credit is also due the prior administration that framed the caging of this international criminal. Because of the war in Afghanistan, bin Laden was forced to take refuge in Pakistan. It is also because of the increased understanding of the Islamic fundamentalist mindset that America is now beginning to wake up to some sense of unfortunate reality. President Obama has a much different view of fundamentalist Islam than did his predecessor.

If the Muslim religion (Islam) did not exist, would we be having a War on Terror?

Would we be required to take off our shoes before boarding an airplane?

Would the State of Israel be under the constant threat of her very existence?

I have never seen a political leader anywhere who talks as fast out of both sides of his mouth as does Barack Obama. Nobel Peace Prize at less than six months in office? They (the "media") bought it all, hook, line, and sinker. That may be changing, but I doubt it will last for long. The "Lame Stream" media is simply way overcommitted to Socialism, at least for the moment. (President Obama recently had an opportunity to rescind the Prize, but of course chose not to do so. Of this much we can be assured: history will never forget this man.)

As a geophysicist, I am privileged to examine a lot of data and information, primarily in support of entities that are in the business of exploration for hydrocarbons and the always challenging attempt to reduce risk in their ventures. It is my job to hunt incessantly for the truth as it relates to subsurface objectives, thousands of feet below surface. This book will be all about the fleshing out of the "truth" as relates to the current political landscape, American history, as well as a bit of world history, of necessity in understanding exactly where we came from.

I seriously doubt that this country has ever been exposed to the extent it is today, with respect to the risk of survival, as a republic. We are being hit from within and from all sides. We have an occupant in the White House whose primary goal is to "fundamentally transform" this country. Just exactly why would he want to do such a thing? I can tell you why he wants to do it, but let's hold that for a bit later.

I was not impressed by his reluctance to provide the Constitutionally required proof of natural born citizenship until more than 27 months into his presidency. What is even more troubling is the fact that he spent untold millions of dollars to intentionally shield the contents of the birth certificate that now purportedly proves his natural born status. Is he Barack Hussein Obama, Barry Soetero, or yet another alias that has yet to surface? Only time will tell. In any event, his lack of respect for adhering to the rule of law, upholding the Constitution from the outset was (is) troubling, indeed. It made me want to call him something like BO for short, but I will go with the title deserving of the office, until otherwise noted, President Obama.

I feel a great burden to address the issues that will be the core content of this book. It is a burden that I cannot shake, and so it goes that the subject matter simply has to come out. I will draw from multiple media sources, multiple scientific sources, and multiple authors who have done a tremendous job of providing a wealth of information that will be weaved into this work.

Above all else, it's my goal to give you a full, unbridled take on the America we have today. We are at a place *we do not want to be* for any length of time. It's my opinion that we can exit this circumstance, but it will not happen if we allow President Obama to maintain his office and further succeed in his above stated goal. He has to be stopped. Trust me, this guy is no Messiah. We've already had the Truth visit this planet about two thousand years ago. He's closer to His return now than He has ever been. When He does make His comeback, He will not be in the mood to deal with the current deceit and misrepresentation.

America is virtually upside down in so many of its current endeavors. Our Congress is full of misguided, "non-representing representatives," as has been so aptly put by the modern-day Thomas

Paine. What a great actor is that Bob Basso; he deserves an Academy Award. November 2010 changed the picture materially, but will it hold?

November 2010 would not have been possible without so many incredulous rulings, passage of new laws, and of course those famous words of Nancy Pelosi, "We've got to pass this (health care) bill, so we can figure out what's in it." She needs to pack up and go back to San Francisco and help Jerry Brown with his yet-to-be-seen plan for a miraculous staving off of California's bankruptcy. I hold no ill will whatsoever for the people of California, but I will say this: Do not come to me to bail you out of your long-standing record of raising tax after tax to stifle what could and should have been free enterprise offering it's wares to the citizens of your great state. You have failed miserably and the chickens have come to roost. Deal with it.

I want you to know that it gives me no pleasure whatsoever to focus so much attention on the "bad side" of America, but if we have any hope of changing the current course, we have to admit there are significant issues that must be addressed, and then we have to address them. These multiple issues, including an allowed drift to Progressivism, will take a gargantuan effort to mete out and correct.

Can we right the ship? "Yes, we can."

America, are we ready to eliminate the overbearing bureaucracy that presently dominates the governance of our lives? I certainly am, but it's going to take many millions of like-minded souls to put a stop to this nightmare and get back to some semblance of the Republic that our Founding Fathers had in mind when they produced the United States Constitution.

That's the document that took all of <u>four</u> oversized pages to scribe out the most effective system of governance the world has ever known.

We now have an Occupant in the White House who believes it's outdated and incapable of providing the guidance necessary to execute the rule of law throughout this land. If we, the People, have anything to say or do about it, The Constitution of the United States will never be out of date.

"O" will never escape the true America that took a break, fell asleep, and temporarily forgot just exactly how precious our freedom actually is. We are now finally awakening, and he is going to feel pressure like he has never felt before, and soon.

His gig is up, he has been found out.

The true America is not interested in Socialism, Marxism, Communism, or any variant that he might want to construct. You see, America was founded to move as far away from all of that as it could possibly get.

I reiterate, Mr. Obama, you may as well know that it was founded on Judeo-Christian principles, not on those Muslim ones you seem to be so fond of. Yes, we are watching his every move, and we strongly disagree that this is a Muslim nation. It never has been, and if we have anything to do with it, it never will be.

Sharia law? I don't think so.

Skyrocketing energy prices, cap and tax? I don't think so.

Socialized medicine? I don't think so—unconstitutional.

Barack, Bill, and Hilary need to stash that concept way down under.

We will be delivering some bad, bad news for their plan, so they may as well start preparing for it now. Start looking for real estate outside of Washington, DC, far away from 1600 Pennsylvania Avenue.

This book is organized to expose the reader to some of the key elements related to both our relative current loss of freedoms on the one hand and what I will loosely term the goals of freedoms to be restored. We have let things slide further than most of us ever imagined. The forces currently undermining our taken-for-granted freedoms have been at work for a long while, and it will take a significant amount of time and energy to reverse the flow, but it can, it must be done. The first chapter speaks to some of the contrasts between those forces at work today.

The core of this book deals with energy, the environment, and the economic relevance and linkages of each. The world we live in today is getting smaller and smaller by the minute. Therefore, a significant element of foreign policy also plays into any significant actions we will need to contend with on these fronts in our future. I have been a student of foreign policy for many decades and have no intention of claiming expertise, but I do have opinions based on observations, and I will share them freely as they relate to the core of the matters touched upon in these pages.

The energy policy in this country is in its most precarious position since I have been a member of the profession that works at it 24/7. It can be dealt with in a very systematic and effective way, but the current administration does not have a clue as to how to protect the interests of the American people and assist in the delivery of the products that drive and fundamentally support our entire economic system. We will certainly deal with that, with specific recommendations as to where to go from here and how to reverse some of the already inflicted damage.

The environment, intricately linked to our energy system, presents us with great challenges—not due to Global Warming—but how we resolve some of the intense misinformation that is currently guiding policymaking on multiple fronts. Upon finishing this book, my hope is that the reader will have had the opportunity to materially advance his / her understanding of some of the science and critical inputs we must consider before making rash, very expensive, highly inappropriate decisions.

The economic consequences of making bad energy and environmental decisions could be very severe, if we fail to recognize the errors far enough in advance, and we are certainly nowhere near where we need to be in our understanding of such consequences. However, we have plenty of current indicators already in play, including individuals and entities who have their eyes on the prize—

the American pocketbook. We also have a government so huge that it must be placed under arrest and significantly modified, or else.

Finally, it will be seen that I do have opinions as to just how we might make a few adjustments with respect to righting this very large ship, a vessel that was designed to withstand just about any storm, just about any disaster that could come her way, if we had followed the recommended and very simple template, aka the constitution. We haven't, so we are suffering the consequences. Laws need to be repealed, belts need to be tightened, and a lot of dead wood needs to be thrown overboard. It's time to trim the sails, find a captain that has his crew's interest first and foremost, and who can properly steer the rudder. There is no time like the present.

The Enemies Within versus The Friends *of* Freedom

The United States of America has never been perfect nor will it ever become so. However imperfect, it remains the last bastion of true freedom on the face of the earth. Just as in her earliest days, she has enemies within who just cannot seem to grasp the incredible value of freedom. Perhaps I am mistaken—they do, in fact, fully understand the value of freedom and are hell bent to destroy it. In any case, they are definitely not on the same page as those of us who would love to simply prosper incrementally each and every day, without undue encumbrance from any source. Two very different pages. Are we now coexisting with two different countries? I hope not, and I hope America's days ahead as a united group of "states" will become closer to the model that our founders had in mind. It seems that that "horizon" is very distant.

Nonetheless, just as one can see the first sense of land while on a ship on the ocean, my belief is that the republic for which we once stood very firmly indeed remains within our sight's distance. May we all get there sooner rather than later.

The Enemies Within

I could list at least a hundred key enemies (of our states) that President Obama has brought out of the woodwork. But, I'm going to try to limit it to the ten worst of the moment. Given the never-ending bag of surprises President Obama brings to the American dinner table almost nightly, holding it to just ten has been a major challenge.

It's one thing to draw upon preferred expertise to fill your cabinet in order to attempt to make the country run as efficiently as possible. Every president has that urgent responsibility the minute he wins the election. It's quite another to load your entire administration with avowed, committed, anti-American men and women who are devotees of the Socialistic mantra that has emanated from President Obama since well before the 2008 elections were concluded.

These appointments are not limited to cabinet positions. They reach deeply into the workings of our government and into the judicial branch, a la Justice Sotamayor and Justice Kagan. These two individuals are clearly relevant to the key debates of the day, and each shielded herself from any measure of relevant screening during Senate Judiciary Committee hearings. What a waste of time and taxpayer money. What a travesty of justice. These appointments are so incredibly ideological that they do not come close to the standard that should equate to appointment to the highest court in our country. That's simply what happens when you have an extreme ideologue sitting with his feet up on the Resolute Desk in the oval office. Arrogance, no concept of respect for the office, pure, unadulterated "Alinsky"esque ideology. That's what it will be until he is removed from office.

I can assure you that none of our Founding Fathers would have approved of either of these high court appointments. That should become a future "litmus test" for any appointee. Would George Washington, Thomas Jefferson, or Ben Franklin have approved either of these nominees? I seriously doubt it.

President Obama has chosen these "leaders" very carefully. However, a few of them were already there before President Obama got to his position. (For a comprehensive list of individuals who have had a profound influence on Obama throughout his childhood, adolescence, college years, pre-legislative/senate days, continuing to this very moment, I highly recommend *The Manchurian President* by Aaron Klein, with Brenda Elliott.) Here's the list of some of his closest current comrades:

GEORGE SOROS, the Hungarian communist that can't wait to help President Obama "transform" America. Don't believe for a second that he, as reported in Wikipedia, helped transform Hungary from communism to capitalism. He's still a communist. He continually pulls the puppet strings to his liking, and his background influence is tacit to the "success" of any future initiatives coming from this administration. The Ultimate Progressive. His *Center for American Progress* represents a major insurgency against what this republic stands for. And that is only the beginning.

CASS SUNSTEIN, the brilliant lawyer who loves to "nudge" the processes of Progressivism ever so gently so that at any given moment, you really cannot detect movement or "change." His current title: Administrator of the White House Office of Information and Regulatory Affairs. If he has his way, animals will have virtually equivalent rights to human beings in the courtroom. And don't forget his wife, Samantha Power, one of BO's foreign policy advisors, who was resurrected by President Obama, who had fired her during his campaign, after unkind remarks about Hilary.

LISA JACKSON, Administrator of the EPA, the chemical engineer who is now charged with reengineering the way America does all manner of business. Of course, that starts with indoctrination of our kids in grade school so they will grow up to be masterful stewards of the environment. This Socialist, multinational adherent is flat-out dangerous and dangerous to the fundamental way of American life, dangerous to our health and welfare. If she gets her way, she will tax you and I out of existence, as we are simply human deterrents to cleansing the environment to the point that it finally becomes acceptable for the Snail Darter and any other beings whose existence has been challenged by we nasty human beings. *Now that the Senate has currently determined that it cannot find the votes to pass "Cap and Trade," she is one of the most powerful individuals in America, armed with nothing but fraudulent and very erroneous information. That is one of the main reasons why I am here, why I will fight her to the bone or wherever it takes us.*

VALERIE JARRETT, that skillful manager of President Obama's governmental affairs. Her official title is Assistant for Public Engagement and Intergovernmental Affairs. Her origins in Iran, later endeavors in Chicago politics, and recent accolades toward that stalwart *Van Jones*, make her very interesting, indeed. Also with communist linkages, she is the daughter-in-law of well-known communist Vernon Jarrett.

VAN JONES, who was released under cover of darkness from the throes of the Obama administration as the "Green Jobs Czar," is now conducting policy analysis at the *Center for American Progress*, as well as a senior policy advisor at *Green for All*. His self-avowed communist leanings place him in a still very tight inner circle with. A true believer in *George Soros*, he was hand-picked by Valerie Jarrett.

T IMOTHY GEITHNER, Secretary of the Treasury, has certainly come of age as the country works its way through the Great Recession. He has been so effective in working with the likes of *Ben Bernanke* and Paul Volker, demonstrating incredible expertise in redefining the place of the dollar in the global environment, helping us to carefully manage the deficit and proving once and for all that we are now finally on the road to financial recovery. Let's not talk about hyperinflation, or other such nasty terms, or about the fact that the national debt is now over $14.275 trillion.

B EN BERNANKE, that loveable little bear of a guy. Now, to his credit, he recently came out publicly and "warned" us that the National Debt "could" present us some very difficult problems to wrestle with in the relatively near future. But, let's not get alarmist about this "thing," as this country has more wherewithal than one can imagine in dealing a knockout blow to hyperinflation, increasing interest rates, increasing energy costs, and multiple other economically sensitive issues that had better be dealt with like *right now*.

A L GORE, "Inventor of the Internet," former Vice President, current co-owner and leader of the cap-and-trade ready international group Generation Investment Management (GIM). Al Gore wasn't satisfied with his Nobel or his Pacific Ocean masterpiece, so he has dug in very deeply with Generation to ensure that the entire world will succumb to the notion that selling hot air, aka CO_2, will become the most lucrative business the world has ever known. He and George have it all figured out, and it is only a matter of time before they have a corner on that quaint little market. They were the fifth largest shareholder in the Chicago Climate Exchange (CCX). Follow the yellow brick road to the wizard. Unfortunately for him, the CCX has gone under as of January 2011, due to the apparent collapse of 'Cap & Trade', at least for the moment. May it rest in peace forever.

TONY PODESTA, more than likely a surprise entry to many readers, the consummate lobbyist, based in DC, and brother of John Podesta, another in the lineup at *Center for American Progress*, and former chief of staff for Bill Clinton. With this dynamic duo fighting for the freedoms of SEIU and ACORN, we can be assured that they will always fight fair and work doubly hard to protect each and every one of our constitutional rights and boundaries. Were it not for *Tony Podesta*, we wouldn't have any reference to Glenn Beck's infamous Crime, Inc. But, of course we do have this prestigious group of completely non-conflicted individuals doing everything in their power to run the republic into places it has never been before. Let's hope and pray they fail miserably.

JOHN P. HOLDREN, Science Czar, Director of the White House Office of Science and Technology Policy. Wikipedia states, "His work has focused on the causes and consequences of global environmental change, energy technologies and policies, ways to reduce the dangers from nuclear weapons and materials, and science and technology policy." Mr. Holdren, please see me after class, we have some things to discuss. Your psychedelic world has no relevance to the world we actually live in, and you need to "come down."

That's the Top Ten List of Individual Enemies Within.

However, we do have a few "entities" that also need to be contended with and brought out into the open repeatedly for the American public to review.

Let's start with *ACORN*, America's poster child for a whole new way to create small business and for arranging credit for needy mortgagees. This entity will attempt to morph via name changes and new URL's on the Internet, but thanks to some very creative investigative journalism, they have been 'outed.'

SEIU has been one of President Obama's favorite "go-to" organizations since well before he was elected. Now that he's in office, the revolving door to the West Wing is continually occupied by his many friends from this esteemed labor organization. You know, the thugs that like to beat up on people if they've congregated for a purpose that may not line up with their own. They recently experienced a changing of the guard, what with Andy Stern taking an inconvenient early exit. Hmmm, I wonder just exactly what caused that little tiff?

Just ask Kenneth Gladney about his memory of the evening of August 6, 2009. His mortal sin was that of handing out "Gadsden" flags at a town hall meeting in Gadsden, a suburb of St. Louis, Mo. The videotape of him being beaten and kicked by clearly purple T-shirt-adorned SEIU "volunteers" is unequivocal as to the intent and purpose of Obama's team—suppress any inkling of discord with his beloved "health care" program. And what a fine job they did in bringing us much closer to "sharing the wealth."

Although this list could go on for a chapter or two, I'm going to finish it with one more entity, one that is cowardly, that will not reveal who they really are. Nonetheless, they are real and another of those enemies within that we need to be very much aware of. They are *"The Invisible Committee,"* who coauthored the spellbinding nonfiction work known as *The Coming Insurrection*. Many of you have probably not heard of this group, so I'm going to give you a glimpse into the masterpiece. From it's next to last chapter, titled "Get Organized" (in order to no longer have to work):

> We know that individuals are possessed of so little life that they have to *earn a living*, to sell their time in exchange for a modicum of social existence. Personal time for social existence: such is work, such is the market. From the outset, the time of the commune eludes work, it doesn't function according to that scheme—it prefers others.
>
> [The Invisible Committee (unidentified insurgents)] [1]

If they (the committee) get everything they want, Newsweek will have to go back and slightly modify their headline to, "We're all communists Now."

Since we're on the subject of sharing the wealth, here is a brief quote that succinctly describes the absolute fallacy of Socialism and the direction President Obama would love to lead this country into:

A powerful, bulleted quote from Pastor / Dr. Adrian Rogers (1931–2005):

- You cannot legislate the poor into freedom by legislating the wealthy out of freedom.

- What one person receives without working for, another person must work for without receiving.

- The government cannot give to anybody anything that the government does not first take from somebody else.

- When half of the people get the idea that they do not have to work because the other half is going to take care of them, and when the other half gets the idea that it does no good to work because somebody else is going to get what they work for, that my dear friend, is about the end of any nation.

- You cannot multiply wealth by dividing it.

America, do we understand where we are today with respect to this set of statements?

Before we give the Progressives any more space about the impact they are currently having on American life, let's move on for a bit to the *Friends of Freedom*.

The Friends of Freedom

GLENN BECK has arguably done more to advance the cause of freedom in this country than any single individual in the past fifty years, bar none. His manuscripts, his continuing dialogues, and his vigilance on the important stuff place him in a category all his own. He and I do not agree on everything, but we are very close on the majority of the important stuff. He has done a masterful job of exposing the dregs of the Obama administration, *incredibly through the very mouths* he is exposing. It's hard to lie about testimony when it is recorded on videotape. This is not light stuff, and he has done a masterful job of educating America, if only She will fully wake up. By the time this book hits the marketplace his TV show will have been disassembled and he will be making hay in a different range of venues. Nonetheless, he has made his mark, and his influence will continue to be felt, rightly so.

RUSH LIMBAUGH, an energetic, highly intelligent commentator has steadfastly defended the tenets of the constitution and has provided America with more than enough facts to circle the globe three times. Were I in a position to do so, I'd nominate him for the Medal of Honor. If President Obama and he were ever presented to the American public together, with objective questions, it would not be in the least bit pretty for President Obama will never let it happen. He would rather deliver an address to the Disabled American Veterans, or the Special Olympics, followed by one to the Alaska Legislature.

MARK LEVIN, a graduate of the Beasley School of Law, Temple University, and a former chief of staff to Ronald Reagan's chief of staff Edward Meese, is author of *Liberty and Tyranny*, a must read for anyone lacking a clear understanding of this country's underpinnings. His daily "Mark Levin Show," played out on more than 150 radio stations, focuses on the facts, and certainly irritates the likes of Keith Olbermann, Chris Matthews, and others cut from the same cloth. They will never, ever catch up to Mark.

SEAN HANNITY, a man who has stood vigilantly by as America has been presented with unimaginable challenge after challenge over the course of the past decade. He has been on the front lines in California when farmers needed to obtain a confirmation of fundamental water rights that could have made an immediate difference in the lives of millions of Californians. The relief appears to be perhaps on the way as we go to press, but California's problems are only likely beginning. Back to the main point: do we actually believe that President Obama will provide a range of viable solutions that help the populace of the United States of America?

ANN COULTER, alongside the syndicated columnist listed immediately below, has provided America with a much-needed female voice to both buttress and finish out the fundamental support Americans need to fend off the insurrection of Progressive Democrats and Republicans who have yet to realize the republic for which the vast majority of us all stand. Ann's consistent and firm stand against Socialism, Marxism, Communism, Islam, and all other counter-American forces places her among the best we have to offer in the battle for freedom. Her work entitled *Godless* [2] couldn't have been more on the mark.

MICHELLE MALKIN, an incredible warrior who daily places the interests of the country above her own and very succinctly brings us up to speed on matters of immediate importance relative to national security, imminent legislation, and a host of other issues. So long as she remains in a position to positively influence the media, America will find a way to move forward, without the undue influence of the (Silent) Progressive Party in America. Michelle knows where these Progressives live, and I am confident she will continue to aggressively fight the battle against them, exposing them over and over and over again.

JONAH GOLDBERG, a fellow Manhattanite. Although he hails from the Big Apple at present, my upbringing comes originally from the Little Apple, back here in Podunk, Kansas. Among Jonah's many accomplishments is his book entitled *Liberal Fascism* [3], (the Secret History of the American Left from Mussolini to the Politics of Meaning). This is one fine piece of work and if you have any doubt as to just exactly where the liberals and the fascists of this country stand, I highly recommend you obtain a copy and become informed. In fact, even if you think you know where they stand, you need to read this book. It covers critical moments of world history that have been compiled in a very informative, provocative summation. It also primes the reader to a much needed, broader understanding of the "hidden" Progressive movement in this country. His syndication as a columnist will only increase with time.

STEPHEN MOORE, member of the editorial board at the *Wall Street Journal* and gifted speaker across the United States, would run circles around President Obama if ever given the chance to share his philosophies related to U.S. and global economics. If President Obama spent one-tenth the amount of time with Stephen Moore as he spends with Timothy Geithner, this country's economy would materially advance within ninety days. Fat chance of that happening, given President Obama's Marxist preferences. In any event, Stephen is a stalwart at the *Journal*, and from my perspective, we need more individuals like he and Bret Stephens guiding that ship. However, I am not swayed by the drift that the general board at the *Journal* has taken toward "post-modernism" and other tendencies away from fundamentals. Sorry, Rupert, just my personal preferences. My advice: go straight back to the fundamentals as fast as you can.

DICK ARMEY, former congressman and majority leader of the House of Representatives, represented the 26th District of Texas. He now leads Freedom Works, based in DC, and materially contributes to the effort to restore America to her fullest potential. He played a major role in the "Reagan Revolution" and clearly understands exactly what the Founding Fathers had in mind when they crafted both the Declaration of Independence and the constitution. The people inside Freedom Works have been key in assisting the movement of the Tea Party and other entities dedicated to preserving our centuries-old experiment intertwining free markets and the enjoyment of life, liberty and the pursuit of happiness (property). That would be Matt Kibbe, Rob Jordan, Brendan Steinhauser, and Wayne Brough, among many others.

THOMAS SOWELL, scholar extraordinaire, currently embedded within Stanford University, where he is a senior fellow at the Hoover Institution. Thomas exudes incredible wisdom across a very broad range of subject matter, especially of course, economics. Among other important contributions, he penned *Applied Economics*[4], which provides highly credible insight into what has worked, and more importantly what has not, in the context of economics in man's endeavors. His achievements are unparalleled in the understanding of how things work in the real world. His experience in Chicago, Los Angeles, and New York have opened him to new horizons, of that I am certain. How else could a former avowed *Marxist* give us the remarkable insight he continues to provide in syndication? Yes, he was a Marxist in his twenties, until he hit the reality of working within the federal government of the 1960s. (The federal government has not improved since the 1960s, unless of course you happen to be a Marxist, in which case your past two years have been like a "dream world.")

JOEL ROSENBERG, a unique contributor to mankind, in that he has the gift of understanding Bible prophecy, bringing it to bear on modern-day conditions, and opening the eyes of the beholder to challenge him/her to delve deeper into the Revelation that exists in the book. His works, such as *Inside the Revolution*[5] and

Epicenter [6], span fiction and nonfiction with remarkable foresight and clarity. Just so you know, what we are currently experiencing is not totally unpredictable. In fact, by some measures, the worst is yet to come. The reality is that we have some very rough sledding ahead. Frankly, I hope that we have a little more time to work on the preparations for the last days, but I have no idea just how close that timeframe happens to be. What I do know is you had better be prepared for the moment virtually all mankind is waiting for, the Second Coming of Yeshua HaMashiach, (Hebrew transliteration of Jesus the Messiah). If you are not prepared for that moment, when He will appear as a "thief in the night," you will very likely have eternal problems that I do not believe you will want to deal with. You need to deal with that issue as soon as you possibly can.

OLIVER NORTH, CHARLES G. KOCH, MARK STEYN, and a whole host of others have played significant roles in the posturing of the best America has to offer to the rest of the world. Isn't this what it's really all about—making this a better place to live and make our respective contributions?

∽∼

One other patriot deserves special mention, President George W. Bush. While I did not agree with every decision he made while in office, he exhibited tremendous courage and made very tough decisions based on the best actionable intelligence available at the time. I applaud him on the release of *Decision Points* and hope every American will lift both he and Laura up as they continue on their paths.

The list above is, as of this writing, filled with living individuals who continue to make significant contributions, but where would we be without the following Founding Patriots?

George Washington, Patrick Henry, John Paul Jones, Thomas Jefferson, James Madison, Benjamin Franklin, John Locke, and so many others truly put this republic in motion.

How wise he was when Franklin was asked what had been produced as he exited the Constitutional Convention of 1787:

"A Republic, if you can keep it."

God, I wish those men were around today to assist in straightening things out a bit.

United States Foreign policy

Israel First

Hillary Rodham Clinton is such a skilled leader. She certainly knows how to put on the best face in support of *her* allies within Hamas, Syria, and the Palestinian Authority. Before we go one step farther, let's not forget who is behind her every move—none other than President Obama himself. With him, we get the added bonus of bowing to political leaders the world over and unabashed support of Islam.

We have multiple, very significant allies the world over: Great Britain, Australia, Canada, and Japan, to name a few. Lesser ties but important relationships exist with many countries that we would tend to describe as Socialist, like Norway, the Netherlands, Germany, France, etc. Then we have the communists, who really do envy our assets and who would sooner turn us inside out than deal with us heads up. Nonetheless, we move forward as best we can, periodically reminding them of these pesky little items like "human rights." But, we're not going to deal with that in this book; we've got too many immediate, otherwise geopolitical items to look at.

When it all comes down to it, there is one ally to the United States that stands out above all the rest—Israel. While she is relatively new at statehood (May 14, 1948), she has continuously inhabited her land for thousands of years. This is archaeologically verified, e.g. the Siloam Inscription in the Old City of Jerusalem, dating back to approximately the 8th century BCE, so I'm not going to waste time here debating the matter as to whether she has the "right" to "occupy" her own land. I will simply state that the land she currently resides in has been transformed at least in part from a barren wasteland to an incredibly prosperous enterprise that only an awesome God could have produced ex nihilo.

While the Balfour Declaration (1920) provided official territorial rights and boundaries to the area known as Palestine, she, through the Creator of it all, occupies today a significantly smaller geographic area than she is actually entitled to. The map below depicts, based primarily on biblical descriptions, the maximum extent to which the boundaries of Israel would have extended. It is followed by some of the biblical quotations, though this listing could have been considerably more extensive. As presented, it provides some sense of the Creator's intents and His defined geographic extents.

It is not my intent to get "religious," but I take the Holy Bible very seriously, and therefore, since Bible prophecy has been shown to be incredibly accurate over the ages, I have no reason to discount its accuracy when it comes to defining biblically significant land boundaries. For example, the emergence of the State of Israel was predicted with great specificity hundreds of years before 1948.

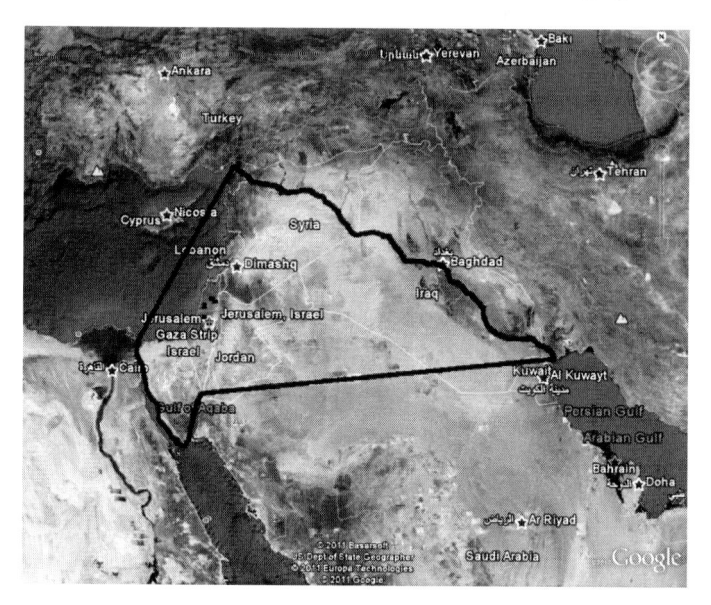

Figure 1: Assigned boundaries of Israel via Biblical definitions
(For a more detailed look, view the colorized version
of this image within the color section, page 145.)

On that day the LORD made a covenant with Abram and said, "To your descendants I give this land, from the Wadi of Egypt to the great river, the Euphrates the land of the Kenites, Kenizzites, Kadmonites, Hittites, Perizzites, Rephaites, Amorites, Canaanites, Girgashites and Jebusites." [21]

Genesis 15:18-21

"I will fix your boundary from the Red Sea to the sea of the Philistines, and from the wilderness to the River Euphrates; for I will deliver the inhabitants of the land into your hand, and you will drive them out before you.

Exodus 23:31

If you carefully observe all these commands I am giving you to follow—to love the LORD your God, to walk in all his ways and to hold fast to him—then the LORD will drive out all these nations before you, and you will dispossess nations larger and stronger than you. Every place where you set your foot will be yours: Your territory will extend from the desert to Lebanon, and from the Euphrates River to the western sea.

Deuteronomy 11:22-24

From the wilderness and this Lebanon, even as far as the great river, the river Euphrates, all the land of the Hittites, and as far as the Great Sea toward the setting of the sun will be your territory.

Joshua 1:4

May he also rule from sea to sea
    And from the River to the ends of the earth.
Let the nomads of the desert bow before him,
    And his enemies lick the dust.

Psalm 72:8-9

"I shall also set his hand on the sea
    And his right hand on the rivers.

Psalm 89:25

It is absolutely the case that the accuracy and canonicity of the Bible is very well documented the world over. That is to say that it has been "vetted" more extensively than any other work in human history; it has stood very well the test of time, and its precepts are unquestionably good for all humanity.

In that context, man has been endowed with a very full, free will. That fact is loaded with a blessing and a curse. It is also loaded with inherent freedom, and our Creator would not have it any other way.

If you happen to be an atheist or an agnostic, then you will have no appreciation whatsoever for the above quotations or the general argument. This book is not written to challenge you to religious contemplation, but I will readily acknowledge that much of what we are contending with in our global systems is much easier to grasp if we understand that we have very real human bounds as to conduct and our relationship to our fellow men. Man has an embedded moral compass, and when he voids that internal guidance, he walks right into trouble and challenges that otherwise would not occur.

These same principles apply to countries and municipalities as well. The United States of America was founded on the beliefs bestowed upon us by our Creator, Judeo-Christian values, as is very well indicated by our Declaration and our Constitution.

The truth matters. The history of our great country has depended on that principle time and again. As has been said before in this old adage, "America is great because she is good. If America ceases to be good, America will cease to be great."

Now, more than ever, America needs to defend every inch of ground in the tiny State of Israel.

The geographic extents of modern-day Israel:

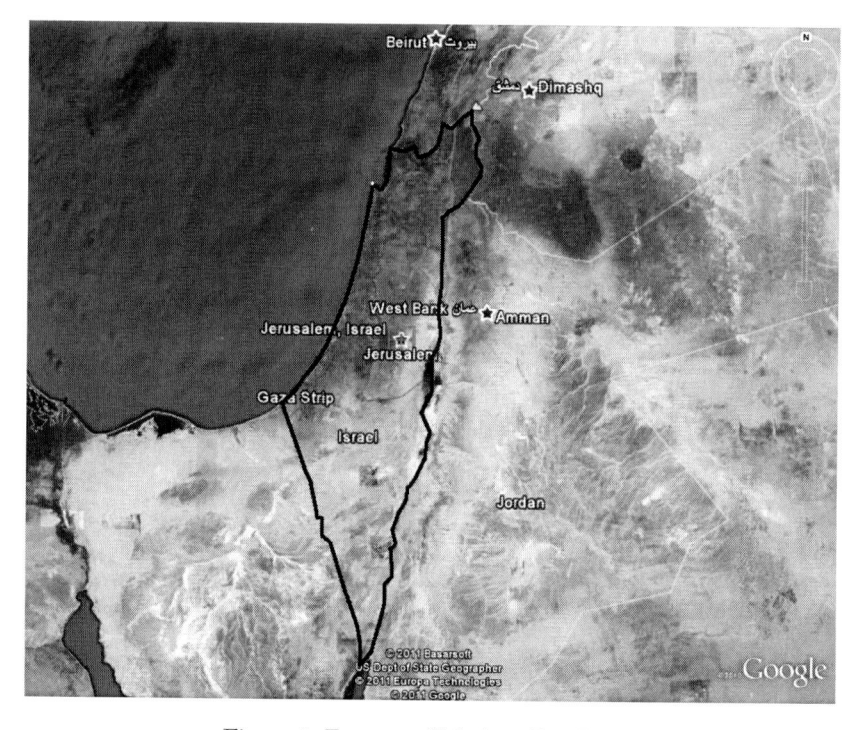

Figure 2: Extents of Modern Day Israel

(For a more detailed look, view the colorized version of this image within the color section, page 145.)

It is also quite obvious that Israel has herself relinquished much of this territory by virtue of historical battles, disputes, mismanagement of her own resources, and her noncompliance with God's instruction, as indicated in the passage from Deuteronomy above. However, the Creator will take care of a lot of pent-up, unfinished business in this immediate area. The Book of Revelation is very specific about that.

Back to the subject of allies.

Harry Truman was president at the moment of Israel's initiation of statehood. I daresay that today's political environment, speaking globally, has never been more sensitive to that small parcel of land between Lebanon, Syria, Jordan, and Egypt.

Much to the chagrin of Great Britain, Canada, Australia, and other primarily English-speaking allies of the United States, these "friends" are simply not as important to our national interest as is the State of Israel.

This *is* a huge spiritual battle. It always has been, always will be. While it may not matter to you, especially if you are an atheist or agnostic, the end of the story is known; it is no secret. The good guys do win, but not without considerable "tribulation," bloodshed, and other manners of discomfort. It will be good to be on the side of Israel when "push comes to shove." This will not turn out at all well for the followers of Allah—and, no, he is not the same god as the God of Abraham, Isaac, and Jacob. In fact he is as far from Him as you can be.

Why is Israel so important to the interest of the United States of America, in direct contradiction to the manner in which she has been treated thus far by BO? Because she is the apple of God's eye. She will, at the end of it all, remain. In direct contradiction to Mahmoud Ahmadinejad, she will outlive Iran or any other member of the appropriately defined "Axis of Evil." According to some biblical scholars, she may well outlive the United States. Do you realize that the United States is nowhere to be found in end-time prophecy?

Israel has been at war since her inception, either physically or figuratively, but mostly physically. She knows how to defend herself.

However, new dynamics are now in play with the nuclear capability of Iran (and by association, Syria).

Intelligence estimates now indicate that Iran may have the ability to "deliver" a warhead to the United States by around 2012, much sooner than many of us imagined even one year ago. Israel has had the capability to deliver nuclear firepower for decades, and we need to be a lot more grateful to her for that fact alone. She is on the frontline of defense in terms of the threat of Islamic Jihad against the Great Satan, a.k.a. the USA. Do you understand the significance of this Jihad?

The Bible tells me under no uncertain terms that I am to "love my enemy." I do, but the same Bible tells me that I am to hate the sin and love the sinner. I do hate the sin that is manifested by suicide bombers and all other acts directed to eliminate the infidels, including the 9/11 event that brought America to her spiritual knees for all of about six months, maybe nine tops.

I guess I'll end up loving those Jihadists to death because I don't see them generally rejecting their coveted "seventy-two virgins" in their Allah-based heaven.

Back to the allies for just a moment.

In the modern definition of matters political, Israel is not a Conservative nation. Does that bother me? Not in the least. At the end of the day, conservative or not, She loves. She tends to wounded Palestinian soldiers before her own; she was first on location in Haiti after a devastating earthquake, when hurting people were desperate for medical assistance. She wasn't just first; she was there with state-of-the-art field equipment that actually mattered in terms of saving lives. She was way ahead of the USA, which fumbled and bumbled in ships offshore for days while people withered under the overwhelming load. *Shame on us.*

Are you connecting with this yet, or do we need another Holocaust to get our attention? Plus or minus 6 million human beings exterminated because some Socialist, Nazi lunatic decided that he was capable of judging who was "adequate" or "superior" in the human race. He deemed it appropriate to construct facilities that would deliver death to innocent men, women, and children because he and his Fascist comrades just knew they had the "Answer." I am here to tell you that a similarly outfitted man has dressed himself as the modern-day Fuhrer, capable of redirecting all of mankind into a "Fundamentally Transforming" New world order. With the election of 2010, however, the Narcissist-in-Chief now has a whole new path ahead of him that he did not predict.

I digress; this is about Israel. If ever there was a time for the United States to take a firm stand for the lone democracy in the Middle East, let alone our deeply kindred spirit, this would be it. Yet President Obama makes move after move, acquiescing to the U.N. at every opportunity, turning his back on the tiny nation-state that has blossomed from nowhere in the desert. This is nothing more, nor less, than additional tantamount evidence that O is a Muslim, pure and simple.

She will take care of Iran, end of story, with or without President Obama.

I also want to make a preliminary comment about energy. Not that it matters so much to the United States, other than noting what can be brought about by proper planning and execution of a strategy, interesting things are happening in Israel's energy sector. Major natural gas discoveries have been encountered by U.S.-based Noble Energy. The discoveries, in Tamar and Dalit fields, have occurred in the Mediterranean, approximately thirty miles offshore in water depths ranging from 4,500 to more than 5,500 feet of water. The total depth of the Tamar structure is 16,680 feet, and the gross mean resource estimate, subsequent to the drilling of a key appraisal well, appears to be 6.3 trillion cubic feet of natural gas. [1]

Israel is now constructing onshore facilities to convert the produced natural gas to electricity. It is probable a very large portion of Israel's electrical energy needs will be met by these discoveries.

In addition, it has also been reported that significant onshore oil reserves have been encountered by Israeli firm Givot Olam, within the Meged license near Rosh Ha'ayin. [2] I will refrain from citing volumetric reserve estimates, due to the lack of credible data, but it does appear that production from the site of the Meged-5 well has yielded daily oil production somewhat in excess of 380 barrels oil per day (BOPD). At a minimum, it confirms additional onshore production, which may lead to additional commercial development.

∽∼

Taking up space right here, right now on Allah, Muhammad, the Ayatollah Khameni, or Jihadists is necessary. Those of you in Detroit know exactly what I'm talking about. You have seen property values plummet; you have seen intense deterioration of your neighborhoods. Those of you in Paris know exactly what I'm talking about. It's not just about property values.

Property values are one thing, but your *life* is another thing entirely. How many of you feel threatened? How many of you feel like you have been backed into a corner that you may not be able to get out of?

My guess: President Obama will not help you out of that corner; he will push you back as far as he can into that corner; that's just the kind of guy he is. I don't care if you are black, white, yellow, or any color in between; you are just a number in his book. He could care less about your plight. That is not his game; his game is the "New World Order." He does not see himself taking a bow on the national stage at the end of his term, except to segue onto the international stage.

I need to get back to Israel.

BO is *telling* Benjamin Netanyahu that Israel needs to give the Palestinians more land in order to preserve peace in Palestine. Bebe is way ahead of President Obama on this one, and I seriously doubt he will fall for President Obama's mandate, coming from American soil, no less. As I pointed out long ago, Israel has every reason to maintain her current borders. Unfortunately, Prime Minister Netanyahu is bending under the strain, considering the results of the "Flotilla" that was cleverly crafted to become a significant public relations nightmare for Israel. Israel should have stood even more firmly on her ground and then turned the tables on the Jihadists.

Even if it were not a biblically-mandated definition, she has defended and maintained her U.N.-mandated borders such that she is entitled to the prosperity she has propagated in the Land. She, and only she, has solved the equation of survival in one of the most hostile territories on earth. I am witness to the land, as I have managed to transect her from border to border, and she is beautiful as she stands today.

Israel, do not fall for the marks of the deceiver. Do not allow a foreigner to dictate to you what is best for you. What the foreigner should provide to you is explicit, not implicit protection of each and every one of your borders.

The United States is failing in its mission to protect the State of Israel. The Knesset needs to study this issue now and in great detail and decide how it plans to deal with America. As you in Israel have discovered, true allies in this country are difficult to locate in today's regime.

We send billions of U.S. dollars to Israel each and every year. Unfortunately, we also send billions of U.S. dollars to geographically close enemies of Israel each and every year. You want the numbers? Estimated foreign aid to Israel in 2009 was $3.1 billion. Estimated foreign aid delivered to Egypt and Jordan was $2.8 Billion each. [3]

While Jordan appears friendly to Israel on the surface, do not count on Jordan to bail Israel out of any conflict. The same holds true for Egypt.

However, they do "tolerate" Israel. Do you think they would come to Israel's defense if attacked by one of those "neutral" states like Syria or Iran? I have been in Jordan, and I have observed King Abdullah's comments on numerous occasions. I seriously doubt he would lift a finger in support of Israel, if it came down to that. Assad? Forget it; he will duly assist Iran in any way possible.

I have an issue with those numbers. Material conflicts of interest cloud every dollar going into any of those entities, except Israel. In Jordan, for instance, $163 million went in the form of a "cash payment" to the Jordanian government. I'm guessing they redistributed that wealth equally among all 6.1 million Jordanian citizens (2008). That's $26.77 per capita, and I'm sure they were happy to receive that moderate supplement. Considering that the GDP per capita is about $3,470, the U.S. gave each Jordanian citizen about a 1 percent raise, assuming King Abdullah granted an equitable distribution to all citizens. Didn't happen, did it? King Abdullah laughed all the way to the bank.

I did visit the Hashemite Arab Kingdom of Jordan briefly a few years back, and I can see that they can use some assistance. However, that assistance (coming from America) needs to have a much tighter string attached. They know nothing of a real democracy, being currently ruled by a monarchy, although they do elect representatives/senators in a quasi-democratic ruling body that answers to the monarch, King Abdullah, who is their chief executive and commander-in-chief. Credit them for having more free trade agreements in play than any other Arab country in the region.

Islam

This section is written for one purpose—to attempt to inform the reader of some of the fundamentally significant tenets embedded within the Muslim "faith." Islam is a tightly integrated facility that includes social, political, military, and religious context and content.

If Muslims want to sit down with the rest of the world's religious leaders and begin to hammer out a virtual complete rewrite of the Qur'an, denounce any notion that they have every intention of wiping Israel off the face of the earth, and denounce the continuing goal of eliminating the infidels, then we can initiate a new dialogue.

Having death, destruction, and domination as your central tenets of faith make it really difficult for the rest of us mere mortals to take your "religion" lightly.

Muslims follow the teaching of a single so-called "prophet" named Muhammad, who lived from 570-632 AD. He claimed to have been the receiver of divine revelations from Allah. These revelations were then transcribed into the Holy Qur'an, which is the Muslim's equivalent of the Holy Bible in the Christian faith. The Qur'an, written hundreds of years after the first manuscripts of the Holy Bible, actually repeatedly usurps passages from the Bible, without ever, of course, providing any reference to it.

The Qur'an is divided into chapters known as Surah. If you have been told that Islam is a peace-loving, equal rights providing religion that was inspired by God, then I suggest you need to seek the truth as to such a claim.

Assuming you may not have the time or desire to delve into the Qur'an, I will pre-empt your research and let you know, under no uncertain terms, that the Qur'an is not inspired by the God of Abraham, Isaac, and Jacob, and that it is, instead, a confused document that, if anything, induces it's adherents to *hate the infidel*. Who is the Infidel? *You*, if you are not a Muslim.

(See 'Holy' Qur'an, Surah 8.12 "…Smite infidels on their necks and every joint and incapacitate them. Strike off their heads and cut off each of their fingers and toes.")

Any Muslim that adheres to his faith cannot deny that fundamental reality. That applies across the board, whether Sunni (approximately 85 percent of Muslims), or Shi'a (approximately 15 percent). The current best estimates of global Muslim population totals about 1.6 billion.

Whether you are Sunni or Shi'a, your Qur'an indicates to me that you are out to "get" me; that doesn't sound in the last bit peaceful to me.

According to the Pew Public Forum on Religious and Public Life in 2009, this was the distribution of Muslims across the globe, expressed as a percentage in whatever country of reference. As of 2009, the U.S. seemed to be in a relatively low percentage, globally speaking, but that is only one metric, or measurement, of the magnitude of influence that can be regionally propagated by Islam.

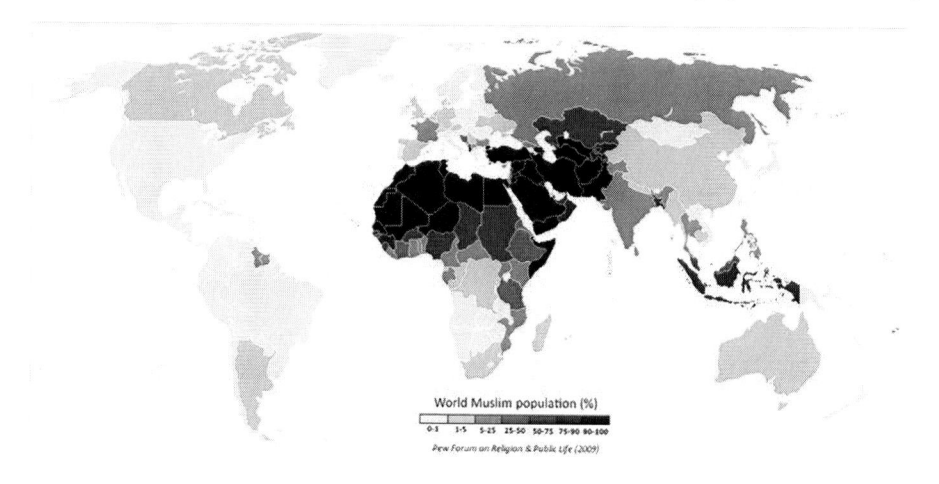

Figure 3: World Muslim population [8]

World Muslim Population 2009

When the Muslim population in any given country reaches approximately 10 percent, multiple significant transformations begin to take place in that country. Ask France how they are liking their increasing Muslim background count, now at about 6 percent, with over 3.5 million Muslims.

Ask the United Kingdom, with its Muslim population now approaching 1.65 million about 2.7 percent of their population. I am guessing that the encroachment of Sharia Law in Great Britain is not providing much added value in either it's context of law, or in it's former leadership in the financial world. The impending difficulties related to Sharia Compliant Finance are only beginning to surface.

This photo was taken at a Muslim demonstration in London:

Photo 1: 3 February 2006 Protests staged in London, demonstration by Muslims angry over the publication in Scandinavian periodicals related to the prophet Muhammad

(For a more detailed look, view the colorized version of this image within the color section, page 146.)

The Muslim population in Canada is currently estimated at 657,000, about 2 percent of their total.
What is the Muslim population of the United States?
The answer is nebulous, but here are some estimates to consider:

American Religious Identification Survey:	1.3 million (2008) [4]
U.S. News and World Report:	5 million+ (2008) [5]
Pew Research Center:	2.5 million (2009) [6]
Council on Islamic Relations (CAIR):	7.0 million (2010) [7]

There are those who estimate that the fraction of Islamic fundamentalists/terrorists within the Muslim faith approaches 10 percent. I have seen conservative estimates placing the limit at more like 7 percent. [9] To be on the safe side, let's use 10 percent. Those are the Jihadists who see this as a "Holy War." If Pew is correct, quick math yields a ballpark number of 250,000 Islamic terrorists now roaming the streets and neighborhoods of America. We have fifty states, with anything but an equivalent population distribution among the states. If it were equivalently distributed, each state would be housing approximately five thousand Islamic terrorists.

Since New York City's population is now about 8.25 million, one could imply that you (New York) have about 6,718 Islamic terrorists roaming your streets. BO wants them to feel very comfortable. If you don't believe me, just ask NASA Administrator Charles Bolden, who has stated that perhaps foremost among his top three responsibilities, as directed by President Obama, he *"wanted me to find a way to reach out to the Muslim world and engage much more with dominantly Muslim nations to help them feel good about their historic contribution to science and engineering."* [9]

Too bad he couldn't reach out and touch Mohammed Atta. Now, that was a feat of engineering: 107 stories with a single Boeing 707, more than 3,000 deaths…what an Islamic feat. Or would you rather we pass that off to some other "religion"?

The Jihadists feel an intense personal responsibility to *kill* the infidels. If you are not a Muslim, you are an infidel. Ask the people of Dearborn, Mich., (Muslim capital of America) how they feel now that their Muslim population is approximately 40 percent of the total population of 100,000. That should give them about four thousand Jihadists, give or take.

Here is some more data.

The Muslim Brotherhood, one of the more dominant Islamic organizations in the United States, has now officially ratcheted up the notion of Jihad in *this* country.

Barry Rubin, director of the Global Research in International Affairs Center and editor of the *Middle East Review of International Affairs Journal,* indicates that the Brotherhood is "ready to move from the era of propaganda and base-building to one of revolutionary action." He gets this impression directly from the recently elected Supreme Guide of the Muslim Brotherhood, Muhammad Badi. According to Rubin, as reported by ACT! for America (October 12, 2010), in a sermon published September 30, 2010, titled "How Islam Confronts the Oppression and Tyranny [against the Muslims]," *Badi said waging Jihad against both Israel and the United States is a commandment of Allah that cannot be disregarded.*

I happen to take Badi at his word, until he directs his vigilant troops otherwise.

The city of Detroit, now with a population of approximately 915,000, (as compared to 1,850,000 in 1950), houses the largest Muslim population of any American city. There is no place in America with a more pathetic-looking future. The unions have wrecked what used to be the world's premier automobile manufacturing complex. Now, the Muslims have virtually overtaken the essence of what is left of that manufacturing shell.

Just exactly what do you think the future holds for Detroit?

To commemorate the onset of Ramadan 2010, President Barack Hussein Obama issued this statement on August 13:

"Ramadan is a time when Muslims around the world reflect upon the wisdom and guidance that comes with faith, and the responsibility that human beings have to one another, and to God…

"…These rituals remind us of the principles that we hold in common, and Islam's role in advancing justice, progress, tolerance, and the dignity of all human beings.

"…And here in the United States, Ramadan is a reminder that Islam has always been part of America and that American Muslims have made extraordinary contributions to our country. [10]

It seems to me that this is the first time I've ever heard that Islam has "always been a part of America." I need to check the roster of soldiers at Valley Forge, then at Gettysburg. I'll get back to you on my findings.

Outline of Recommended U.S. Foreign / Defense Policy

The last section touched upon matters focused largely on Israel and her archenemy, generalized as Islam; I do not relish that necessary fact. Perhaps the Muslim world will do something of an about face in the near future and cause all those images to become relics of a forgotten distant past. Please forgive me for considering that to be a very low probability eventuality.

With Hillary Rodham Clinton managing the affairs of the State Department, I do not expect her to move anywhere close to these recommendations. Former Secretary of Defense Robert Gates made a decision to remain with the Obama administration through 2010, after serving somewhat briefly in the later stages of the Bush administration. He actually made it almost halfway into 2011. His focus had been to hold the line on defense spending, and given the difficult economic times we are currently experiencing, I find no fault with that strategy. However, one must assume that he had been in very substantial communication with the secretary of state, the president, etc., and therefore had been in general agreement with most foreign-policy decisions during his tenure. For that reason, I will assume he would not have been in general agreement with most of the content below.

- *Understand the negative impact of the European Union (EU) on the United States and the consequences of becoming bound with them on a multitude of socio-economic levels.* If we allow it to happen, the consequences will be severe. For example, Greece. (By the way, *The Invisible Committee* was all over the situation in Greece.) We're already committed to a portion of the bailout of that Socialist democracy, via the International Monetary Fund (IMF). The U.S. share of IMF transactions is approximately 17 percent, give or take. U.S. Congressman Todd Tiahrt (who happens to have been my representative) had it right when he said, *"It is simply unfair—as a matter of principle—to force American taxpayers to use their hard-earned money to prop up failed policies in relatively wealthy nations,"* [11]

A group led by the EU, the European Central Bank, and others involved in the Greek Bailout have committed approximately $145 billion, as of May 2010, so the approximate take from the U.S. is about $24.65 billion. The EU is proving in real time just how problematic the notion of interlinking sovereign nations can become. There is, of course, a significant move afoot among leading Socialist thinkers surrounding BO to link us tighter and tighter with this group, as part of the bigger plan for the "New World Order." Copenhagen 2010 was merely an opening act toward bringing global compliance to the table relative to "climate" issues. The reader needs to be assured that climate issues are but a piece of the bigger pie that will ultimately reach to the pocketbook of every economically viable individual on this planet. If we allow it to happen, it will be a global transfer of wealth unlike anything people could ever imagine. The drag on the global economies is incalculable, certain to wreak havoc and depression on every continent.

- *Materially modify the U.S. Atomic Weapons Arsenal*, and do it without telegraphing internal strategy to the international community. I realize this will not set well with former Secretary Gates, who expressed strong support for the outcome of "new and improved" START negotiations with Russia. Did Mr. Gates actually trust the Russian administration to fulfill its side of the bargain? During the Reagan administration, the U.S. had approximately 25,000 nuclear warheads stockpiled. That number dropped dramatically during the first Bush presidency to approximately 12,000. According to the U.S. Department of Defense, as of May 3, 2010, we have broadcast to the world that we now have 5,113 warheads operationally deployed, in active reserve, or held in storage. [12] According to the Nuclear Threat Initiative, a U.S.-based research organization, estimates of Russia's current stockpile range from 15,000-20,000. [13] Getting an actual verifiable number is something we cannot seem to accomplish at present. Do we somehow believe we are now less vulnerable to outside threats than we were in 1980? I can understand the logic that would suggest that the damage resulting from even 5,113 warheads would be catastrophic, if deployed in almost any short-term scenario. However, it will be virtually impossible to anticipate the full range of potential incoming hostile warheads if the likes of Russia, Iran, North Korea, and others, join forces against us. If they do, a number like 5,113 seems highly questionable in view of safeguarding our national defense.

- *Dramatically reduce foreign aid to countries deemed inconsistent with principles that define our republic* and the democracy related to it. Translated, this means we should not support Socialistic, Marxist, Communist, Totalitarian regimes that generally oppose the principles of individual freedom. According to the state department, *excluding our military support in Afghanistan, Iraq and a relatively minor host of additional countries*, the United States is estimated to have spent around $23.5 billion for foreign economic aid during FY 2008.[14] In terms of our proposed total budget of outlays for 2010 ($2.98 trillion), this is a relatively small number (about .8 percent of our budget.) However, we have significant national problems to solve with respect to our own unemployment, for instance, that deserve a very high priority, and I'm not referring to the "stimulus plan," which is not stimulating anything other than most people's nerves. While foreign aid needs to be directed to multiple deserving countries, we need to do a much better job of monitoring progress in the deserving target countries.

- *Enforce existing immigration laws.* Thank you to Arizona and Governor Jan Brewer for drawing a line in the sand. There has already been weeping, gnashing of teeth, and street demonstrations at various SEIU outposts across America. They are the quickest to organize truly Socialist groups on very short notice. If an individual comes into this country without legal documentation, they should be immediately deported to whatever country they infiltrated from. Then we have Eric Holder holding the water for the ACLU and what must be some of the most brilliant constitutional scholars on the federal payroll, who are standing up for the rights of the poor, downtrodden, drug smugglers, and parents of "anchor" babies, those automatic citizens.

Our Canadian border is just as porous as our Mexican, and the probability is very high that transgressors from the North will be linked to Islamic terrorists, as compared to the Mexican insurgents, who are more likely to be related to drug-runners. (But let's not assume for a moment that Islamic Jihadists will ignore the southern border.) Neither case is good for America, and both need to be choked off to the maximum extent possible, as soon as possible. This almost incomprehensible daily, weekly, monthly influx of illegal immigrants verifies that the federal government is out of control and incapable of satisfactorily resolving one of the vexing problems in our country's history. *Amnesty* is not a solution. Start with the wall.

An acquaintance has an excellent idea with respect to the wall. He believes we should not just apprehend those who come into this country illegally but that we should put them into labor camps that we could then use to construct the wall. I'm all in favor of that. You don't think that would slow down the flow of illegal immigrants coming across the Mexican border?

- *Wake up to the reality of Islamic terrorists.* The current administration has demonstrated an astounding aversion to dealing with what used to be obvious to Americans:

Terrorism is very hazardous to our health, and it is no unproven secret that the *vast* majority of terrorist-sponsored activity in this country and around the world is sourced from Islamic entities. Those within the current administration that propagate the misinformed notion that "moderate" Muslims have no beef against the United States do no service whatsoever to the citizens of this country.

Moderate Muslims have the same incentive to do away completely with the "infidels," and their beliefs will not change, especially if they have the freedom to roam as they please within our borders.

As indicated earlier, some research indicates that 10 percent of Muslims consider themselves "extremists," i.e. ready and willing to take aggressive action against the infidels, wherever they happen to be. That translates to a mere low-side estimate of 130,000 potential armed and ready Islamic fundamentalists within our borders, many, if not most of them probably illegally. Recent history has brought us a bit closer to reality with incidents at Ft. Hood, the "Christmas Bomber," and most recently the failed assailant at Times Square. Note the silence from President Obama on this entire last incident.

President Obama is a Muslim at his core, and it matters. (I am not buying for a minute the claims coming out of his mouth, as well as multiple Christian clergy, that he is a Christian. Show me the evidence of his actual faith walk.) Combine that with his Marxist background, and tell me what you see. The worldwide population of Muslims is approaching 1.6 billion. Do the 10 percent math on that number (160,000,000), and tell me that our foreign intelligence services need to be more restrained on their methods of extracting valuable actionable intelligence. In the event that you have not properly registered that number, 160 million is more than half the population of the entire

United States. That is one estimate of the number of Islamic terrorists roaming the planet. Based on known results from New York, Madrid, London, Tel Aviv, Frankfurt, Paris, Jakarta, and a host of other cities across the globe, that number is probably conservative.

- *Avoid any and all global Climate Change initiatives.* They will be long-term traps of inestimable economic proportion, all of which, if approved, will be signed to incorporate a transfer of wealth from developed to developing and undeveloped countries. All will be damaging to the global economy, and all will fail miserably in the attempt to control "greenhouse gases." Why would I make such an astounding statement? Because it's based on factual data, not models and inference. There is a significant difference between the two, and the establishment of the moment does not appear to have a clue as to this fundamental difference. The IPCC is not the second savior of the world, behind BO. Finally, at long last, the solar scientists are weighing in on this issue. They have become emboldened by the revelations provided through "Climate Gate," as well as those provided earlier by whistleblowers within the EPA, namely Alan Carlin and his internal review entitled, *"Proposed National Center for Environmental Economics (NCEE) Comments on Draft Technical Support Document for Endangerment Analysis for Greenhouse Gas Emissions under the Clean Air Act,"* dated March 2009. The internal document was suppressed until after the vote on House Bill 2494 took place. The document contained multiple well-documented challenges to the EPA's unfounded conclusions related to human-induced Global Warming and the purported consequences related to this global phenomenon. *America, we have some serious problems to contend with, and Climate Change is absolutely not on the list, not now, not likely ever.* Please quote me on this, far and wide.

Greenpeace, FYI: Man's current influence on global climate is miniscule, barely measurable. We will visit that issue in detail in later chapters.

- *Win the Wars in Afghanistan and Iraq.* Do you actually believe that pulling out of either of these countries at this critical juncture is in the interest of the United States of America?

  The Soviet Union lost its war with Afghanistan before the U.S. arrived in 2001. They have been licking their wounds ever since.

  The United States has developed the trust of millions of Afghani's since 2001, and they happen to border Iran and Pakistan. These two countries are very important in our War Against Terror. I am not going to elaborate here, but please investigate if you have any doubts as to the importance of ongoing engagement in both of these countries.

  The U.S. has now pulled "combat troops" out of Iraq, leaving 50,000 military advisors and soldiers to protect resident Americans and to oversee a hoped for transition to democracy. I openly question the wisdom of leaving a major void in that country at this delicate stage of its development. The U.S. has invested billions of dollars in that country, and I simply do not see the obvious evidence that the Iraqis are in a position to move to the next stage without a substantial, well-armed military presence.

  Iraq and Iran have been at war for centuries, and the United States has been involved nearly every step of the way for many decades, for reasons of global strategic importance: Hydrocarbons.

United States Energy Policy

If you think that the United States can compile all the energy assets necessary to run this place entirely on its own recognizance, you are misled. That includes the forced and mandated expansion of all the "renewables" that are seen to be the solution to our energy puzzle. Diverting attention and resources into wind power for electricity and ethanol for mixing with gasoline will prove to become very costly disasters, if we allow it to happen as planned by current policy planners. We will deal with both wind and ethanol in greater detail later in this chapter. Hydroelectric: won't happen, not "green" enough.

This country has never been, in its entire history, more *interdependent* on the global energy delivery system than it is today. Our sources are disparate, some hostile, and such that we will be unable, within my lifetime, to materially alter them.

We currently *consume* approximately 20 million barrels oil per day (BOPD) in this country.

At the same time, we currently *produce* approximately 5 million BOPD.

Here are the primary external contributors, (in order of contribution), to our energy supply, as of June 30, 2010, as reported by United States Energy Information Agency [EIA] August 30, 2010):

Total Imports of Petroleum (Top 15 Countries) (Thousand Barrels per Day)

Country	Jun-10	May-10	YTD 2010	Jun-09
CANADA	2,733	2,527	2,562	2,538
SAUDI ARABIA	1,353	1,097	1,121	959
MEXICO	1,208	1,428	1,242	1,190
NIGERIA	1,109	1,026	1,061	830
VENEZUELA	899	1,109	1,225	1,256
RUSSIA	760	719	580	618
IRAQ	630	394	505	390
ALGERIA	550	518	491	433
ANGOLA	425	448	442	447
COLOMBIA	407	315	351	313
BRAZIL	308	320	315	299
UNITED KINGDOM	269	176	293	268
VIRGIN ISLANDS	244	193	285	276
KUWAIT	217	225	206	179
ECUADOR	211	160	184	154

Table 1 [1]

Of this group, one is most closely aligned with American interests and policies: Canada.

Of this group, one is currently providing the largest import volume: Canada

Many, if not most, entities in this group are not necessarily aligned with U.S. interests. You can make the case that Saudi Arabia is very interested economically in what we are accomplishing.

Venezuela is fundamentally Socialist and is working overtime to undermine the strength of the United States. They are not only supported by the Obama administration; they are waiting patiently to fundamentally assist in the transformation of the USA. They will be only too happy to see our system of private enterprise fail miserably. If they and Obama get their way, that is exactly what will happen, provided of course, we let it happen.

Free enterprise relates very directly to freedom. Do you cherish freedom? Then start acting like it. Participate in real polls; show up at Tea Parties. These Americans actually believe that they can influence a largely corrupt and ineffective government. I am unquestionably and unashamedly one of them, among other political facets, and I absolutely believe that there has never been a better time to take a stand for freedom.

The results of the historic election of 2010 speak volumes about how Americans truly feel about their individual freedom and their displeasure for any notion of regime change that would further limit any aspects of our freedoms. Our freedoms are many, and each and every one of them is worth waging a battle over.

Energy, that's presumably why you're in this chapter.

Do you like light at night?

Do you appreciate cooling in the summer months and heating in the winter?

Do you appreciate that your energy costs in this country are among the lowest in the world?

We must *stop* the nonsense that has been matriculating since Greenpeace and like-oriented entities have been materially undermining a very substantial stockpile of your freedoms. These freedoms have been providing you and your children the opportunity to participate in a society where we absolutely enjoy the prosperity that ingenuity, competition, and free markets have brought us. We have incentives to excel, to become more efficient, and to be the most substantial purveyor of freedom the world has ever known.

Let's talk about Greenpeace for a moment. It was supported early on by Patrick Moore (who claims to be a founder), who has since absolutely renounced what the organization has become. What it has become is an entity that is dedicated to disrupting virtually any enterprise that attempts to earn a profit from any activity coming in contact with mother earth. You can sort out what that means. They had noble beginnings, from Vancouver, British Columbia, attempting to curtail nuclear testing in Pacific waters (a worthy cause if they had left it at that), but they quickly moved to limit a plethora of other activities and are viewed as hostile to a wide range of American enterprises.

Can we continue to prosper in this republic? That is up to you and me, all 310 million of us, *if* we choose to do so.

Do you know where the electricity flowing out of your wall socket is actually coming from?

On a current usage basis, these are the sources and the ballpark numbers from about 2009:

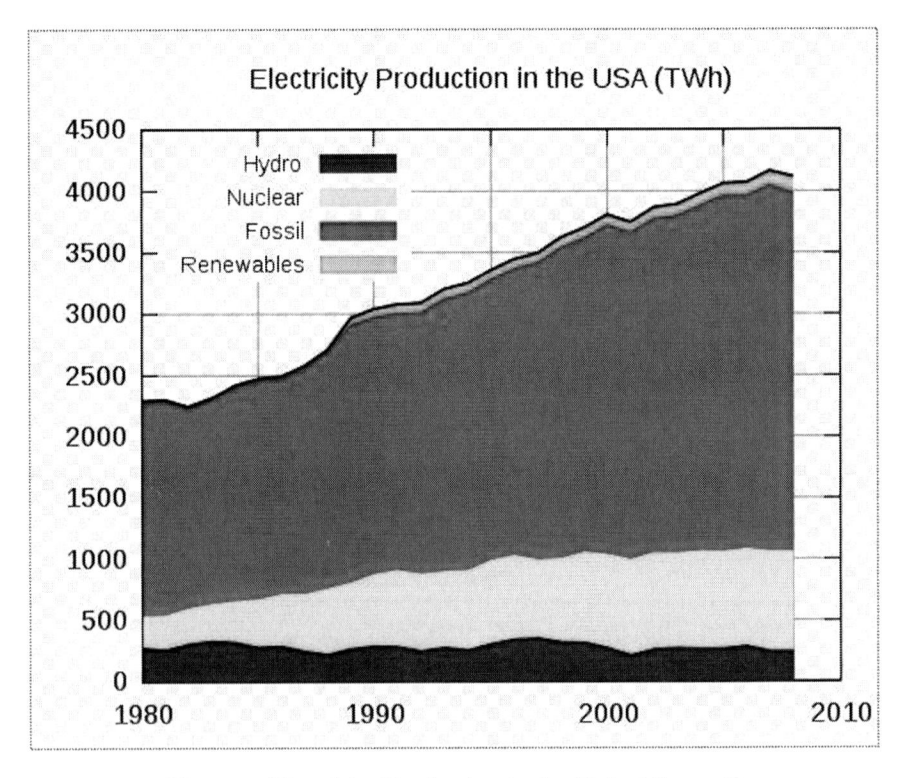

Figure 4: Electricity Production in the United States [2]

(For a more detailed look, view the colorized version of this image within the color section, page 147.)

I simply want to point out that the narrow sliver at the very top includes wind, solar, biofuels, and any other "renewable" source you wish to add to that piece of the pie, combined.

Do you understand the magnitude of the contribution coming from those EPA-designated "hazardous" CO_2-generating fossil fuels?

Do you understand the realistic timeline that will be required to displace that very substantial piece of the pie? If you buy the suggestion that it can happen by 2020, as BO would have you believe…

Do you understand why that piece of the pie has developed to the extent that it has? It's called efficiency and economy. We use that piece of the pie as we do for a very good reason. It fuels the electrical component of our economy better than any alternative that has been available for many decades. It fuels the transportation sector better than any commodity this country has ever seen to date. If there is a viable replacement, outside of the impostors in "renewable energy," please bring it forward immediately. That includes electric cars, first introduced by Henry Ford, who rightly concluded then, as we should now—due to incredible battery limitations—they cannot perform economically.

There are inherent risks involved in producing the raw energy supplies that come from any given component in that diagram.

The environmentalists' "fave" is windfarms. That source will continue to kill thousands of birds and utterly destroy thousands of square miles of landscape to provide incremental, non-baseload, unsustainable power to but a portion of America's power grid.

Enter the Renewable Electricity Standard. This legislation (House Resolution 890, introduced February 12, 2009), would strive to achieve that all electricity generated in this country be supplied by at least 25 percent renewable sources by 2025, a big part of that coming from wind. I strongly disagree. It (wind energy) is extremely costly and will become more so. Study after study, on a global basis, have shown it to be inefficient, very high maintenance, and just a plain bad investment. As reported by the Heritage Foundation's Conn Carroll on October 21, 2010, [3] based on BO's own Energy

Information Agency estimates, here are some numbers to ponder, for projected energy costs per megawatt hour in 2016:

- Conventional Coal Power: $78.10
- Onshore Wind Power: $149.30
- Offshore Wind Power: $191.10
- Thermal Solar Power: $256.60
- Photo-voltaic Solar Power: $396.10

Yet, don't try to tell that to Siemens or General Electric. They do not see the world the same way you and I do. They see the world through massive subsidies and the momentum of the "green" movement. It remains to be seen just how realistically the new Congress will view the fundamental facts of thermodynamics, the core of the energy issue.

By the way, the focus of the Heritage piece was none other than *jobs*, i.e. the jobs that will be lost due to increasing energy prices.

One of the best, most succinct treatises I have seen with respect to wind energy, entitled "Speaking Truth to Wind Power," was compiled by Trebilcock (2009).[4] I highly recommend it to anyone interested in a clearcut, deliberative assessment of this issue.

You don't believe me about the landscape?

See for yourself (below); this is unretouched. It's probably just me, but I do not find this to be the least bit appealing. If I were a California resident paying higher energy costs for the privilege to have this revised landscape, I would be a very unhappy camper. California, let me warn you right now—I have no desire to "bail you out" of your financial mess. You have brought every penny of it on to yourselves, and the other forty-nine states have no business absorbing your propensity for legalizing illegal aliens, NIMBY policies as to hydrocarbon extraction off your coast, NIMBY policies as to nuclear power alternatives, and NIMBY policies as to disallowing viable farming (highly proper water use) in your Great Valley at the expense of a fish.

It's only money, financial wherewithal, prosperity, economic growth, debt reduction/elimination, and yes, freedom.

Photo 2: Windfarms—Palm Springs, (San Gorgonio Pass) CA [5]

(For a more detailed look, view the colorized version of this image within the color section, page 149.)

The subsidy you, as an American citizen, are paying for this sort of assemblage, on a dollar-for-dollar basis, is a mere $23.34 per megawatt hour, as compared to $0.25 for natural gas. Let me help you with the math; that's about a factor of 100 difference, in favor of the windmills, that generally die at night, just when you like lights and television. I can guarantee you that without that very substantial subsidy, wind power would be dead in the water. Period. Please forgive me, but other than for individuals who insist on that form of energy, it needs to die.

Do you care about those subsidies?

Let's see about that.

> "Under my plan of a 'cap and trade' system, electricity rates would necessarily skyrocket…even regardless of what I say about coal is good or bad, because I'm capping greenhouse gases, coal power plants, natural gas…you name it …whatever the plants were, whatever the industry was, they would have to retrofit their operations. That will cost money…they *(energy providers)* will pass that money *(cost)* on to the consumers." *(Emphasis added)*

Many of you know where this quote came from, but for those of you who are unaware, the source is your current commander-in-chief, President Obama, on the occasion of a campaign speech in San Francisco, January 27, 2008. Do you think he has changed his opinion about 'cap and trade'? (We will deal in more detail with "cap and trade" later in this chapter.)

Please pardon me, but I do not like this kind of talk directed at me and 310,000,000 other Americans.

Many of you agreed with this guy on November 2, 2008. In fact, 69.45 million Americans voted for President Obama, as opposed to 59.93 for John McCain.

Some of you were somewhat skeptical in November 2008, but you were not satisfied, and you had some apparent reasons to be dissatisfied. Now you have, or soon will have, if you read ahead, plenty of credible scientific and otherwise related facts, with which to judge our country's energy situation. Henceforth, you will not be uninformed.

Still fewer of you were where I was then, and still am today, very irritated that he could get away with what amounts to fraud and a very misleading indication of where we could or should go as to our energy consumption and sourcing.

Back to then candidate Obama's statement about cap and trade, and electricity.

If he gets his way, this is what you get:

- Skyrocketing costs to refrigerate your food or to have a restaurant do it for you.
- Skyrocketing costs to heat and cool your home or your rental unit or office.
- Skyrocketing costs to use your computer at home or in your office.
- Skyrocketing costs to watch your TV.

- Skyrocketing costs to bake a cake in your oven or for your baker to make that special wedding cake.
- Skyrocketing costs to do your laundry in your home or for the Laundromat to provide that service to you.
- Skyrocketing costs to automate the power grid (so that your electricity usage can be controlled by external monitors) and expand it to meet remote wind farms.
- Skyrocketing costs to transport vegetables form California (if the EPA lets them grow crops) to New Hampshire.
- Skyrocketing costs to create new infrastructure that will replace heretofore low cost, higher efficiency energy delivery systems.

What part of that list makes us in any, way, shape, or form happy about skyrocketing energy costs?

There is a constructive way out of all this. It will be entirely up to us to do what it takes to execute the plan. That includes those of you in California. This plan will be minimally legislative, maximally market driven, exactly as it should be. However, we may have to overturn some already enacted legislation in order to reset the system back where it belongs.

There is an aggressive move afoot to force every American citizen into "energy submission." This is the simplest way I can describe what is materially underway, and there is only one way to stop it:

Demand that policymakers recognize that free markets have always worked and that they always will. Further, that they (policy makers) work for us, and that it is their responsibility to act in accord with our wishes, our preferences, and our desires for a return to the most efficient energy delivery system the world has ever known.

I am sick and tired of the federal government interfering with, intervening where it has no business whatsoever, and generally creating "policy" that is absolutely counterproductive to our long-term energy needs. The private sector has done an incredible job of creating infrastructure, jobs, virtually uninterrupted energy service, and it did it in an environment that was not conducive to any of it. It was not conducive to it because of onerous regulatory bureaucracy, headed by two principal agencies, the United States Department of Energy (DOE), and the incredibly long, obfuscating arm of the EPA.

In mid-October 2010, the EPA pronounced that the ethanol mixture mandate into American vehicles can now reach as high as 15 percent, raised from a previous high of 10 percent, another gigantic victory for the special interests and another huge loss for American citizens. Why am I so critical of this latest move? Two primary reasons: cost and thermodynamics. It will cost you more to power and move your vehicle from point A to point B because ethanol is far less efficient as a fuel, which is thermodynamically defined. I could go a lot further with this, but not right now.

DOE should be materially altered. (You may recall that there was, not that long ago, a move afoot to eliminate DOE entirely.) It is not functioning on behalf of the American people. It is functioning on behalf of itself, and there is a huge difference. The people need energy, delivered in the most efficient manner possible, regardless of source. As you will soon see, "renewables" are certainly not all they are cracked up to be.

Since the inception of the DOE, America's dependence on foreign oil has done nothing but materially increase year after year. Please believe me when I tell you that our dependence would not have been one barrel higher without the DOE. The amount of money that American taxpayers have paid for this largely ineffective agency is a staggering *(number unavailable, due to Obama administration transparency, but I am going to guesstimate no less than $200 billion)* since 1980. The DOE budget for FY 2012 is a staggering $29.5 billion, up 76% in the past decade. It has absolutely nothing to show for it, other than employing today approximately 14,950 American citizens. They need to find their way back to the American mainstream and use their intellectual energy in the competitive marketplace.

As a matter of full disclosure, our firm has been engaged within a larger consortium, managed by the Kansas Geological Survey, in a research project funded by the U.S. Department of Energy. Our firm's role has been to design 3-dimensional seismic imaging support, related to subsurface problems in enhanced oil recovery, and the Survey/DOE further investigation of saline aquifers for potential CO_2 capture and sequestration (CCS). I will refrain from offering an opinion as to CCS feasibility within that project until I see the full measure of the data. In general, I am opposed to the notion of attempting to control the emission of CO_2, regardless of method.

After Jimmy Carter promised to "win the war" against energy dependence, he was ousted in 1980 for good reason, and this country should never, ever revisit any policy that remotely mimics anything he ever introduced, especially his incredulous "Windfall Profits Tax." Please forgive me for having to come out and say this, but the DOE is run by individuals who do not actually know how the energy industry operates or at least how it should and would operate if not obstructed by inappropriate barriers and regulatory mazes that offer virtually zero protection to the consumers in the marketplace.

Instead, the policies, as have been demonstrated by the recent disaster involving the Deepwater Horizon, absolutely circumvent the free market. The result is ineffective controls, which in all probability would have been implemented by industry in the course of competition, to ensure safety and requisite backup and control systems at the Horizon site. Do you actually believe it would be in a company's (shareholder's) interest to *not* be very deliberate in careful execution of a plan to protect and defend that platform?

With the hindsight of numerous published reports, let me be clear that both BP and Transocean each sidestepped what should have been standard practice and operating procedure. BP had a history of cutting way too many corners, and Transocean personnel should have responded much differently, given the downhole indicators they were aware of during certain pressure buildup tests that were conducted prior to the blowout. My point is this: If true market forces were at work in the decades of "policy" that purportedly guided wellsite processes, the competitive market would very likely have served to extinguish the risks that were allowed to be taken, due almost exclusively to U.S. government policy manuals.

If you are reading this and believe that the reams of OSHA, NOAA, EPA and now, of all entities, Department of Homeland Security (DHS), regulations somehow "protect" Americans from disasters such as occurred at the Macondo wellsite, I beg to *strongly disagree*, and I will openly debate you anytime, anyplace to make my points.

Oh, I almost forgot that the Minerals Management Service (MMS), the former federal entity charged with oversight on Gulf of Mexico (GOM) oil and gas drilling activities, has now been replaced (upgraded of course) to the newly created Bureau of Ocean and Energy Management (BOEM). While they officially lifted the Moratorium on deepwater drilling in the GOM on October 12, 2010, the myriad of new, largely unnecessary, and ill-defined procedures required of offshore operators and contractors will effectively and significantly limit the pace of exploration that is necessary to fight the battle of natural reservoir decline across the GOM resource region.

Forget about the New Deal, (especially the "New" New Deal), and forget about Social (In)Security. Instead, get ready to replace Medicare and Medicaid, and especially ObamaCare, with real market, limited-government solutions. George Washington, Thomas Jefferson, and every other Founding Father wanted nothing to do with big government. It was never a part of their plan, and it will never be a part of the plan of patriotic Americans who believe in their republic.

This is no time for weak-kneed, uninformed, non-technical neophytes to be dealing with fundamentally important matters of energy delivery. This is the time for experienced, highly technical expertise to be engaged in the most complex problems of our time. That expertise is available in the private sector; it is not hiding behind the curtain of our government.

The Energy Delivery System we currently utilize in this country could be much better. However, policy decisions running many decades have materially skewed our supply toolset away from what it could and should have been. These policy decisions were made by bureaucrats who simply do not understand the practicalities of what we are dealing with here. I'm sure they have had good intentions, but they do not comprehend reality.

What's worse is that a new genre of energy policy fantasy has now permeated not just the White House but every "green" industrial entrepreneur waiting to reinforce Al Gore, Boone Pickens, George Soros, and President Obama.

Let's move on to some real data, since those folks clearly understand it but choose to skew it so that the average American simply has no defense against their fraud and misrepresentation.

With the help of scholarly gentlemen like Robert Bryce, Michael Economides, and others who actually pay attention to the data and attempt to grasp the fullness of what it portends, we are no longer going to be in the dark. Let there be plenty of light on this crucially important subject.

Given his voluminous and highly technical research, I feel led to summarize various tidbits from his most recent book, *Power Hungry*, where Mr. Bryce provides critical insight on a number of matters relating to energy supply, demand, and policy.

Drawing significantly from Bryce, here are a host of *myths* that you must recognize and work incessantly to dispel. If you are not willing to fight the fight at this level, you may as well put this book away, because you are wasting your time. Go watch CNN, CBS, NBC, or ABC:

Before we move into this subject area, I need to provide advance commentary.

I am personally friends with, acquainted with, or otherwise professionally associated with a number of people who are involved in "green energy," including ethanol, wind, and other "renewable" sources of energy.

One can certainly make the case that the United States' energy product spectrum needs to contain every possible form of energy as we move into an uncertain future. However, I think it very important that we very carefully consider, especially in our energy policy formulations, the ramifications of "mandates" in any energy sector guidelines.

With that pretext, please view the following fact-based considerations relevant to the marketplace of energy ideas today in America.

For the thousands (perhaps millions, by now) of Americans gainfully employed in the "green energy" movement, I encourage you to bear with me as we examine the implications of overemphasizing the perceived "Green Economy" of the future.

I can assure you, the content below is not personal but based entirely on facts.

I have reviewed the content of numerous competing writers who have weighed in on the subject of Climate Change, including one released by Krupp and Horn, entitled "Earth, The Sequel: The Race to Reinvent Energy and Stop global warming."[6] Instead, I lean very heavily on what lies ahead, based on very sound research and real, unequivocal data.

Thirteen Very Costly Myths Surrounding Green Energy
Wind and Solar are "Green"

So, what exactly is "wrong" about the green emphasis on "renewable" energy? If you're a farmer and you want to pump water with a windmill and then take advantage of that substantially intermittent supply of wind to create some watts to light your house during the daytime when the wind is blowing, then knock yourself out. And you can certainly take advantage of "selling" your excess electricity back to the "smart grid." Just don't give up your night supply of electricity so you can continue to read with those high-efficiency but potentially dangerous mini-fluorescent (mercury) GE light bulbs. (Have you built your stockpile of incandescent bulbs for when the EPA wisely reverses itself on its current encouragement of fluorescents?)

Energy density, that's where it's at, if you can find it.

In this country, we have gotten very good at that, better than any country in the world. But that's not good enough for Al Gore, BO, or a whole assemblage of "energy gurus," who actually know virtually nothing about energy, except how to market the least efficient, least dense, and the most expensive energy they can sell you on their new market, known as the Chicago Carbon Exchange (CCX). We will deal with that in more detail later, but for now, let's get on with energy density.

Energy density relates to the amount of energy that can be contained in a given unit of volume, area, or mass. We can also talk about power density, which is the ability to harness power in a given unit of volume, area, or mass. Power (usage) equals energy (usage) per unit of time.

We also need to define a few more units of energy and power:

1 watt (W) = 0.00134 horsepower (hp)

1 kilowatt (kW) = 1,000 watts = 1.34 hp

1 kilowatt-hour (kWh) = 1,000 watts delivered for 1 hour

1 megawatt (MW) = 1,000 kilowatts = 1 million watts

1 gigawatt (GW) = 1,000 megawatts = 1 billion watts

1 terawatt (TW) = 1,000 gigawatts = 1 trillion watts

1 ton of oil = 7.33 barrels (bbls) of oil

1 bbl of oil = 42 gallons

1 bbl of oil equivalent = 1.64 megawatt-hours (MWh) of electricity

1 bbl of oil equivalent = 5,487 cubic feet of natural gas [7]

So let's rank various energy sources to see where they fall with respect to energy density/deliverability:

Fuel Sources Ranked According to Energy Density and Deliverability

Fuel Source	Horsepower Per acre	Watts per square meter	Area (sq miles) to produce 2700 Megawatts
Nuclear	300.0	56.0	18.8
Oil well*	289.0	53.5	19.6
Natural gas well*	287.5	53.0	19.8
Solar#	36.0	6.7	156.0
Wind#	6.4	1.2	896.0
Biomass#	2.1	0.4	2606.0
Corn Ethanol#	0.25	0.05	21,267.0

Table 2: Fuel Sources ranked according to energy density and deliverability

Source: Calculations for energy densities of "renewable" sources from Jesse Ausubel, "The Future Environment for the Energy Business", *APPEA Journal* (2007), http://phe.rockefeller.edu/docs/ausubelappea.pdf. Other sources include Energy Information Administration. (after Bryce, 2010)

Renewable energy sources. Solar and wind are intermittent, requiring significant redundant backup systems. *They are absolutely incapable of delivering reliable base load electricity.*

* Assumes wellsite area of 2 acres, average production for gas well = 115,000 cubic feet per day (MCFD), and average oil well producing about 19 barrels per day (BOPD).

Note that data relating to corn ethanol is not included in the graph (Figure 5). The energy density for corn-based ethanol is so low that it is virtually indetectable, and the area required (21,267 square miles) would require a graphic scale about seven times that shown here if the vertical scale were held constant.

Power Density Comparisons of Various Fuels

(Chart showing Nuclear, Natural gas well, Wind with bars for Horsepower per acre, Watts per square meter, and Area (sq mi) to produce 2700 Megawatts)

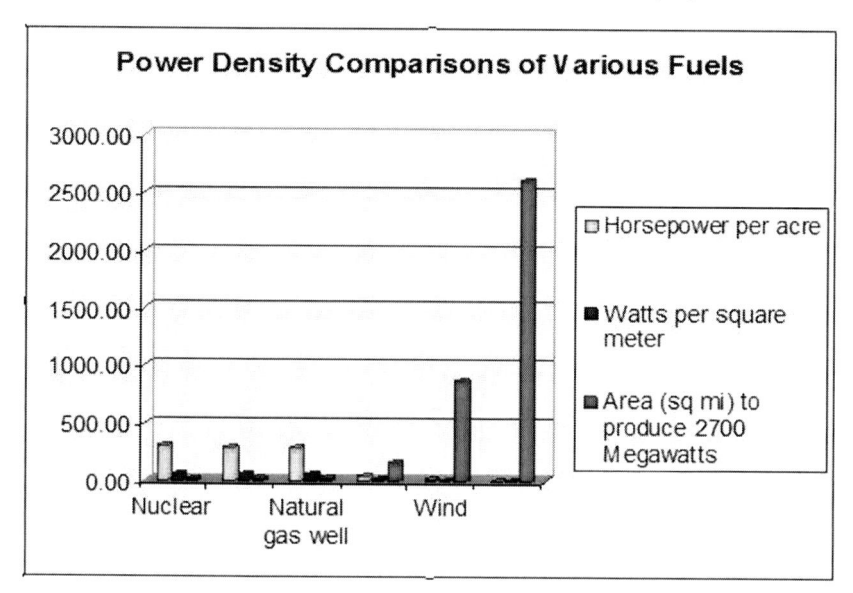

Figure 5: Power Density Comparisons
Please Refer to the Table for Additional Information
(For a more detailed look, view the colorized version
of this image within the color section, page 147.)

Exactly how much land in this country do we wish to dedicate to corn ethanol production? Ethanol is damaging to all but the most recently designed internal combustion automobile engines. Further, *ethanol production is a net energy consuming* enterprise, given the energy required to grow, tend, and harvest the crop, and then the refinery processes to produce it. In addition to that, the water resources that are consumed in the irrigation and refinement of the product are very significant. A study conducted by Argonne National laboratory on the use of all biofuels, released in 2009, yields the following result:

> "…Water consumption for biofuels production is projected to increase by 19 billion gallons per day (bgd), or by 2.5 times, between 2005 and 2030. Most of this increase is for the production of corn-based ethanol, which is projected to increase by nearly 13 bgd and *accounts for roughly 60 percent of the total projected nationwide increase in water consumption over the projection*

period. It is more than double the amount of water projected to be consumed for industrial and commercial use in 2030 by the entire United States."[8]

Corn ethanol is a bad, bad deal for America.

What's worse is that existing federal mandates have placed onerous demands on the country's already dwindling and significantly overregulated refinery industry, such that even though it makes very little to no economic sense to bring ethanol mixing into play at all, they are likely going to be required to increase their already mandated input of ethanol and thus generate more demand for corn ethanol.

We can change this picture.

We must change this picture.

I know you "Iowans", and you "Nebraskans" do not want to hear this, but you will do the country (and the rest of the developing world) a big favor by producing your corn and selling it to the global agriculture industry, as opposed to the ethanol industry.

Subsidizing this industry is fundamentally irresponsible, on many levels. One of the early research papers I reviewed came from a 2001 Cornell University study, which delivered a direct and comprehensive evaluation of the facts surrounding ethanol. Here is a glimpse at findings in that study: "It takes more energy to make ethanol from grain than the combustion of ethanol produces."

At a time when ethanol-gasoline mixtures (gasohol) were touted as the American answer to fossil fuel shortages by corn producers, food processors, and some lawmakers, Cornell's David Pimentel took a longer-range view.

> Abusing our precious croplands to grow corn for an energy-inefficient process that yields low-grade automobile fuel amounts to unsustainable, subsidized food burning," says the Cornell professor in the College of Agriculture and Life Sciences.[9]

To summarize, solar and especially wind and corn ethanol are not in any sense of the word "green" but rather raise real "red flags" as to any meaningful, broad-based contribution to our national power needs. If certain of you citizens want to plant your $1.25 million windmill, go right ahead, be my guest. If certain of you citizens want to install leaky, high-maintenance solar panels on your roof, go for it, but please *do not* ask me to pay for half of it; I will fight you on that proposal. We have better options that are time tested and which have absolutely no justification for being replaced, fossil fuels. We haven't even talked materially about coal as of yet. We will, now.

Wind power reduces CO_2 emissions— (ABSOLUTELY NOT)

And I'm guessing you (in the wind industry) thought that if you simply built those horrific monstrosities that are now dividing the California landscape, that we would come. No way. In case you haven't noticed, the migration out of California (by legal U.S. citizens) to places like Nevada, Colorado, and the like, has been significant. Though, I would say this—that it appears that the native folks in those states are not actually all that pleased that you are bringing your high-priced real estate mentality to these neighborhoods. We'll have to wait and see how this plays out, now that Barney Frank and Christopher Dodd have "restructured" Freddie Mac and Fannie Mae (*not*).

I am so grateful for their dedication to "protecting" me from those evildoers on Wall Street and the banks they so carefully regulated before the residential real estate meltdown they themselves propagated through their "creative legislation." Mr. Dodd, apparently you saw the writing on the wall and decided to get out while you could still take down a very healthy pension and then embark on a new career as one of America's top lobbyists. Those federal pensions you had a hand in designing are just incredible!

Let's get back to that enviable wind power. It is so green that I just don't understand why they paint all those blades and turbines white. I'm guessing they want to match the color of the clouds.

The U.S. government has now committed billions of your and my hard-earned tax dollars to subsidize one of the most unreliable, inefficient, and lowest energy density sources known to mankind. If we do not take action *now* to curtail the actions of Congress, it will get much worse. On a global basis, the numbers are now headed for the trillions of dollars. And you can count on the U.S. taxpayer subsidizing multiple countries that are cooperative with the green movement.

Reducing CO_2 emissions? Just exactly how will President Obama, Al Gore, and the U.S. Congress accomplish this feat? They won't. It's been tried and tested in other markets, especially Western Europe. Here's why, in one word—Redundancy. Due to the fact that wind supply is extremely intermittent, it is rated to deliver at most about 30 percent of the time, with many areas actually only capable of deliverability 10 percent of the time. So, the reality is that *if* you, or your municipality, is foolish enough to buy into the "green" mantra of wind, you or your municipality will also have to construct either a natural gas-fired base load facility, or, God forbid, a coal-based plant that just might be a better fit for your local structure.

You think a natural gas plant is emissions-free? Of course it's not. I'm certain you have seen the pictures of smokestacks associated with coal plants. Guess what you are not seeing coming out of those stacks? You are not "seeing" CO_2 because, you see, CO_2 is *colorless, odorless, tasteless,* and for the most part virtually *harmless* at concentrations emitted from those facilities.

Here are some real numbers to place in your back pocket when you are actually able to speak with some authority on campus, in the coffee shop, on the street in a discussion, or perhaps with diehard family members who simply cannot fathom that CO_2 is *not* harmful to their well-being.

The current average global concentration of CO_2 in earth's lower atmosphere is approximately 390 parts per million (ppm), as measured at Mauna Loa [10]

That's equivalent to 0.0039 percent of earth's atmosphere. You breathe it in and out all day long. Plants love the stuff, especially at concentrations much, much greater than current average atmospheric. Ask any greenhouse manager about that dangerous CO_2, that the EPA has now classified as an "endangering," gotta-be-controlled substance.

For those of you who wish to refer me or the reader to the "Global Wind Energy Council," which has declared that "a reduction in the levels of carbon dioxide being emitted into the global atmosphere is the most important environmental benefit from wind power generation," I will simply have to inform you that their famed report entitled "Global Wind Energy Outlook 2008" patently ignored the concept of "redundancy."

We will revisit CO_2 in greater detail in a later chapter, but for now, let's take a look another "big picture" related to energy use:

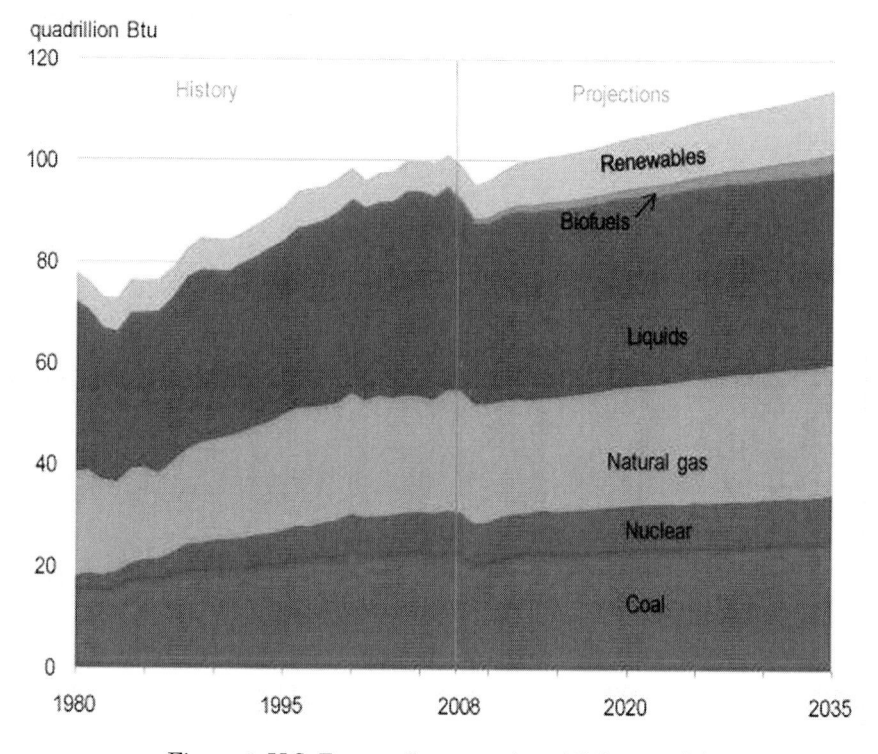

Figure 6: U.S. Energy Consumption-All Sources [11]

(For a more detailed look, view the colorized version of this image within the color section, page 150.)

By our own government's projections, the contribution of fossil fuels to our total primary fuel consumption will continue to gradually increase from today to 2035 (and beyond). Contributions from renewables are projected to double, but where is the supposed reduction on CO_2 from fossil fuels, due to wind power? *There will be none.*

This model projects an overall increase of energy consumption of 0.5 percent per year from 2010-2035. I think they've hit the low side on that estimate.

I would not count on U.S. energy consumption materially declining anytime soon. However, if the current administration succeeds in its attempt to "fundamentally transform" this country into something no one recognizes, then energy consumption in this country will absolutely decline, right along with our standard of living, manufacturing, jobs, and everything else that has made this country great. Count on it. Then thank Saul Alinsky, who will have succeeded tremendously in his training of the ultimate community organizer.

Denmark Provides an Energy Model for the U.S.

Niels Gram of the Danish Federation of Industries says *"...windmills are a mistake and economically make no sense."* Aase Madsen, the Chair of Energy Policy in the Danish Parliament calls it *"a terribly expensive disaster."* [12]

The Danes, for that matter virtually all of Western Europe, bought into wind energy hook, line, and sinker. (So has Texas, much to the chagrin of the residents of Austin, who are seeing firsthand the costs associated with wind power to the tune of many billions of dollars, so far). I think I see some signs of it letting up in Western Europe. And, by the way, they have yet to decommission a single coal-fired electricity facility, understanding all too well just how precious lights at night can actually be.

President Obama wants the U.S. to look a lot more like Denmark:

> "Today, America produces less than 3 percent of our electricity through renewable sources like wind and solar—less than 3 percent. Now, in comparison, Denmark produces almost 20 percent of their electricity through wind power. We pioneered solar technology, but we've fallen behind countries like Germany and Japan in generating it, even though we've got more sun than either country…' [13]
>
> BO, *Earth Day Speech, April 22, 2009, delivered at the Trinity Structural Towers (wind) manufacturing plant, Newton, Iowa.*

I don't think we should be followers of any of the above-mentioned countries as to energy matters either, but I sure don't want to lead the world down the path of the some of the costliest energy the world has ever known. Not me, not for an instant longer than it will take to halt this current frenzy to "green," wind-based energy.

The Danes have pumped massive subsidies into their wind infrastructure, and here is what it has brought them:

According to the International Energy Agency (IEA), Key Energy Statistics, 2008, residential customers in Denmark paid an average of $0.38 per kilowatt-hour. We, in the United States, paid about $.10 per KWh. Can you imagine a fourfold (400 percent) increase in your electricity bill just so you can become as "green" as Denmark? Well, that's exactly the path BO wants to take you down. Denmark does not import a drop of oil, due to the fact that they have invested heavily in offshore drilling in the North Sea, and it has paid off. Yet, according to EIA statistics, they continue to import about the same amount of coal as they did back in 1981, well in advance of their wind energy boom.

In spite of the fact that they are net exporters of oil, they still obtain about 51 percent of their primary fuel supply from crude oil (the U.S. is at about 40 percent).

Bryce provides data to support the claim those hydrocarbons overall provide the Danes with forty-eight times the energy they receive from wind. That ratio is very unlikely to change anytime soon. Further, due to the subsidization of their wind energy, and I'm sure a whole host of other "user-friendly taxes," the Danes managed to pay about $5.83 per gallon for gasoline during 2008, while the U.S. consumer paid about $2.12 per gallon.

If BO has his way, look for us to get a lot closer to the Danish number for a gallon of gasoline. Trust me; it does *not* have to happen. If you and I have anything to do with it, it *will not* happen.

Here's something to ponder, as cited by Bryce, coming from the Danish Center for Political Studies (CEPOS), a Copenhagen-based think tank, in 2009:

> The Danish experience also suggests that a strong U.S. wind expansion would not benefit the overall economy. It would entail substantial costs to consumer and industry, and only to a lesser degree benefit a small part of the economy, namely wind turbine owners, wind shareholders and those employed in the sector."
>
> [14] Bryce, page 114

For me, that's enough about Denmark for a while. I wish them luck, but I will tell you that under the energy plan I would prefer to see developed (later in this chapter), they would not get one dollar from the United States to support their wind dreams.

I almost forgot another very important element related to wind energy. Wind proponents are going to wish I had forgotten this, regarding the absolute "safety" of those 300- to 400-foot wind turbine towers. Those turbines have transmissions within them to attempt to regulate the sometimes overpowering force generated by Mother Nature's wind. People have now begun to find out about this, as of yet, unsolved problem. Research is desperately underway to resolve this very significant issue. But until that solution comes around, here is what has happened in far too many cases around the world:

Photo 3: Wind generator fire [15]
(For a more detailed look, view the colorized version
of this image within the color section, page 148.)

As a final matter of reference with respect to the risks and dangers associated with wind turbines, please take a look at the following forty-second video clip, demonstrating the failure of a turbine that could not control the intense energy generated when wind speed exceeded the limits of this particular system:[16]

To say the least, you do not want to be anywhere close to these monstrous facilities when the wind is up.

T. Boone Pickens' Plan will save us all (NOT)

Since his days as a corporate raider at Mesa Petroleum, I have had very little respect for Mr. Pickens. Yes, he knows how to make a buck. But that is far from the only game in town. I care a whole lot about people and wonder if he actually does, excepting those few in the uppermost echelon in government, in world politics and those in the upper, upper echelons of the energy business.

I can say this about his plan, without any hesitation: It is illogical.

He wants to greatly expand the wind-power grid for America, (and, of course, he has invested other people's money (OPM) heavily in this enterprise), in spite of what was just developed on point three above regarding actual experience in a live environment (i.e., not a model). He then wants to take all that natural gas that "won't be needed for electricity generation" (forget about redundancy requirements), and convert the U.S. automotive fleet to natural gas. This will, of course, relate well to those semitrailers traversing the Rocky Mountains each and every day, who transport those California fruits and vegetables to the rest of America, which just loves that stuff. I'm just picking that one example for starters. I do not wish to imply that natural gas cannot make a meaningful contribution to the transportation sector; I simply see it as a long way into the future before it becomes anywhere close to viable.

The plot only gets better when you include General Electric (GE), that stalwart receiver of billions from President Obama and additional bailouts and subsidies for that wonder-wind energy that you and I are now subsidizing. Jeffrey Immelt really appreciated that bonus he got last year for making GE tons of money, largely through your assistance.

In May 2008, Pickens ordered $2 billion worth of wind turbines from GE.

In July 2008, he began selling his Pickens plan, which has been a flop.

Since that moment, both he and GE have had a tough run. While GE stock has recovered to about $20 per share from its low of about $8 in February 2009 (as compared to its 5-year high of over $41 in September 2007), the road ahead for GE is anything but certain.

Wind Power Reduces the Need for Natural Gas (NOT)

We have already touched on this preliminarily, back in that Danish discussion, but this matter has wheels to it.

In fact, the exact opposite is true—if you increase the installation of wind-based power plants, you must also install natural gas-fired power (or, alternately coal-fired) to support the redundancy required for base load. There is no way around that reality, and T. Boone Pickens and Jeffrey Immelt both know it, but you will not hear about it from them.

I happen to live in Kansas, right next door to my "green" friends in Colorado, who are in for a rude awakening, not too unlike that experienced in Denmark, nor that experienced recently in Austin, Texas. Their electricity rates are about to skyrocket, consistent with President Obama's wishes, due solely to their newfound commitment to wind energy. In Colorado, they voted in 2004 to mandate that at least 10 percent of their electricity be sourced in renewable (wind) energy.

In fact, they liked the idea so much (without testing the price reality), that their legislature has now mandated that by 2020 they achieve a 20 percent average input from renewable energy. One of their primary grid providers is Xcel Energy, a natural gas and electricity provider operating in eight states. An internal review regarding their Colorado assets resulted in the fact that it expects "the costs of integration to be predominantly fuel costs resulting from 1) the inefficiency of generation due to wind generation uncertainty, and 2) the cost of additional gas storage."

We in Kansas have our share of trouble on the horizon. The Kansas Corporation Commission has approved regulations that will mandate that utilities operating in Kansas will have to deliver 15 percent of their power from renewables by 2016 and 20 percent by 2020. The regulations took effect in November 2010, fulfilling the law passed by the 2009 Kansas legislature, all in the name of a deal cut between then-Governor Mark Parkinson and Sunflower Electric Power, who plans to build an expansion unit in its Holcomb, Kans. power plant. [17]

The utility rightly anticipates the extremely cyclic nature of the wind source and therefore recognizes that it will not only have to bring gas generation into play, but they will also have to create gas-storage facilities close to the gas-fired generators in order to maintain proper pipeline operating pressure for the feedstock. Natural gas storage facilities are not easy to construct and have significant geological parameters that must be met simply to operate.

It is never easy, and it is never cheap.

The final point that needs to be made about these mandatory renewable requirements relates to our old friend, coal. If mandatory requirements come into play, for example in West Virginia, Indiana, and Wyoming, our top three states for coal-fired electricity generation (also the least expensive in the country), guess what they will have to build to support their "green" wind farms? More natural gas plants, more redundancy, more expensive…

Going Green Will Reduce Imports of Strategic Commodities and Increase jobs (NOT)

This is really getting good, redundancy, inefficiency, and "skyrocketing costs."

Unfortunately, that's only the beginning. We have some other very significant, strategic reasons to avoid overly aggressive commitment to this new, green, clean energy. One of the biggest ones is China. Yes, that same China that now holds more U.S. debt than any country on the face of the earth. Unfortunately for us, they are also sitting on top of some of the most important, strategic minerals in the world, with respect to wind farms, solar fuel installations, and electric cars with those unique batteries and other components. [18]

The only thing I can say with absolute certainty about "green" energy is that it has not been in any way, shape, or form well thought out.

Aside from the ignored redundancy expenses elucidated above, the total lack of emissions reduction related to changeover from coal-to-wind or gas-to-wind, the problem related to our lack of certain strategic materials may eventually overwhelm everything else. Let me give you another translation for strategic: *hard to get and very expensive if held in the hands of unfriendly stewards.* That's exactly where virtually all of them are.

Ever heard of neodymium? How about praseodymium? Lanthanides? That's primarily what we are talking about, the "rare earth" elements. China sits on the most abundant supply of this group of elements in the world. Some would suggest an "endless" supply, like the U.S. and coal. Only their "endless" is a whole lot more "endless" than ours.

Neodymium-iron-boron magnets supply a major component in the Toyota Prius engine. To quote Bryce,

> "Analysts have called the Prius one of the most rare-earth intensive consumer products ever made, with each Prius containing about 1 kilogram (2.2 pounds) of neodymium and about 10 kilograms (22 pounds) of lanthanum. And, it's not just the Prius. Other hybrids, such as the Honda Insight and the Ford Fusion, also require significant quantities of those elements…The American wind sector is almost wholly dependent on neodymium-iron-boron magnets, which are used inside wind turbines."
>
> Bryce, page 134

It's not just lanthanide elements that are crucial to "green" energy. Ask First Solar about "tellurium," one of the elements in the compound known as cadmium telluride. Without it, their solar cell manufacturing business would be materially compromised. While tellurium is produced as a byproduct of copper mining/refining and their supply needs are being met today, *the world's only currently active tellurium mine is located in China.*

Suffice it to say that we have significant strategic materials limitations in virtually every corner of the "green" domain. The fundamental difference between these strategic materials and the "oily" ones we are used to is that the crude oil market is globally diffused and likely to stay that way for about as far as the eye can see, while the "green" materials supply is highly concentrated.

To finish this segment with another quote from Bryce:

> Consider a deal that the City of Austin's municipal utility, Austin Energy, made in 2009: The utility agreed to build a solar farm that will use 220,000 solar panels. *All of them will be made in China.* Or consider wind turbines: In late 2009, the backers of a $1.5 billion wind project in West Texas announced that they were planning to install 240 wind turbines on the 36,000 acre site (150 acres per turbine). The project backers were seeking $450 million in federal stimulus money to make the deal happen. *All of the wind turbines for the project are to be built in China.* (Emphasis added)
>
> Bryce, page 137

The United States Lags in Energy Efficiency (DOES NOT)

Once again, we need to straighten out the facts, right here and right now. The United States of America is easily one of the most efficient energy delivering and consuming countries on the face of the earth, bar none. If you have evidence to the contrary, then bring it forward. I would be very happy to review it with you.

These are the facts, as obtained from the U.S. Energy Information Agency (EIA):

From 1980 to 2006, the U.S. decreased its "energy intensity" by 42 percent. (Energy intensity is defined as "Total Energy Consumption per Dollar of Gross Domestic Product"). Only one country beat that mark: China, at 63 percent. China? Their improvement involved major equipment upgrades across their entire spectrum of energy delivery and consumption. Give credit to the U.K., which matched us over this same period. Also, from 1980 to 2006, The U.S. per capita energy use *decreased* by 2.5 percent. The only countries that fared better were Switzerland and Denmark, which registered 4.3 and 4.2 percent, respectively. That does not mean that the U.S. used less energy per capita; we did not. We used 334.6 million Btu per capita in 2006, compared to a world average of 72.4 million Btu. [19]

The facts speak loudly and clearly that as the U.S. matures, its per capita energy use, the best metric available, will likely continue to decline as we increase overall efficiency. That's what happens in a competitive marketplace. Free markets work; communism does not.

The U.S. Can Cut CO_2 Emissions by 80 percent by 2050, and Carbon Capture and Sequestration (CCS) Can Help Achieve that Goal
(NOT)

What an unbelievable mandate. It actually does not meet the standards of a suggestion, let alone a mandate.

Here is the reality:

The probability of the U.S. backing up (receding) to a level of CO_2 equivalent to 80 percent of that prevailing in our atmosphere in 2005, by 2050, due to mankind's influence, is approximately equal to the U.S. landing a breathing human being on the surface of the sun.

Mankind does not have any material effect on the production of CO_2 entering earth's atmosphere.

If the trend of the past hundred years continues (and there is no certain evidence that it will), earth's CO_2 concentration will probably be somewhere around 470 ppm by the year 2050, with or without any intervention whatsoever on the part of mankind. [20]

This estimate is based on real data, not the modeled contrivances of the infamous Intergovernmental Panel on Climate Change that should, frankly, be dismantled. I make that statement based on the obvious, that the true science that *could and should* have taken place under its purview to study earth's complex and intricate atmosphere, was clearly displaced by heavy political hands. These hands are so dirty and contaminated that it will be virtually impossible to consider any of their conclusions on a foregoing basis.

I know people who are on the inside of the IPCC, and I can assure you that I am not in the least "bloviating" with respect to the political machinery, chicanery, and all else that goes on behind closed doors as they prepare their periodic "reports" to the world. They have some very good scientists participating in real research. Unfortunately, the results of real research conducted by some top-level scientists does not support most of the claims that IPCC reviewers would want the world to see, and therefore, their opinions do not make it out of the cutting room floor. That is really bad news, and it will affect real human lives, most of them outside the USA.

Why will it be impossible to cut emissions by 80 percent by 2050?

Let me be very straightforward about this question. It will be impossible for that to happen in this country because we choose to prosper. With prosperity comes demand on energy systems. As was clearly pointed out at the beginning of this chapter, the vast majority of the electricity we consume will be derived from fossil fuels. It will take decades to transition away from that picture, if we, in fact, do it at all. The wisest path to reducing fossil fuel-based electricity would be to significantly expand our nuclear energy base. On the other hand, the least efficient, most costly, and the least worthy of our capital input into energy systems would be that of "renewables."

Due to this propensity for prosperity and the fact that we will continue to drive primarily gasoline-powered motorcars, we will continue to emit CO_2. So what?

But did you know that with our prosperity of the past couple of decades, our country's carbon emissions have virtually flattened at around 7 billion tons per year? The indications are that we in the United States will remain flat in spite of the fact that our population is slightly increasing because we are becoming yet more efficient with our advancing technology. I do not see this country taking steps backwards as pertains to our prosperity, our technological advancement, or whatever else provides us with those comforts we have come to enjoy. There are, however, plentiful forces at work who believe that this is exactly what should happen, if for no other reason than to reduce our "carbon footprint." I very, very, very strongly disagree with anyone in that camp. We are not the primary culprit driving up the emission of CO_2. The data on that point is very clear, and here it is:

> Members of the Organization for Economic Development (OECD), at last count 30 countries, have also flattened their trend related to carbon emissions. Those countries primarily reside in North America, Western Europe, Australia and Japan. Everybody else on the face of the earth is in the Non-OECD group, and that is where the real action in carbon emissions is heating up—big time. In 2008, carbon emissions for the Non-OECD countries surpassed those of the OECD, and by 2030 they are projected to be double the OECD, totaling approximately 26 billion tons per year. The rate of growth for the Non-OECD from 2000-2030 is projected to be 160 percent, while that for the OECD is projected to be about 6 percent. [21]

Here is what the data is projected to look like out to 2035, according to our DOE/EIA, as of May 2010.

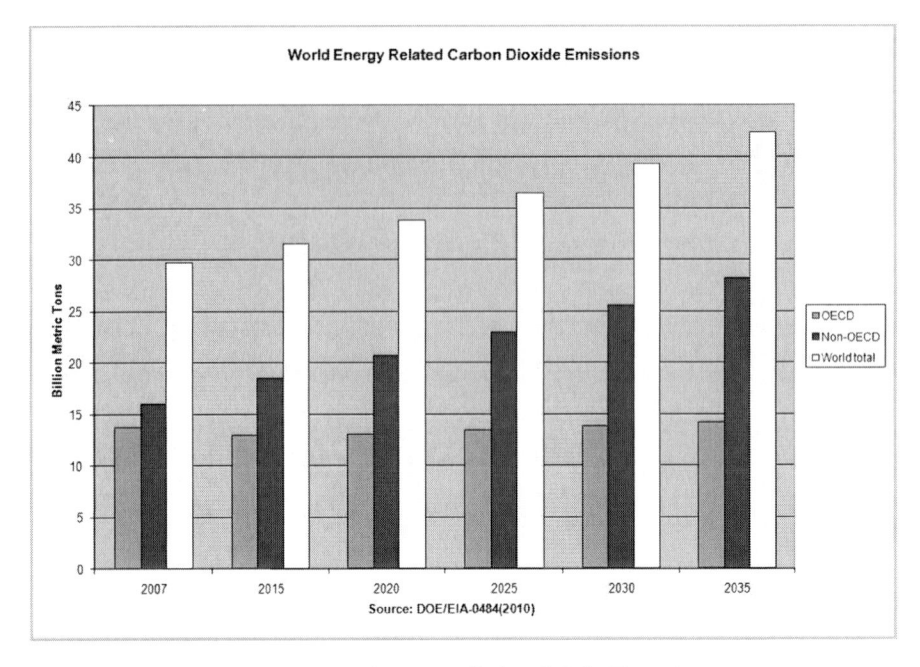

Figure 7: World Energy Related CO_2 Emissions

Carbon emissions will not stay where they are emitted. Guess where they are going to go? Everywhere. Who's going to stop them from migrating wherever the winds will blow them? Nobody: not the IPCC, not NOAA, not the EU...especially not the EPA.

So, even if we were able, through some miraculous, magical, ingenious devices capable of mitigating our emissions in the USA, just exactly where will it get us against the likes of China, India, Russia, and the Middle East? We will be absorbing as much of the non-OECDs, and the remainder of the OECD's carbon as is humanly possible. That's where it will get us.

Carbon capture and sequestration (CCS)...For those of you unfamiliar with the terminology, it relates to the injection of CO_2 into a subsurface rock system that will supposedly contain it ad infinitum, so that some purportedly significant amount of CO_2 can be taken out of the atmosphere.

The saline (salt water) aquifers that are now the subject of research to test whether subsurface injection will "permanently" seal injected CO_2 are substantially loaded with fractures, nearly all of which are connected in some ultimate path to the surface.

If that technology continues to draw capital away from real problem-solving issues in this country, it will simply extend the economic pain we are about to experience, due to the already scheduled environmental "protection" that Al Gore, Henry Waxman, Barbara Boxer, John Kerry, and the like want to wish on the American people.

Don't forget; they know what's best for each and every one of us energy-consuming, taxpaying, carbon emitting, citizen-slaves. As they have been desiring for so long, they now have it where *we* are working for *them*. They have finally arrived.

Taxing CO_2 (aka 'Cap and trade') Will Work (ABSOLUTELY NOT)

Notwithstanding the 2010 elections and the decreased probability of moving this legislation forward, I remain very uncomfortable about where it stands at this moment. When it is actually killed, I will rest my case. At this moment, I consider it live.

But I do need to admit a mistake in the title for this subchapter. Taxing the American people, American industry, and any moving thing, including cattle, for emitting CO_2 will work—for all those dutiful employees of the U.S. government who now find themselves in dire need of cash. If they get what they want—and again, I will commit to you that I will dedicate myself to seeing that they don't—*you* will be taxed like you never knew you could. Oh, I know "they" who know what's best for you have told you that Big Oil, Bad Coal, those Bad, Bad Trucks and Trains, and the like, will be paying through the nose for their carbon footprint, and if you are good little citizens, you will be exempt.

There is a big problem with their suggestions. *We* will pay for the increased cost of energy associated with all those bad emissions that those entities will be consuming and paying a lot more for, just so they can obtain those prized carbon credits. And don't forget those mandates associated with wind power.

Given that my entire career has been spent in both the energy and environmental industries, I am utterly amazed that the "technical experts" on what I will loosely term the "wrong side" of the carbon issue have somehow allowed themselves to become mesmerized by outright fraud. Alas, I believe the day may be coming in the not too distant future where Al Gore may, in fact, get to have "his day in court." I simply want to remind him and his devotees that in the long run, the truth will win out.

What does "cap and trade" really boil down to? It simply provides the U.S. government the authority to effectively tax all energy by defining first a "cap" related to some arbitrary amount of carbon dioxide emitted by any given entity. If the entity produces (emits) more CO_2 than it is calculated to be allowed, then it can "trade" from another entity credits for the CO_2, which that entity did not produce in the normal course of its activity.

The proposed scheme dealing with emissions caps would be placed on electric utilities, oil refineries, natural gas producers, iron and steel industries, and cement and paper industries, to name but a few.

Emission caps would begin at a reduction of 3 percent compared to 2005 levels by 2010, 17 percent by 2020, 42 percent by 2030 and 83 percent by 2050.

Approximately 15 percent of the emission (pollution) permits would be auctioned by the federal government in the initial years, gradually increasing over time. The revenue raised from these auctions would be "distributed" back to consumers through a combination of refundable tax credits and some sort of benefit payment schedule to offset the impact to low-and middle-income wage earners. (I have no idea how they can or will manage that chain of transactions, and I doubt they do, either.)

But there are other places these auction receipts will go:

- Prevention of international deforestation
- Helping the U.S. adapt to the negative effects of Climate Change
- Helping other nations adapt to the negative effects of Climate Change
- International clean-technology deployment

Regulated companies would be "allowed" to purchase carbon offsets to meet a portion of their emissions overruns. They could fund "clean" energy ventures to substitute for emissions they cannot reduce on their own account.

New coal-fired power plants will be subject to intense emission performance standards, making CCS mandatory.

According to the non-partisan Congressional Budget Office (CBO), here are the projections related to the auctions:

> "...enacting the legislation would increase revenues by $873 billion over the 2010-2019 period and would increase direct spending by $864 billion over that 10-year period. In total, CBO and JCT estimate that enacting the legislation would reduce future budget deficits by about $4 billion over the 2010-2014 period and by about $9 billion over the 2010-2019 period..."

So, there you have it, a virtually revenue neutral bill. If I didn't know better, I would have thought that Barney Frank and Christopher Dodd had thought this up. In reality, they were down the hall fashioning up the real handling of the money.

Thankfully, the US Congress began to come to its senses and the US Senate did not allow cap & Trade legislation to advance as had been the hope of Al Gore, Barack Obama, General Electric, Duke Energy, T. Boone Pickens and a host of other individuals and entities worldwide. Trading at the CCX would have been so profitable for a few insiders and so painful for the bulk of Americans who would have seen their energy costs drift steadily upward to match the capital being drawn into the trading machine. The general public would scarcely have noticed, exactly as planned by the 'traders'.

Auctions would have commenced in 2012, with a starting price for a "credit" of $10 per ton, rising at 5 percent per year, plus inflation, in subsequent years. Talk about a manipulated market.

The interesting thing is how and where they intended to move all that money. The how would have been through the hands of "traders," who would have made a commission on the sales of "air," through an auction process.

The answer to the question of where would have been an entity that was already constructed and active, known as the Chicago Climate Exchange (CCX).

See more about it below. However, before we get there, the answer to the second question is that these "trades" will directly induce a significant cost increase related to energy consumption, increasing through time. The government-defined thresholds allowable for any given entity will be materially reduced in time, making it more and more difficult and expensive to produce their product. The government's fundamental goal *is* to drive carbon-related energy prices ever higher, with the goal of eventually quashing the production of what have been historically the cheapest fuels known to mankind. They just don't happen to be "green" enough.

However, the market changed materially on November 11, 2010. That's when an announcement came forth indicating that at the end of 2010, the CCX would be shutting down. [22] As it turns out, the CCX had been acquired by an Atlanta entity known as the Intercontinental Exchange. They also bought the Chicago Climate Futures Exchange and the European Climate Exchange for the sum of about $634.5 million in April 2010. Although it is in effect defunct as of this writing, I submit we need to have a brief discussion about the CCX. After all, that was one of the primary drivers behind the urgent need to get this monstrosity of cap and trade passed in the Senate (now termed "Energy for a Clean America" or some such misnomer).

The European Climate Exchange continues to arrange for the buying and selling of air, and I only wonder if that part of the world will recognize the futility of that activity. Fat chance. The article that cited the shutdown of CCX implied that regional exchanges in the U.S. may continue to operate. In the eastern U.S., that would be the Regional Greenhouse Gas Initiative (RGGI); in the West, we have the Western Climate Initiative. My advice—find something else to do with your time and money. (As this book goes to press, it has just been announced that the New Hampshire House of Representatives has just passed a measure to halt that state's participation in the RGGI, by a vote of 246-104. However, two republican state senators co-sponsored the original bill, bringing New Hampshire into the RPPI, so the final outcome is not certain.)

While it has been dismantled, it is worth noting that the primary players are busily engaged worldwide to make another pass at 'managing' emissions.

CCX was also intricately linked to Climate Exchange PLC, the European Climate Exchange, and Mr. Richard Sandor. While membership and participation in the exchange was voluntary, please note that it was "legally binding" in its activities. Not surprising, since real money is involved.

Let's not forget how this really got started. The Joyce Foundation, who had a Board Member named Barack Obama, funded the Tides Foundation, led by none other than that Hungarian-Communist turned Socialist–American George Soros, which provided the first real capital, something in excess of $1 million, to seed it's growth. Then we have London-based Generation Investment Management, which had become the 5th largest owner of CCX. Generation was founded in 2004 by none other than Al Gore himself, along with partner David Blood. Generation's self-stated vision is to "embed sustainability into the mainstream capital markets…" With offices in London, New York and Sydney, they certainly cover a lot of ground.

But, that's not all, not by any means. Let's not forget about Peter Harris and Mark Ferguson, Goldman Sachs employees, who have been appointed to serve as members of a newly proposed (February 2010) Obama agency to be known as "Climate Service." The group will operate in tandem with NOAA's National Weather Service as well as the National Ocean Service. I guess I forgot to mention that Goldman Sachs was also a significant shareholder in CCX.

Oh, I think I also forgot to mention that Barack Obama was a shareholder in CCX.

In the event that you didn't connect with earlier comments about the Smart Grid, it's time to elucidate on that a bit. *Climategate* author Brian Sussman puts it this way:

> The Smart Meter is going to run your life. And it will be the tool allowing a handful of elites to become filthy rich.
>
> Citizens will be muscled into participating in this program via government giveaways. Upgrades to appliances and weatherization improvements will be partially offset with rebates. Likewise, reductions in energy use will be rewarded with up to $8,000 in cash.
>
> Sussman, 2010

There is one more player involved in the background who must be highlighted before we leave this item. Remember Franklin Raines, former chairman of Fannie Mae, until he was set out to pasture due to multiple improprieties? He just couldn't seem to get a handle on accounting principles, such that he was sued by the Office of Federal Housing Enterprise Oversight, following an investigation by the SEC. The OFHEO sought $110 million in penalties and $115 in returned bonuses from Raines and two other Fannie Mae executives. Raines and the three executives agreed to pay $3 million in fines, which will be picked up by their insurance policies at Fannie. Eventually, Fannie Mae reached a settlement with the OFHEO for $400 million.

This same Franklin Raines, while still at the helm of Fannie Mae in 2002, applied for two patents pertaining to a "System and Method for Residential Emissions Trading." Eventually, the patents were granted in 2005. Assignees for the patents were Fannie Mae and CO2e.com, LLC. Raines was forced to leave Fannie Mae on December 21, 2004.

This activity has not gone unnoticed by Representatives Darrel Issa (CA) and Jason Chaffetz (UT), who have written a letter to the U.S. Patent and Trademark Office, as well as Michael Williams, current CEO at Fannie Mae, which reads in part as follows:

> We are troubled by evidence that, while Fannie Mae was funding hundreds of billions of dollars in risky mortgages that were a primary cause of the financial crisis, it was simultaneously pursuing a patent to capitalize on the potential of legislative efforts that would have the effect of increasing energy costs to millions of Americans.

During Barack Obama's campaign, John McCain inferred that Raines was one of his primary economic advisors, a claim that Obama never refuted.

CCX is a thing of the past.

Oil is 'Dirty,' as measured against other commodities.

Crude oil is generally darker in color than gasoline, although certain "high-gravity" oils are as clear as jet fuel. High gravity refers to an American Petroleum Institute (API) metric, where a low number on the scale relates to heavy oils and a high number relates to light oils.

In 1859, Seneca Oil Company's Manager, Colonel Edwin L. Drake, led a team in the discovery of oil in the Oil Creek Valley near Titusville, Pa. One can make the argument that no other single event has had the impact on the world that this exploratory venture had that day in America. It led to the gradual transition in this country of burning a much higher energy density fuel for most purposes, even to this day. While natural gas and coal play a very significant role in our current energy mix, crude oil dominates worldwide.

Africa contains multiple developing countries that desperately need to move from an energy supply dominated by dung, charcoal, straw, and other clearly lower density, and in some cases high toxicity substances that they cannot seem to shake. Why? Because the oil that is produced in Nigeria, Angola, Guinea Bissau, Togo, Congo, Chad, etc, is largely controlled by corrupt governments that manage to keep the resources out of the hands of the people who desperately need them, instead keeping it for themselves to barter on the global petroleum market, pocketing billions of petrodollars while the people perish.

And what do Greenpeace, the World Wildlife Federation, and others in that "green" group propose for these desperate people? They propose and fight nearly to the death for animal rights well above human rights, such that it becomes virtually impossible for the people to gain access to crucial raw resources that could truly and beneficially "fundamentally transform" their unassuming lives.

Why is Barack Obama not insisting that Edriss Debye of Chad direct billions of dollars worth of newfound petroleum wealth toward to the building of electrical power infrastructure to reach some of the poorest people on the face of the earth?

Crude oil and natural gas are among the highest energy density products available to man, with the lowest expense. They should be used wherever possible to lift the people into a new paradigm of living without fuel toxicity, without carbon monoxide poisoning due to burning wood inside tents. Given the intense government controls in many of these nations, pressure should be brought to bear on policies in desperate need of change in favor of the people.

In Indonesia, rainforest is being ravaged at the expense of harvesting "palm oil" as a preferred "renewable resource." What idiocy, propagated by European policies that favor these green fuels. Since 1996, nearly 10 million acres of beautiful forest has been replaced in favor of the low energy density, high cost palm oil.

[23] That is simply one more example of a "renewable" biofuel that displaces a higher energy density, lower cost direct hydrocarbon, imminently available in one of the world's riches hydrocarbon provinces.

Those of you concerned about CO_2 need to know this fact:

In 2008, the World Bank issued a report that estimated that this deforestation activity caused the release of 2.6 billion tons CO_2 per year, making Indonesia the third largest emitter of carbon dioxide on the planet, behind China and the United States. How's that for a clean, renewable fuel placing ridiculous influence on a previously pristine and incredibly valuable home for what is now an endangered species?

I say it's high time that these European profligates get off the back of the previously pleasant and natural resource-rich Indonesians and allow them to produce to their own energy at maximum efficiency. Get out of their way, and figure out a way to scrub your coal-generated power stations. You can do it; trust me.

Oil is nowhere nearly as "dirty" as you have been led to believe by a myopic and very substantially uninformed media. For that, you can begin to thank Al Gore, Michael Moore, Andy Stern, Van Jones, Lisa Jackson, Carol Browner, Henry Waxman, Joe Lieberman, John McCain, Lindsey Graham, and any others you may wish to add to the list of coconspirators who had been fighting *for* "cap and trade," clean energy, or whatever misnomer they want to place out there. Don't forget.

They have chosen to deliberately ignore and distort fundamental facts related to our energy 'condition'.

Cellulosic Ethanol Can "Scale Up" and Cut U.S. Oil Imports (NOT).

Aside from "grain" ethanol, this is the next biggest scam perpetrated on the American people. According to a 2008 study conducted by the University of Colorado (one of the greenest universities on American soil), production of cellulosic ethanol requires 42 times as much water and emitted 50 percent more CO_2 than gasoline, which it is "destined" to replace. Look at the power density. Cellulosic ethanol produces 0.4 Watts per meter squared (W/m²), whereas a marginal natural gas well will yield 28 W/m². [24]

Let's talk about replacing that dirty oil from the Middle East. Ten percent of our daily consumption, rounded to 2 million barrels oil per day equivalent, translates to about 32 billion gallons oil per year, which, due to energy conversion, will require that we produce 48 billion gallons cellulosic ethanol per year to replace the "dirty" oil. These 485 million tons of cellulosic ethanol will require that we displace about 42 million acres of arable cropland in the U.S. to provide room for that beloved switchgrass to grow, not to mention the water required to keep it alive. That's about equivalent to the size of the entire state of Oklahoma. I doubt they are going to willingly give up their entire state to produce *your* beloved switchgrass. I want it to be very clear that it will never, ever be *my* beloved switchgrass.

Electric Cars Are the Next Big Thing (NOT).

How wrong can Honda, GE, Toyota and Nissan be? Real wrong. They know the numbers, and yet they think they can somehow beat Tesla's Law and simultaneously beat China's domination on crucial Rare Earth elements/alloys.

No way; the Chinese control that market, and they always will. That case is closed. Oh, President Obama didn't tell you that Rare Earths are crucial components of electric cars and solar panels? Here, I thought he was supposed to be the most transparent leader we have ever seen. I wonder if he has some kind of "back door" deal cut with China, given that Anita Dunn (his fired communications director) has such admiration for Mao, let's not forget that.

I want to close out this section with first a quote from an official in the U.S. Department of Energy, [25] and follow up by pointing you to an MIT (Massachusetts Institute of Technology) classroom, via a web video link.

Here is the quote from the DOE Office of Vehicle Technologies, summarizing the case against electric-powered vehicles, based on four areas of consideration: cost, performance, abuse tolerance, and life:

> Cost: The current cost of Li-based [lithium-based] batteries (the most promising chemistry) is approximately a factor of three to five too high on a kWh [kilowatt-hour] basis. The main cost drivers being addressed are the high cost of materials and materials processing, the cost of cell and module packaging, and manufacturing costs.
>
> Performance: The performance barriers include the need for much higher energy densities to meet the volume/weight requirements, especially for the 40-mile system, and to reduce the number of cells in the battery (thus reducing system cost).
>
> Abuse Tolerance: Many Li batteries are not intrinsically tolerant to abusive conditions such as short circuit (including an internal short circuit), overcharge, over-discharge, crush, or exposure to fire and/or other high temperature environments. The use of Li chemistry in these larger (energy) batteries increases the urgency to address these issues.

> Life: The ability to attain a 15-year life, or 300,000 HEV [hybrid-electric vehicle] cycles, or 5,000 EV [electric vehicle] cycles are unproven and are anticipated to be difficult. Specifically, the impact of combined EV/HEV cycling on battery life is unknown and extended time at high state of charge is predicted to limit battery life.#
>
> Howell, pg 4 [26]

I strongly encourage you to take a look inside an MIT classroom on January 11, 2010, being led by Professor Donald R. Sadoway, one of the best in his field of materials science. The essence of what I want you to capture will occur within the first ten minutes of the video, but I predict you will go further into the hour long presentation. With people like him leading the way, we may well achieve an economic opportunity in battery storage technology, but it will take a significant period of time and a lot of money to get there.

Here is the link: http://www.videosurf.com/video/high-performance-rechargeable-batteries-for-sustainable-transportation-and-large-scale-storage-of-electric-power-111922573

We Can Replace Coal with Wood (ABSOLUTELY NOT).

Yes, there are adherents to this notion. Please just go back to the reality of energy density, and try to think this thing through. It simply cannot and will not work. It would end up introducing far more beloved CO_2 into the atmosphere, and we will deliver far less energy than we would otherwise. We will find a way to dispose of nearly all of the lead and mercury emitted during coal combustion. I will visit this subject in greater detail below.

U.S. Energy Policy For the Twenty-First Century— A Proposed Template

Every American president since Richard Nixon has declared his form of mission toward energy independence for this country. Nixon had "Project Independence." Barack Obama has his "New Energy for America." Optimism is a good thing for any leader to have; it's deeply embedded in the American spirit, and we need it to move us to ever more creative endeavors. However, we also need, I daresay, to come to grips with reality, moving somehow to realism. As to our energy policy, we have been avoiding realism since 1973, nearly four decades ago. Reality is just around the corner, and Barack Obama is nowhere near ready to deal with it. If we do not take steps to significantly alter his perception, along with the full bevy of devotees he is leading, the gas lines we experienced in 1973 and 1979 will seem like a cakewalk compared to what lies ahead.

This is not a Republican or Democrat issue. Nixon, Ford, Carter, Reagan, Bush 1, Clinton, and Bush 2 each contributed to the path we are currently on. This is a global issue, and the United States is playing into this marketplace as an all too willing participant in the green movement, a movement that is very seriously misguided. It is highly probable that what might work well in America may not be a good fit at all for Western Europe or West Africa. That's fine; they can work out their own bugs. As for us, we have spent well over a couple hundred years testing components, seeking efficiency, and discarding most of what doesn't work for us.

We need very soon to come to grips with refining the efficiency function in our energy policy. And I do not mean engineering efficiency, but rather policy efficiency. If the government of this country is serious about providing real solutions to Americans, they will wisely seek counsel from multiple industry veterans and experts who actually understand thermodynamics and how things work. So far, government has been a lot more focused on getting in the way of industry, by way of onerous environmental law, egregious handouts (subsidies) into some very inappropriate firms and organizations, and other misguided policy. If we have any hope of righting this country as to a realistic energy policy, that must change.

First of all, no one has all the answers tucked away in a vault, ready to be unleashed at just the right moment to save the world from its energy and environmental woes. However, there is no doubt in my mind that competitive private enterprise, coupled with *wise* foreign policy, can and will succeed in providing this country with the best opportunity for energy security. A properly constructed public-private commission dedicated to creating new forward-looking energy supply strategies has a chance to work for America.

The current administration has seemingly ignored the considerable effort conducted by the National Petroleum Council (NPC), organized by President Bush 2. Their report entitled *"Facing the Hard Truths about Energy—A Comprehensive View to 2030 of Global Oil and Natural Gas (2007)*, contains excellent reference information and some policy recommendations that are consistent with reality. The NPC of today, I submit, needs to reiterate the hard truths, and move that message further into the open. Admittedly, that may not be possible under the current administration. I have recently spoken with a board member of the NPC, who prefers anonymity, and he confirms that conditions today in that body are in no way conducive to moving realistic policy forward, unless you happen to be very, very green, indeed.

The reader will notice that the foregoing template does not include "conservation" as a major element of policy recommendations. The reasoning behind that is based on the belief that citizens are forever, through the free markets, seeking ways to conserve their own resources. It is automatic, and it is something that is already engrained into our way of thinking at the individual level. Some individuals choose to ignore that advantage, but this is a free country. I will say this one thing—we in our household tried "compact fluorescent lights" (CFLs). They do not work with dimmer switches, which truly give the user absolute control of how many watts he/

she wishes to use. (I understand they have now produced a model that accommodates dimming.) Additionally, the risk associated with breakage, the concomitant mercury contamination, and EPA cleanup guidelines make these "conservation" items a total non-starter for us.

Each element in this proposed template is imminently testable. If any given element fails, it needs to be discarded in favor of a more attractive method, source, or strategy. Detailed discussions follow the template outline. This is not intended to be an exhaustive plan but rather the ten best immediately applicable opportunities to move this nation forward in its energy sector.

Ten Point Plan for Energy Security for the United States of America

(Note that this plan assumes we will also continue to construct and make maximum use of multiple natural gas-powered power plants nationwide.)

1. Permit and build as many coal-fired power plants as possible in the next two decades.

2. Permit and build as many nuclear energy power plants as possible in the next two decades. In spite of recent events in Japan, there is absolutely no reason to panic. See below.

3. Open more U.S. offshore regions to oil and natural gas exploration and development.

4. Open more Rocky Mountain basins to oil and natural gas exploration and development.

5. Open the North Slope of Alaska, specifically the Alaska National Wildlife Refuge (ANWR) to oil and natural gas exploration and development.

6. Strengthen our ties with friendly regimes across the America's; reduce, wherever possible, encumbrances to unfriendly regimes, e.g. Venezuela.

7. Focus major industrial and academic research attention on the conversion of Hydrogen, the simplest element in the Periodic Table, to usable energy in all sectors: electricity, transportation, storage, and defense.

8. Eliminate subsidies for "wind power" generation—it will be costly, inefficient and a long-term detriment to U.S. energy supplies.

9. Eliminate any and all activity associated with trying to manipulate greenhouse gases for purposes of temperature and other environmental control—it will be futile.

10. Abolish any notion of the concept of "cap and trade"—the ONLY winners will be Traders, Insiders, and Bureaucrats—every American citizen will be subject to major, ongoing and growing financial burdens, and gain nothing.

Energy Policy Discussion

1. ***Permit and build as many coal-fired power plants as possible in the next two decades.***

    Many cringe at the thought of more coal-fired power plants. However, if you have studied up, then you know that we can wipe clean about 90 percent of the harmful toxins that may be emitted by certain coal types, including mercury, arsenic, lead, and the like. So I will not buy the argument that coal cannot be clean. It can be, and it *will* be. This commentary will not be "music in the ears" of those housewives interviewed on "60 Minutes" on August 15, 2010, whose property was affected by the rupture of retention ponds at the Tennessee Valley Authorities' facility at Kingston, Tenn.

The Jeffrey Energy Center is located about twenty-five miles down the road from Manhattan, Kans., where I grew up. That facility contributes measurably to the 130 million tons per year (350,000 tons per day) of coal ash, or "fly ash" as it was called when I worked on a construction crew where it was used to stabilize the soils or subgrade beneath paved Manhattan streets. That is one way to dispose of the coal ash—bury it under concrete or asphalt-paved streets. I can envision others, like transporting it to appropriately designated remote, non-arable lands that currently serve no known useful purpose. Oceanic dumping is not feasible, due to the concentration of the elements mentioned above that could impact our food supply.

Let's figure out a way to dispose of coal ash; coal will be a necessary and essential contributor to our future energy needs for many decades to come.

2. *Permit and build as many nuclear energy power plants as possible in the next two decades.*

Still others, perhaps many in the group immediately above, have justified concerns about how we will contend with nuclear waste. Are you aware that the country of France, the global leader in nuclear power generation, stores *all* of its waste, accumulated since the 1960s, within a site covering no more than ten acres? Trust me; we will figure this out, in spite of billions of dollars spent at Yucca Mountain and other sites. We can, and we will figure this out. It should have been done already, but we have this problem called NIMBY. I'll leave it to you to research the acronym.

While the people of Japan are suffering and recovering from the devastating earthquake of March 2011, it must be noted that the Fukushima Dai-ichi nuclear plant survived the earthquake with almost no damage. The factor that dramatically increased the risk at the facility was the tsunami, which severely damaged cooling systems and related facilities. Other nuclear facilities in Japan have been able to recover, and while they are under very close surveillance, they were not faced with the incredible misfortune of both earthquake and tsunami within a very short period of time.

With respect to U.S. facilities, real risks remain, most significantly at the Diablo Canyon reactor astride multiple faults near the California coast. However, if that facility is as capable of withstanding the shock of a major earthquake as did those in Japan, it is likely it will not suffer the catastrophic damage those in Japan did, for the simple fact that it is situated well above the elevation to which a tsunami is likely to reach.

The crustal zone (including in many cases a significant sedimentary rock cover) upon which most U.S. reactors rest does contain faults and fracture zones. It would be virtually impossible to locate a facility anywhere in the continental U.S. that was not located within some relative proximity to such a zone. However, most are not in the high state of tension and/or compression as those in California, and while movement continues to occur along many of these slip surfaces, they are generally minimal in the context of producing possible damage to a nuclear power plant.

3. ***Open more U.S. offshore regions to oil and natural gas exploration and development.***

By the time of this document's release, some sense of sanity may well have been restored with respect to the Gulf of Mexico, and particularly the Deepwater Horizon disaster. Sixty years into the exploration and development of one of the world's most lucrative hydrocarbon provinces, a foreign operator with very significant U.S. interests made a series of bad decisions that will cost them dearly for decades to come. This incident occurred within the same year that America heard from one of its former Speakers of the House the admonition, "Drill baby, drill." The collective national attitude did support that notion at that moment, and I still do today, along with millions of other

Americans. As was the case with Ixtoc (Mexican Gulf Waters), and the Exxon Valdez in the Cook Inlet of Alaska, the Gulf of Mexico will recover from this incident. The only immediate question is, will the people of America be successful in properly addressing the power-hungry forces inside Washington, D.C.?

That is the question. The answer is yes, if the people will follow a wholly new (yet to be determined founding, fundamental) group of leaders. Are you ready to get behind this type of leadership? Are you adequately educated on the key issues? If not, then the answer will be no, and the people will succumb to the undesired and unintended "transformation of America."

4. ***Open more Rocky Mountain basins to oil and natural gas exploration and development.***

I have a lot of friends in the Rocky Mountain region. Had I not landed in the mid-continent U.S., that is where I would have chosen to live. I may still end up there, breathing the absolutely beautiful scent of pines blowing in the high country wind.

As a citizen of this country, we need to be aware of the very significant hydrocarbon resources that exist in that very beautiful province. In case you have not noticed, there has never been a significant issue encountered with respect to the exploration for, or development of hydrocarbons, in that entire onshore region. Yet the Rocky Mountain region contributes a substantial amount of both oil and gas production to this country on a daily basis. In March 2010, this region produced approximately 770,000 BOPD (approximately 14 percent of U.S. total). The average daily natural gas production for the year 2008 was approximately 11,316 million cubic feet per day (MMCFD), or about 11.3 billion cubic feet per day (BCFD), which was 20 percent of the U.S. total. Production in the Bakken shale has been significantly increasing since approximately 2005, such that today's rate is approximately 310,000 BOPD between North Dakota and Montana. North Dakota dominates with 246,000 BOPD.

Both states' daily oil production changed dramatically with the discovery of Bakken reserves, but Montana's has peaked as of August 2006, as can be seen below. North Dakota will experience a similar phenomenon, but the peak will likely be more drawn out, and obviously at a much higher level. [21]

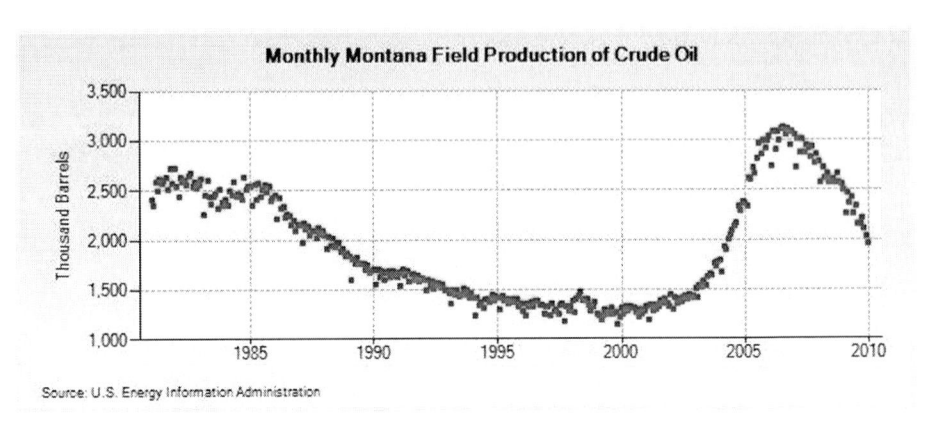

Figure 8: Montana Crude Oil Production 1980-2010 [27]

For comparison, here is the recent data for North Dakota:

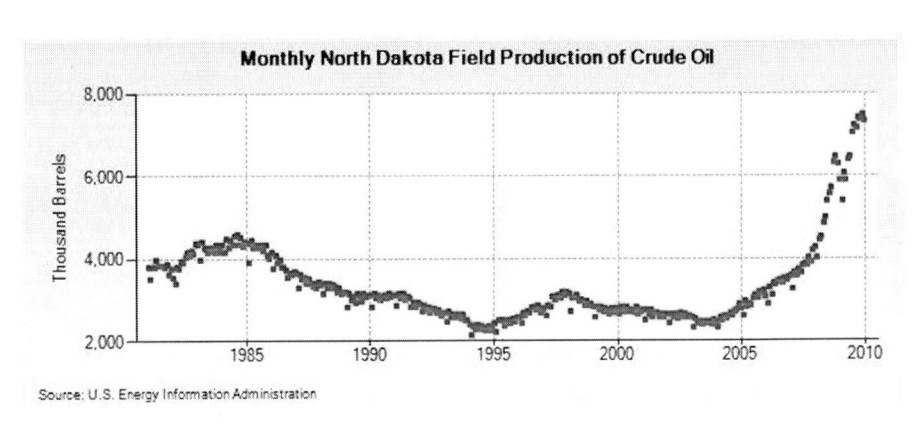

Figure 9: North Dakota Crude Oil production 1980-2010 [28]

While I do not want to minimize the importance of the Bakken discovery and development, I urge caution as to the overall impact this has on U.S. daily production of approximately 5.5 million BOPD as of March 2010. In other words, the entire Bakken play currently contributes about 5 percent of U.S. daily production, or alternately about 1.5% of U.S. daily *consumption*. The play still has legs to it, but peak production is probably not too far into the future. Count on the decline rate to be significant. The decline rate for the Montana play was 30 percent over the three years from August 2006-August 2009.

Unfortunately, the environmentalists have had a real heyday with respect to energy resource development in particularly that region. It has become one of the most difficult in terms of permits, regulations, and wholly unwarranted protests related to exploration and development issues. If the EPA succeeds in banning "hydraulic fracturing" of reservoirs, you can go ahead and add at least 1 million BOPD to the U.S. oil imports equation, perhaps significantly more.

There is no justification whatsoever for the hijacking of a viable and essential component of America's energy supply of both oil and natural gas. I implore the resistance that is deep and wide to come to its senses and make a contribution to America's energy challenges rather than hold hostage thousands of jobs, along with quadrillions of Btu's that this country needs to gain energy security.

I submit the following to provide the evidential reality of this country's crude oil supply, per the EIA database:

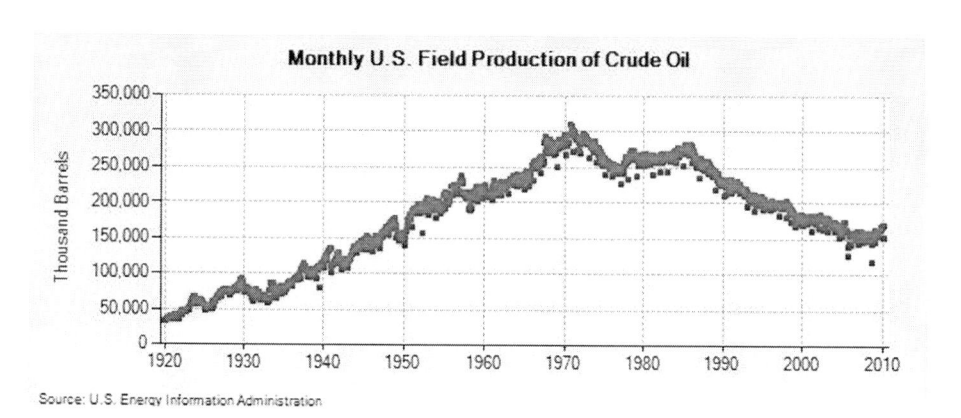

Figure 10: Monthly U.S. Crude Oil Production [29]

Crude oil production in this country peaked the month of my eighteenth birthday, October 1970. It has been in a long downhill slide ever since. While we placed incredible effort toward arresting this decline after the Iranian Revolution in 1979 (America's second taste with gas lines), we were unsuccessful. The slight upward tick at the beginning of 2010 is not due only to the Bakken, but rather the combination of that play, coupled especially with deepwater exploration in the Gulf of Mexico.

The Deepwater Horizon incident, which commenced on April 22, 2010, and was brought under effective control on July 19, 2010, was a colossal disaster. If proper intra-company constraints within BP had been applied, it never would have happened. They will pay dearly for the mistake. Early reports within a month of the disaster, which were never covered by the conventional media, gave very clear explanations of what caused the disaster. I'm not going to bore you with detailed technical drawings, but I can summarize the path to destruction fairly simply:

1. When a potentially productive well reaches what is known as Total Depth, or TD, then the operator of the property (in this case, BP) instructs the drilling Contractor (Trans Ocean) to run casing to the bottom of the well and then to place cement behind the casing (in the annular space between the casing and the freshly drilled earth), to seal off any fluids and gases from entering the wellbore environment.

2. BP had tested the wellbore environment after "cementing the casing." They encountered unusual pressures and some sense of gas compromising and potentially weakening, the cement, yet they did not take action.

3. They had additional warning signs in the ensuing hours, indicating preliminary natural gas blowback to the surface. This precarious condition should have resulted in an immediate effort to secure the wellbore, but no such action was taken.

This occurred because BP elected to displace relatively higher-density drilling mud (which remained inside the casing after placing the cement) with much lower density salt water.

4. The preliminary blowback was followed by the real load that blew mud and water out of the hole. Eventually a high concentration of methane (natural gas) made its way to the rig floor environment, encountered a spark, and exploded into the uncontrollable fireball that eventually took the rig down below the surface of the ocean before the flames were extinguished. It was all due, in essence, to a poorly planned and executed cement job, one of the least expensive activities taking place in the sequence of a well being "completed."

It all amounted to cutting corners. At least three parties bear some responsibility for the failure as described above:

a. BP bears primary responsibility, and company representatives on the platform should have taken the first steps to counteract preliminary warning signs;

b. Trans Ocean Horizon employees should have taken action, in conjunction with BP onsite managers, recognizing the preliminary warning signs;

c. U.S. Minerals Management Service employees should have paid much closer attention to the Well Plan and disallowed what should have been recognized as an inadequate Plan, related to the cement job.

Corners that BP cut in this case have reinforced a very unenviable reputation for it not only in Gulf waters, but in other industry activities as well. The *Wall Street Journal* ran an interesting, fact-based article on June 30, 2010. Here is what they found with respect to BP's OSHA scorecard on refineries:

During the period of June 2007—February 2010:

- BP received 760 "Egregious willful citations."
  The remainder of the industry received 1 citation.

- BP received 69 "Willful citations."
  The remainder of the industry received 22.

- In the case of "Serious citations," BP fared better than the remainder of the industry. BP had thirty; the remainder of the industry received 1,521.

The BP incident is the only one of its kind since exploration began more than fifty years ago in the U.S. Gulf of Mexico. It is unique, uniquely horrible, and uniquely irresponsible on the part of BP as well as the government regulators.

Are you aware that natural seeps occur routinely in every ocean basin on the face of the subsea earth? Every one of them—that's what causes tar balls to wash up on Miami Beach. It is not due to leakage from tankers heading to port. The La Brea Tar Pits in Los Angeles are a perfect example of a naturally-occurring onshore seep.

I want to lay a little energy trivia on you to contemplate, now that the Macondo well has been brought under control.

Firstly, no one knows exactly how much crude oil was released into the Gulf of Mexico during the blowout. That is because flow rates, even once the well was brought under control, were not actually tabulated. Various news services reported that the containment vessel at the surface was capturing at some point approximately 30,000 barrels of oil per day (BOPD) and that they were flaring (burning) significant volumes of natural gas that was surfacing with the oil. Did you ever hear a number, in thousand or million cubic feet per day, as to the volume of natural gas that was being flared? I did not hear any such number. There was also a significant amount of crude oil that was being burned because flow rates exceeded the capacity of the containment vessel.

I say all of that to bring these figures to your attention:

It was inferred (never actually measured) that Macondo leaked 207 million gallons of oil (approximately 5 million barrels of oil), without reporting any number for the natural gas component that was also leaking significantly.

Over the period of a hundred days of leakage, 207 million gallons of oil translates to about 50,000 BOPD. I have my doubts about that number, but I do not have any data to support my contention, other than my own observation of the effluent coming out of the wellhead once they finally severed the damaged riser. I did my own calculations and came up with a range of between 20,000—40,000 "barrels" of oil, which contained a very significant mixture of natural gas and oil. My ballpark guesstimate of actual crude oil leaking into the Gulf was about 30,000 BOPD, which is plenty significant and not to be minimized in terms of damage related to the leakage.

Do you remember the "deep plume" that was of grave concern?

The plume was essentially gone by August 25, about three weeks after the well was brought under final control. Microbes ate it up like piranhas. This was proven by researchers from Lawrence Livermore National Laboratory. Here is what researcher Terry Hazen had to say, "We've gone out to the sites and we don't find any oil, but we do find the bacteria."

It has been calculated that approximately 500,000 barrels of oil leaks into the Gulf of Mexico each and every year, due to absolutely natural causes, fractures in the seabed linked to leaky hydrocarbon reservoirs. That's 21,000,000 gallons per year, or about 1,300 BOPD, each and every day.

So, what are we going to do about that?

Absolutely nothing.

It's time to think a lot harder about our real alternatives as to energy supply.

Regulations governing the industry in deepwater environments will be modified in an effort to ensure no such incident is repeated. But there are no guarantees in that extremely hostile subsea setting; let no one lead you to believe otherwise. Is it worth the risk to address the reserves hidden beneath "subsalt" geological/geophysical impediments? I say, unequivocally, yes, it is worth the risk to attempt to soften the landing we are headed toward as we begin to wean ourselves of the fossil-dominated energy supply system we currently enjoy/endure. I say we enjoy it, others say we endure it. I seriously doubt that anyone who believes that it is a matter of "endurance" has any idea whatsoever what a truly "cooling" earth would be like. We have not seen anything like it since the Little Ice Age. The real data indicates we may very well be headed into a repeat of 1550-1850, sooner than you think. Believe me, I hope I'm wrong.

5. ***Open the North Slope of Alaska (ANWR) to oil and natural gas exploration and development.***

Every American citizen should have already reached the conclusion that we should be taking full advantage of opening up ANWR to appropriate exploration and development. There is no question that this region is special in its natural beauty and that it is situated in one of earth's most intricate and sensitive ecological settings. But that does not mean that fully adequate safeguards have not already been developed or could soon be developed, whereby seasonally appropriate exploration and development should not be allowed to progress. It is way past high time to address the energy potential that this region has to offer the United States. We should already be moving product from this energy-rich region into the U.S. energy marketplace. It is shameful that we have allowed special interests to dominate the discussion of the scientific merits of this matter. They simply do not know what they are talking about, and they need to be stood up on end.

6. ***Strengthen our ties with friendly regimes across the America's; reduce, wherever possible, encumbrances to unfriendly regimes, e.g. Venezuela.***

Look at some additional data that relates directly to our condition as to hydrocarbon supply. Do you remember way back at the beginning of this chapter the list of countries that currently provides the U.S. with the highest percentage of our daily crude oil imports? I'll refresh your memory to let you recall that Mexico is near the top of the list.

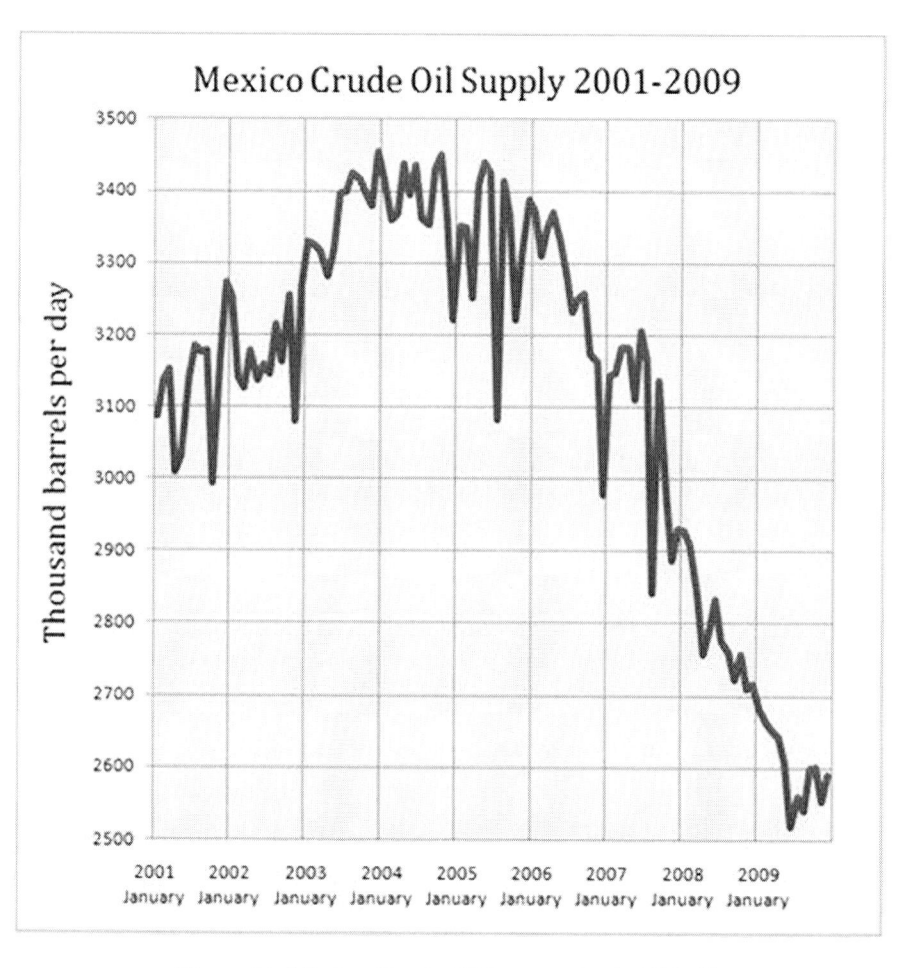

Figure 11: Mexico Crude Oil Imports in the U.S. [30]

I want you to fully understand the significance of this data. This is Peak Oil for Mexico, and unless and until they encounter highly unlikely major new discoveries, this picture will continue. Mexico's production declined approximately 25 percent from mid 2005 to the beginning of 2010. That is a very significant decline rate.

I was wondering why our daily imports from across our southern border went from 1.83 million BOPD in 2006 to the present rate of about 1.2 million BOPD—here's the reason: Mexico no longer has the capacity to service our needs. Let's be thankful that our supply from Canada has been able to keep pace with the decline from Mexico, at least for the time being.

Our current intake from our northern border neighbor is approximately 2.73 million BOPD. Canada's total daily production amounts to about 3.4 million BOPD. Canada's daily production is currently on an incline rather than a decline. That is due entirely to an intensified effort at addressing tar sands (Athabasca Tar Sands). This mining operation requires increasing amounts of natural gas to fuel the heating required to free the oil from the sand. While natural gas is relatively inexpensive at the moment, that condition can change quickly, as was experienced during the timeframe 2003-2007, when prices increased from about $4.00/mcf to about 6.50/mcf. Natural gas prices reached a local low in October 2009 of about $3.00/mcf, as compared to $5.00/mcf in December 2009.

Current pricing hovers around $4.00/mcf.

We need to grow up very quickly in our understanding of the total energy system in this country and how we move *realistically* into the future. We do not have the luxury of "pipe dreams," and we certainly cannot afford the "fundamental transformation" of America via "cap and trade" or any other such approach that will drain the pocketbooks of every single citizen in this country.

I wish I could tell you that corn-ethanol can solve all, or even a small fraction of our supply needs. Unfortunately, as has been demonstrated, it is a net energy loser. Man cannot beat the Laws of Thermodynamics, and that is the battle corn-ethanol is fighting. It does not improve significantly for cellulosic-ethanol. Expect it to be a high probability net energy loser and major water consumer.

I wish I could tell you that wind energy was free. It is anything but free, and while it might supplant some of our non-base load electricity needs, it is a very expensive alternative and will *never* become a part of base-load power. The wind is simply very unreliable, making good about 30 percent of the time, max.

We can, and we must do better.

The oil and gas industry, both independents and major integrated companies in this country, do the bidding for and the capturing of energy resources outside our borders. So, when I indicate that we need to enhance relationships with other entities, I am referring to private sector relationships with outside countries that actually are materially addressed in the real business world, not the massively political world of Washington, D.C. Nonetheless, the government can play a role in assisting companies in a variety of ways, such as:

- Producing a stable, unchanging model for dealing with resource exploration and extraction; our country should be a model for others to view in creating or modifying their laws, their royalty structures, and so on.

- Providing incentives to address these out-of-country reserves that may be located in hostile environments, both politically and geographically. For example, relationships with Colombia, Ecuador, Bolivia, and Argentina could be materially enhanced by proper handling of negotiations relating to energy, environment, and overall policy. *What I am not talking about are negative, anti-U.S. capital activities such as paying ("loaning") great sums of money to assist Brazil in its offshore endeavors, while restricting U.S. offshore activity in the Gulf of Mexico. These policies could not be more counterproductive.*

- Beyond the Americas, the African continent is a bountiful region that should be addressed to significantly enhance its resource base to raise it out of poverty. The United States should be materially addressing opportunities to assist them in creating better legal definitions related to exploration and production licensing and all related activities. If we don't address the issue, we are leaving the door wide open to China and others much closer by to convert energy assets that will become only more valuable with time. I repeat—the United States must address every available avenue of realistic energy capture in the very near future. If we neglect the opportunities that are currently available, we will pay a much steeper price for it in the future. Windfarms, solar energy, and electric vehicles are not the answer to our long-term energy needs.

7. *Focus major industrial and academic research attention on the conversion of Hydrogen, the simplest element in the Periodic Table, to usable energy in all sectors: electricity, transportation, storage, and defense.* While it may seem that this source should be a given, what with vast oceans, a vast atmosphere, and other apparent sources from which to draw nature's most fundamental element, a gas no less, it is anything but a simple task. It has certainly seen its share of research, but it will require a far greater effort to solve the problem of harnessing and effectively utilizing hydrogen as a routine fuel. As it stands right now, we can construct a hydrogen bomb, but we are a long ways off in taming hydrogen as a fuel.

8. *Eliminate subsidies for "wind power" generation—it will be costly, inefficient, and a long-term detriment to U.S. energy supplies.* Earlier discussion above dealt with this issue.

9. ***Eliminate any and all activities associated with trying to manipulate greenhouse gases for purposes of temperature control—it will be futile.*** A more detailed discussion of this issue follows in the next chapter.

10. ***Abolish any notion of the concept of "cap and trade"—the only winners will be traders, insiders, and bureaucrats—every American citizen will be subject to major, ongoing, and growing financial burdens and gain nothing.*** This issue was dealt with in part above, and additional discussion ensues in the following chapter.

Geothermal Energy Considerations

As an additional potentially significant renewable source, I suggest serious consideration be given to the benefits of expanding geothermal energy systems for especially electricity generation. While it is a minor contributor to the grid at the moment, that could change with research to confirm appropriate subsurface systems.

The United States' net winter electrical generating capacity from all sources in 2008 was 1,048.3 Gigawatts (GW). The dominant contribution came from natural gas-powered plants, which provided 427.7 GW, followed by coal-powered plants, which provided 315.5 GW. By comparison, renewable sources such as wind produced 24.7 GW, unsustainable, and geothermal sources produced 2.25 GW, sustainable. [31]

For startup cost comparison, in 1980, Sunflower Electric Cooperative created its Holcomb coal-fired plant, which cost $465 million [32] (1980 dollars), and produces a capacity of 362 Megawatts (MW), for a cost of about $1.28 per MW. The EIA estimates the cost of a new geothermal plant at $60 million, with a capacity of 50 MW, or a net cost of about $1.20 per MW, 2008 dollars. With inflation considered, the cost per unit is significantly higher for the coal-fired plant.

In view of a metric known as "overnight cost," which is primarily related to capital expenditures required to bring a plant online, we have the following comparison [33]:

Advanced Nuclear	$3,820/kW
Integrated coal-gasification with combined cycle and carbon sequestration:	$3,776/ kW
Advanced gas/oil combination Combined cycle with carbon sequestration:	$1,932/kW
Wind (renewable, unsustainable, non-base load):	$1,966/ kW
Geothermal (renewable, sustainable, baseload):	$1,749/kW

Based on statistics from ClimateLab.org, in 2005 the United States led the world in geothermal-generated electricity, producing 17,791 GWh, followed by the Philippines with 9,253 GWh and Mexico with 6,282 GWh. The world total that year was 56,786 GWh.

Most of the current electrical generation from geothermal resources in the U.S. comes from deep western reservoirs. Among the group of renewable sources readily available in this country, it would seem prudent to place an increased emphasis on geothermal, with research dollars focused on better definition of deep-seated reservoirs capable of delivering feedstock to flash-steam plants that pull superheated steam from hot reservoirs, or Enhanced Geothermal Systems, which circulate less than superheated water into natural or induced fractures within hot rock to generate steam that can be used to generate power via turbines.

DOE funding already supports each of these endeavors and on the face of available data, it would seem quite feasible to increase, a hundredfold, the existing capacity of geothermal energy in the United States. If the technology were proven efficient, the access to geothermal resources could be very significant, delivering baseload power to a large portion of the U.S. grid.

Thermal (heat pump) applications of geothermal energy are well established and apply to both residential and commercial facilities throughout the U.S.

The Audacity of Freedom — *145*

Figure 1: Assigned boundaries of Israel via Biblical definitions

Figure 2: Extents of Modern Day Israel

Photo 1: 3 February 2006 Protests staged in London, demonstration by Muslims angry over the publication in Scandinavian periodicals related to the prophet Muhammad

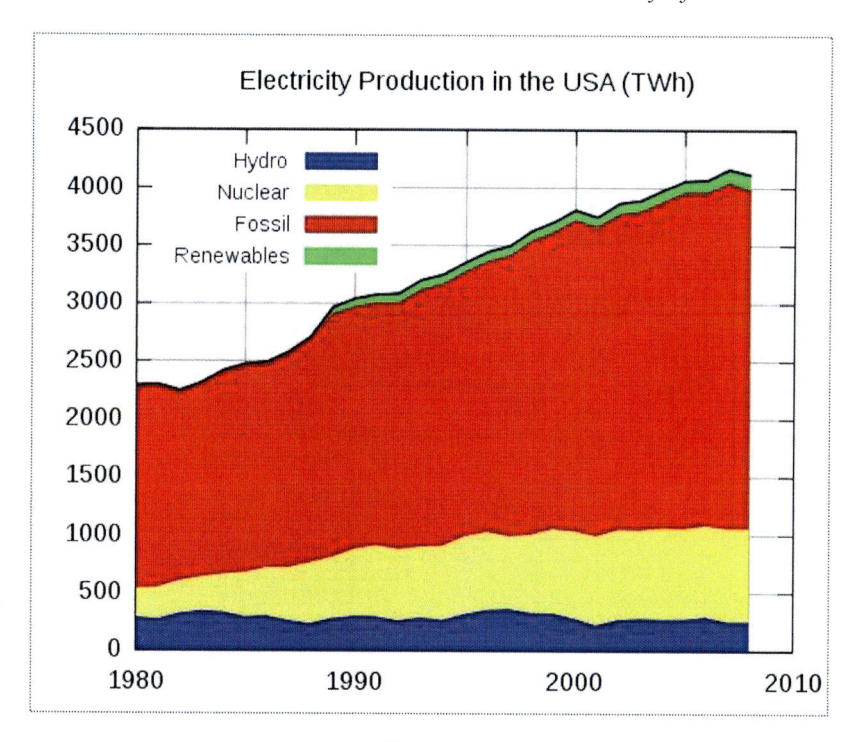

Figure 4

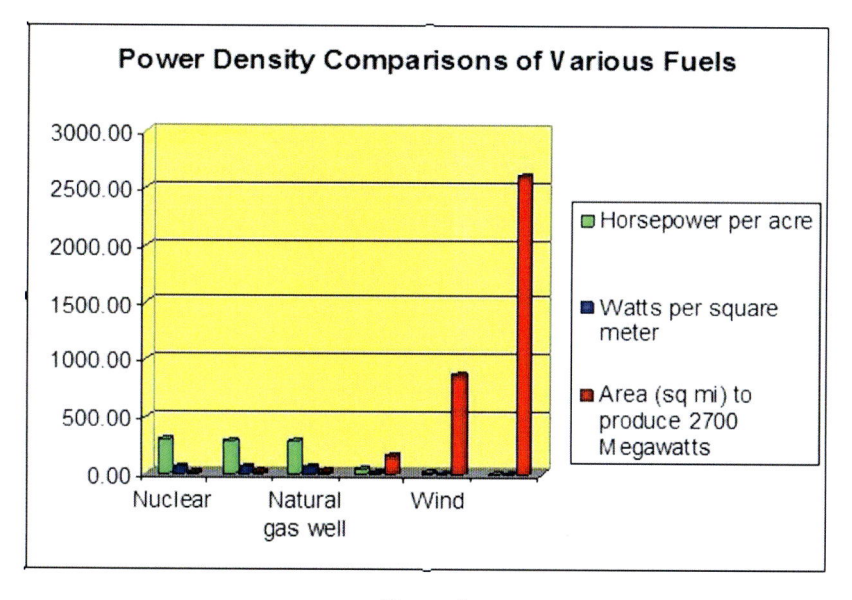

Figure 5

Photo 3: Wind generator fire-enlarged

The Audacity of Freedom — *149*

Photo 2: Windfarms—Palm Springs, (San Gorgonio Pass) CA

Photo 4: Coal-fired Power Plant

150 — *Color Photographs & Figures*

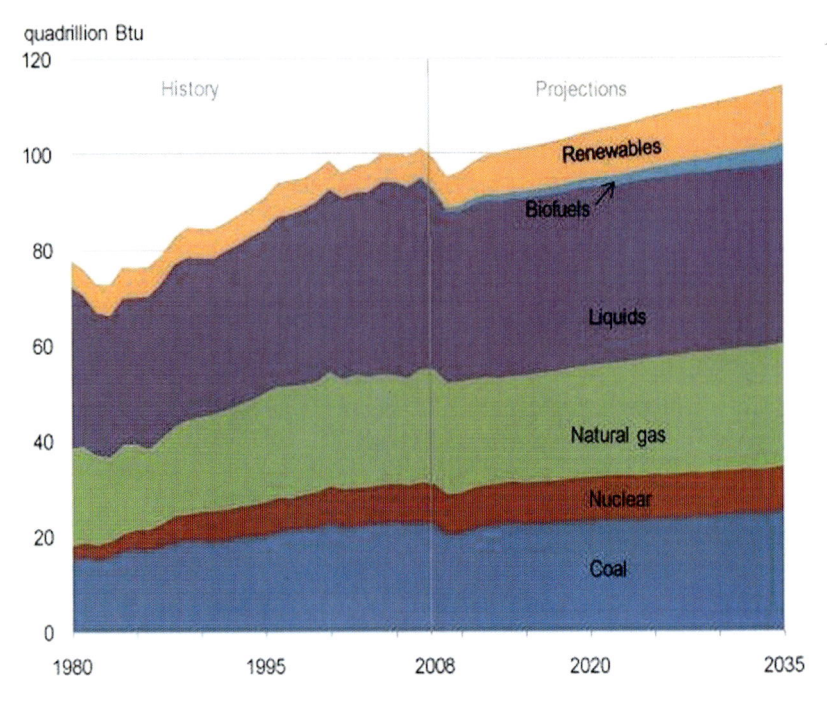

Figure 6: U.S. Energy Consumption

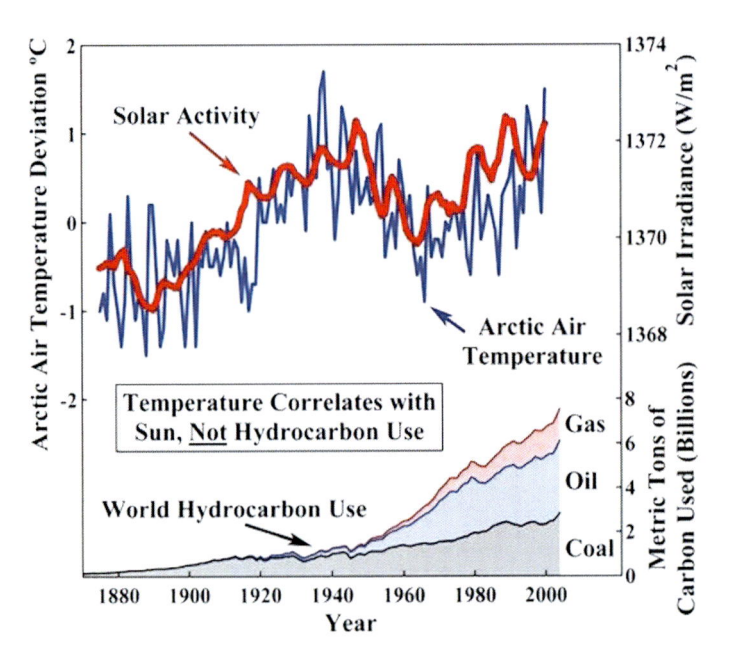

Figure 15: Solar Activity, Temperature, Hydrocarbon use, 1870-2006.

The Audacity of Freedom — *151*

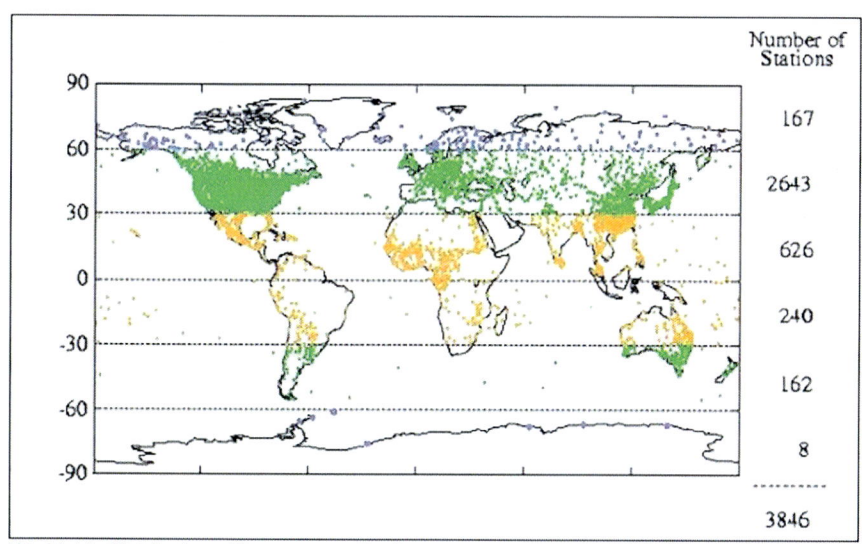

Figure 12: Global Temperature Measuring Stations

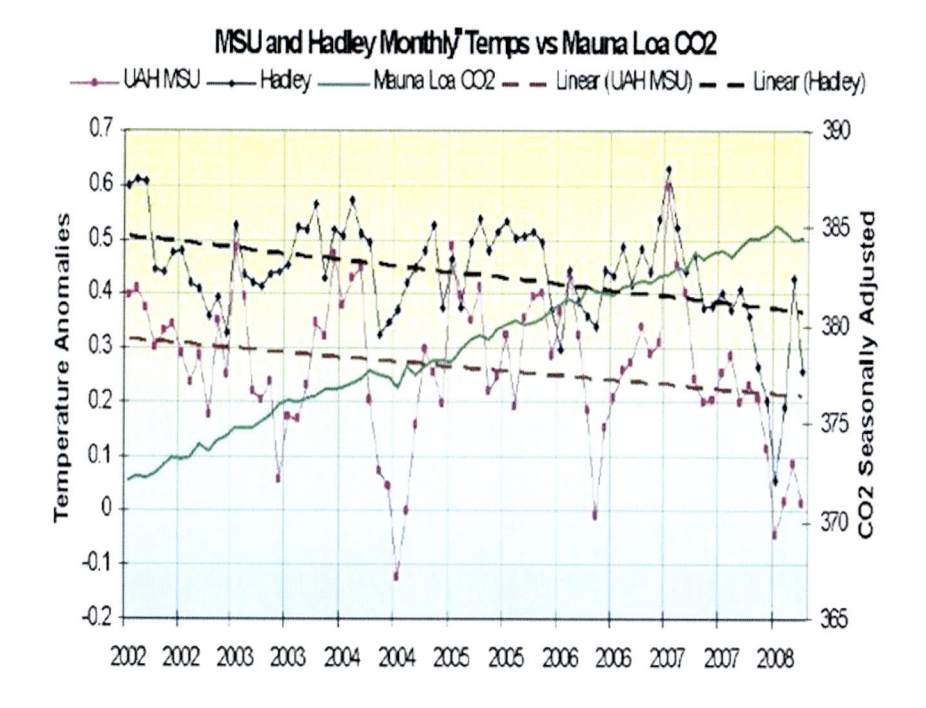

Figure 16: Monthly Global Temperature Records vs CO_2 at Mauna Loa Volcano.

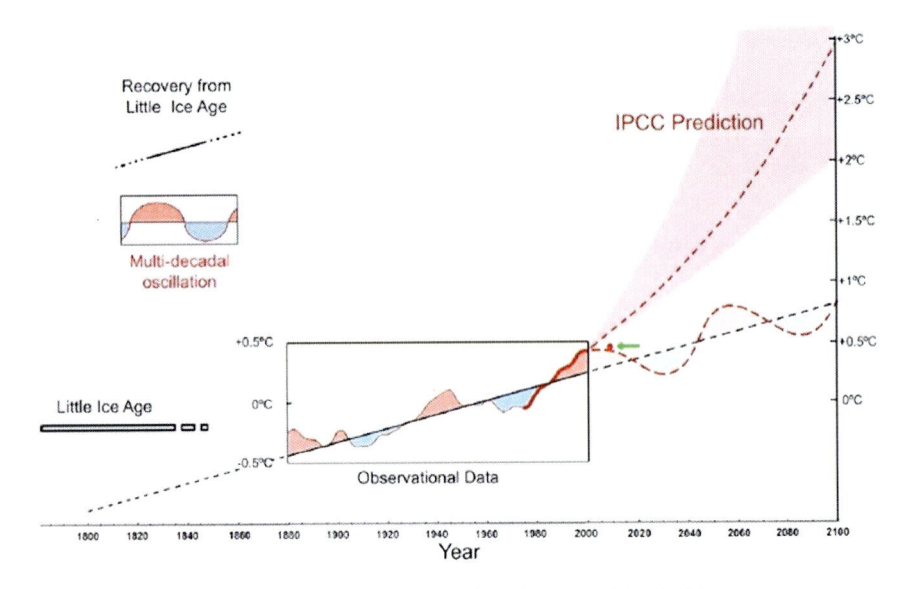

Figure 19: Multi-decadal Oscillation, 1880-2100

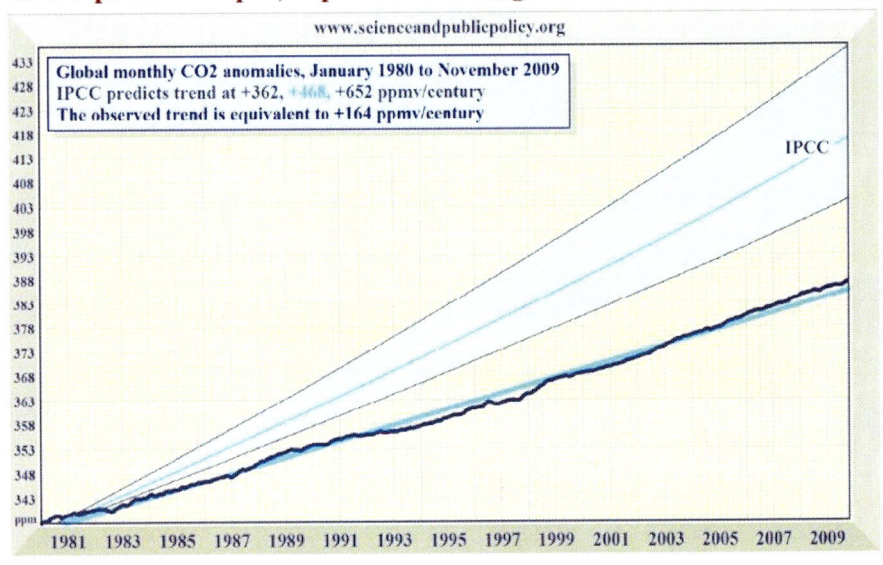

Figure 20: IPCC Predicted CO_2 Exponential Growth, 1982-2009

Figure 22: Lieberman, Warner, Boxer Regulation-Mandate Chart, Small Scale

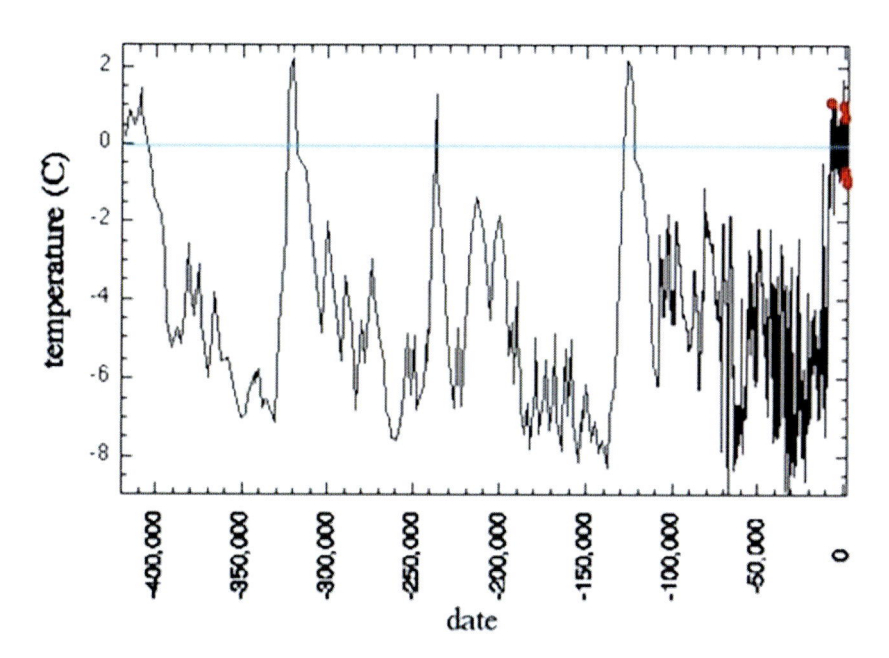

Figure 24: 400,000 Year Global Temperatures via Ice Cores

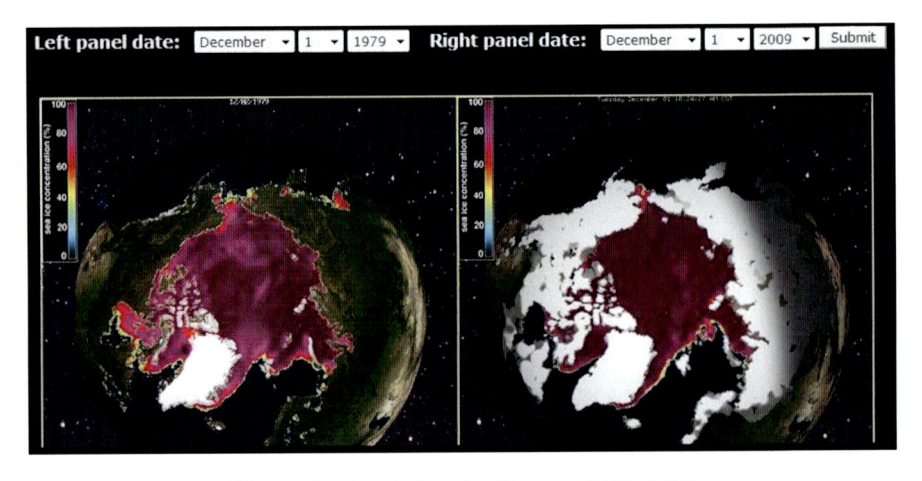

Figure 26: Arctic Sea Ice Extent, 1980-2009

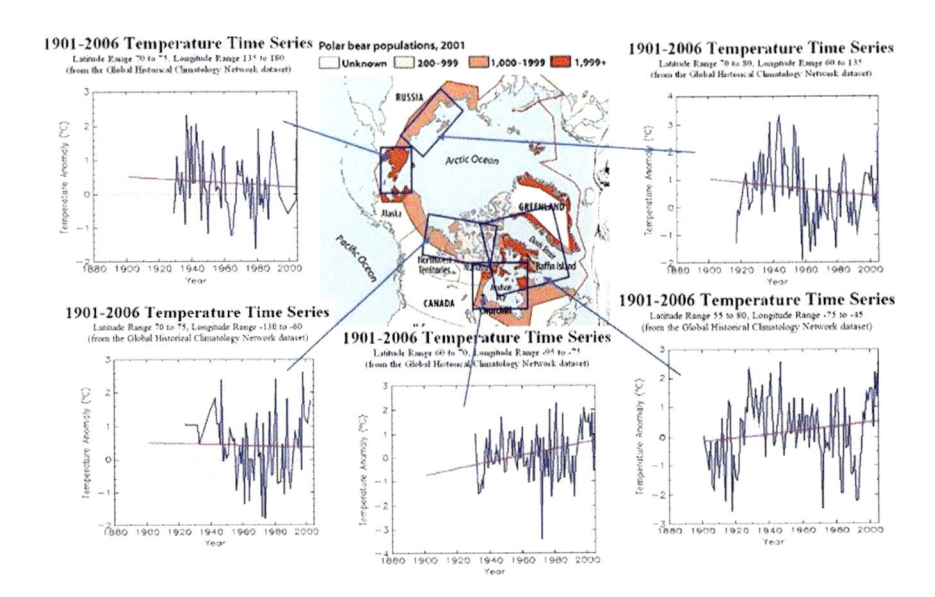

Figure 27: Arctic Temperatures 1901-2006

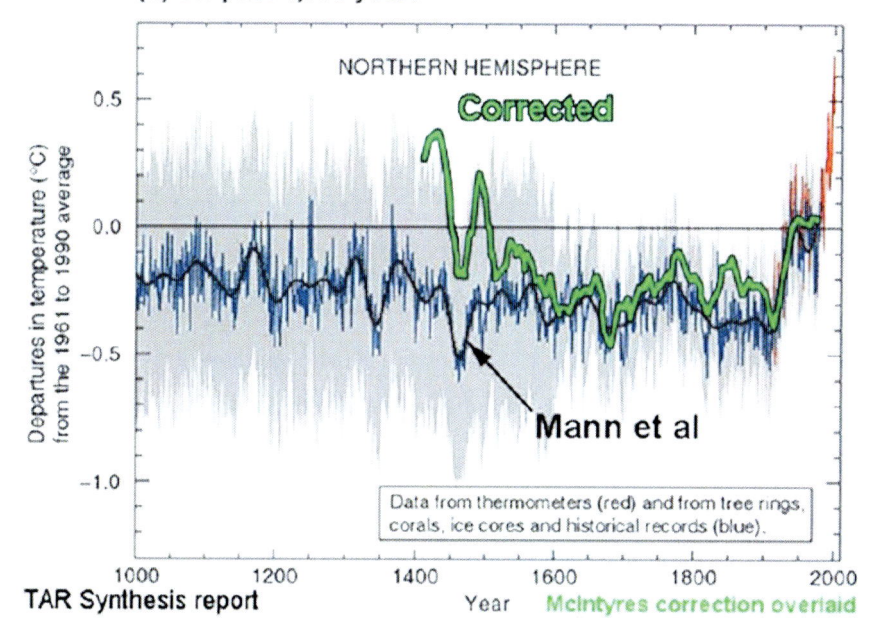

Figure 30: 1,000 Year Earth Temperature History: Corrected Hockey Stick (Color Image with Correction in green)

156 — *Color Photographs & Figures*

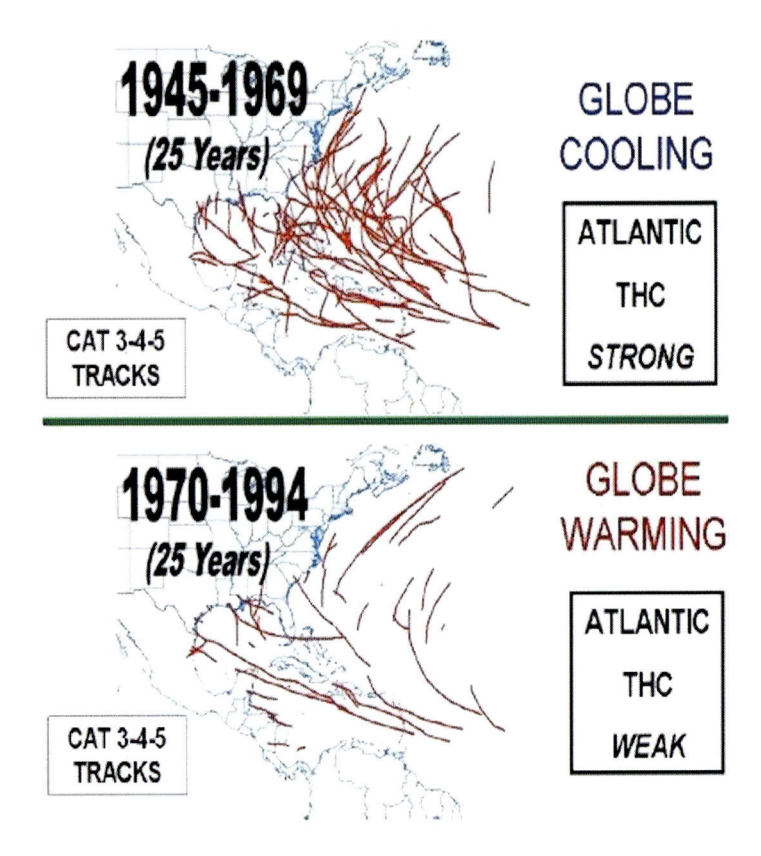

Figure 31: Atlantic Hurricane Tracks: Globe Cooling vs Globe Warming

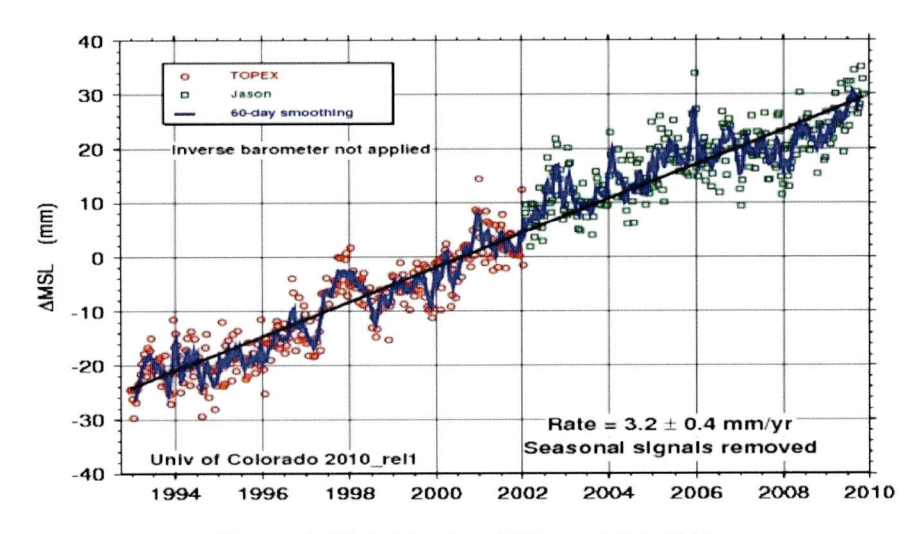

Figure 36: Global Sea Level Change 1992-2010

The Audacity of Freedom — 157

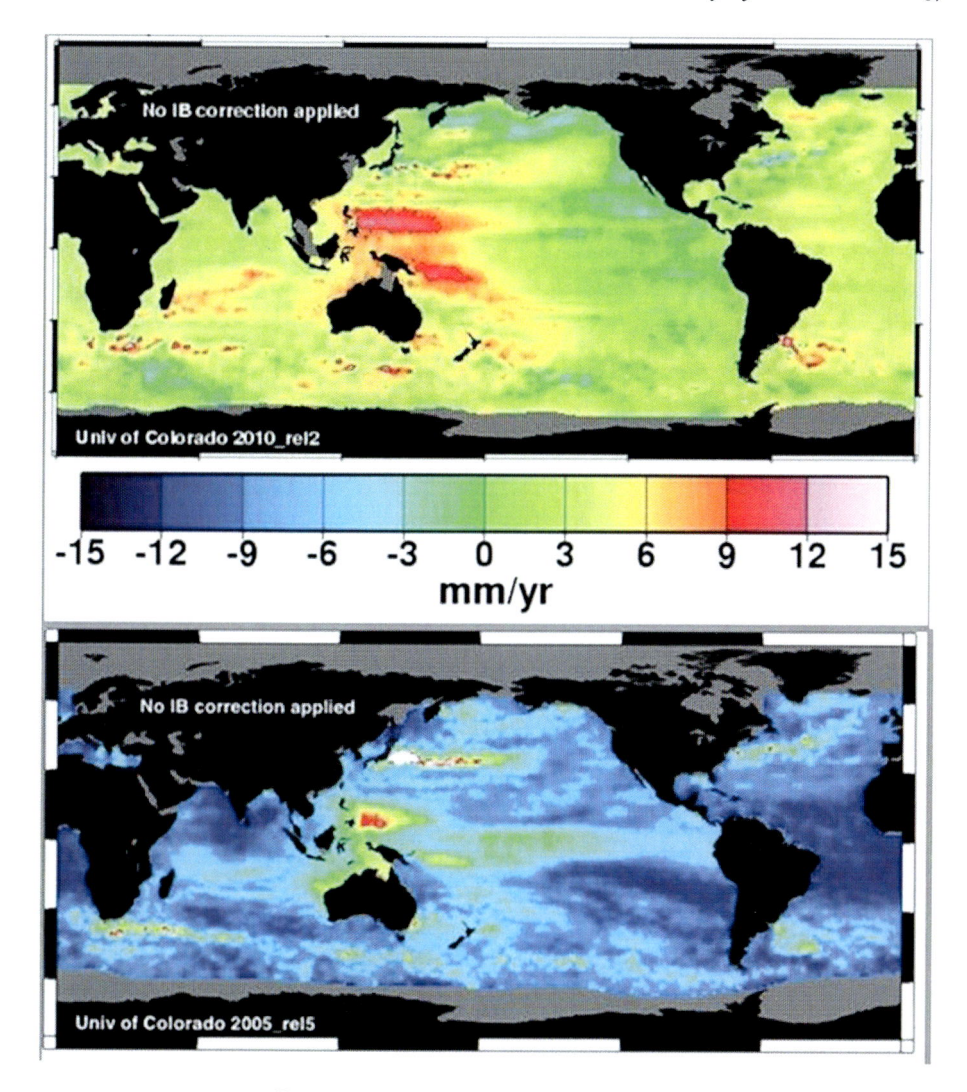

Figure 37: Global Sea Level Corrections

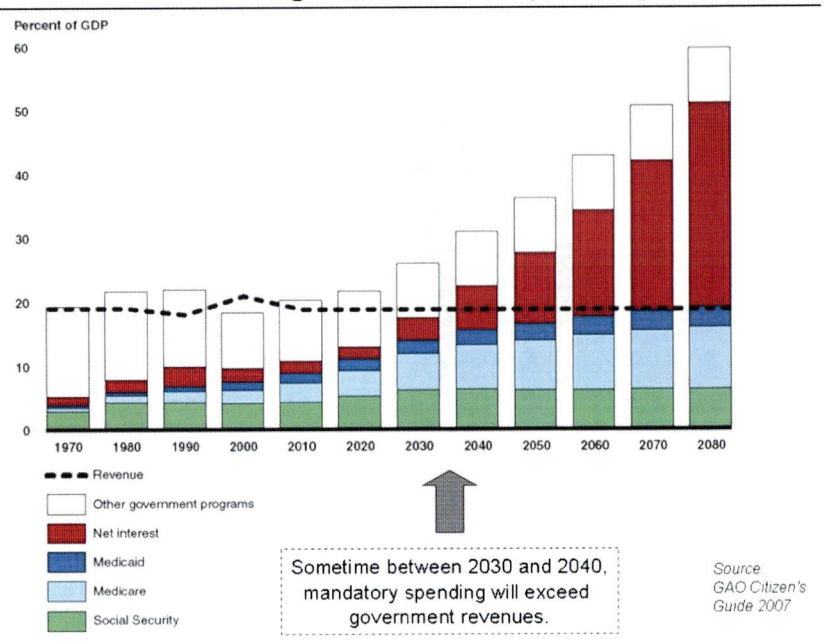

Figure 42: Medicare and Social Security Deficits through 2040

GLOBAL ENVIRONMENTAL SURVIVAL—
The New Green Earth

Two years ago, I never would have believed Americans would so readily relinquish so many of their hard-fought freedoms. Yet, at that moment, then-candidate Obama openly professed his plans to "transform America." He flat out told American that he expected "...energy costs to skyrocket..." (Interview, San Francisco Chronicle, January 17, 2008), and the majority apparently did not take him at this word. I was not one of those people; I will never become one of those people, and I will fight with every fiber of my being anyone who ever attempts to force me to become one of those people.

The next defining battle related to our freedom will relate the substance of what was discussed in the previous chapter with what will be discussed in this chapter. In fact, the battle has been underway for about six decades now, but most of you had no idea what was coming until perhaps around 2005, when Al Gore and his allies really started to raise the volume on "Global Warming." That's about when we first started hearing that "the science is settled." Of course, now the science is "really settled," such that the U.S. Senate simply needs to rubber stamp that underwhelming victory on cap and trade Obama strong-armed in the House Of Representatives during the fall of 2009, just before he Chicago-styled his victory for Obamacare. We are beginning to understand the full magnitude of that monstrosity and the monumental loss of freedom it represents. It must be repealed and replaced with real reform that helps Americans fix their health problems.

Some new perspective may have already been gained with respect to the new law of the land regarding environment and energy. That's aside, of course, from what we already know about the findings of the EPA with respect to their new definition of "hazardous."

The EPA had plenty of help in arriving at their materially erroneous conclusions, which I predict will be roundly overturned by the United States Supreme Court. It will take a while, but *We the People* will get it done. So, Lisa Jackson, prepare yourself for that eventuality. As I testified in Arlington, Va., on May 19, 2009, the American people will hold you accountable for the fraud and misrepresentation you have aided and abetted through your taxpayer-funded organization.

The Scam Artists

As John Coleman, the founder of the Weather Channel, so eloquently put it on March 2, 2008, at the International Conference on Climate Change, in New York City: "It is the greatest scam in history. I am amazed, appalled, and highly offended by it. Global warming; it is a SCAM."

John knew all about the sort of data that I will be presenting below with respect to misplaced weather stations, falsified/manipulated data a la "hockey stick," and the whole scheme of it all. But of course he was nowhere to be heard, except for that "mini-media market" known as San Diego. He's still there as of this writing, handling the goods and doing the day-to-day reporting of this fine globe's weather.

He stands out in stark contrast to the group I am going to highlight below. They certainly stand out as well, in a whole different meaning of "stand out." Take a look at this excerpted summary, as developed by the Washington Examiner on December 4, 2009. The full article was produced by Barbara L. Hollingsworth.[1]

> **Geoff Jenkins,** Chairman of the United Nations Intergovernmental Panel on Climate Change's first scientific group and self-described "frontman explaining Climate Change." Jenkins admitted in 1996 to a "cunning plan" to feed fake temperature information to Nick Nuttall, head of media for the United Nations Environment program. At the time, Jenkins predicted temperatures in London would hit 113 degrees Fahrenheit and the Thames River would rise three feet even though 1996 was, in fact, cooler than 1995.
>
> **Phil Jones**, director of the CRU (University of East Anglia Climate Research Unit), controlled two key databases …
>
> Jones e-mailed instructions to colleagues to "hide the decline" in temperatures and to pressure editors of academic journals to blackball the work of "climate skeptics."
>
> After claiming that the original climate data had been destroyed in the 1980s, Jones was caught urging his CRU colleagues to "delete as appropriate" data requested under Britain's freedom of information laws.
>
> **Michael Mann**, director of Penn State University's Earth System Science Center, is one of the lead authors of the U.N.'s Inter-governmental Panel on Climate Change report…"
>
> In 2003, Canadian statistician Steve McIntyre exposed the flawed methodology behind Mann's hockey stick. The recent e-mail leak led another scientist, Dr. Timothy Ball to quip: "Dr. Mann is in transition from Penn State to State Pen. We can only hope he does a better job with license plates."

Mann has been a committee chairman for the National Academy of Sciences and a member of multiple NAS panels and committees.

James Hansen, head of NASA's Goddard Institute for Space Studies, whose records were also cited as evidence, second only to the CRU data, of incontrovertible manmade Global Warming. McIntyre also caught Hansen engaging in the same sort of statistical manipulation in which past temperatures were lowered and recent ones "adjusted" to convey the false impression that the nonexistent warming trend was accelerating. *After trying to block McIntyre's IP address, NASA was forced to back down from its claim that 1998 was the hottest year in U.S. history.*

Al Gore... Gore's case rests on the now-discredited theory that carbon dioxide emissions (which are increasing) are heating up the Earth's atmosphere, even though actual global temperatures have been declining for at least a decade.

These five, though far from being the only ones, are among the top perpetrators of the Great Global Warming Hoax. They should never be taken seriously again.

Thank you, Barbara Hollingsworth, for your assistance in the attempt to set the record straight.

Deep in the mix of this fraud are multiple senators and representatives in the U.S. government, as of fall 2010. They, collectively in lockstep with the group above, have been largely "successful" in swaying public opinion on this crucial issue:

Sen. Joe Lieberman (I-CT), co-author with John McCain of original "cap and trade" model

Sen. John McCain (R-AZ), co-author with Joe Lieberman

Gov. Arnold Schwarzenegger[+] (R-CA), who has repeatedly caved in to special interests

Sen. Barbara Boxer (D-CA), always a warrior for "green" causes

Rep. Henry Waxman (D-CA), instrumental in passing the House "cap and trade" legislation

Rep. Edward Markey (D-MA), able assistant to Henry Waxman, new partner with L. Graham

Sen. Lindsey Graham (R-SC), a RINO (Republican in name only), until proven otherwise by actions yet to be seen

+Gov Schwarzenegger has been replaced by Jerry Brown, who makes Schwartzenegger look like a radical right-wing fundamentalist.

This group is about equally balanced among Republicans and Democrats. While it is largely a party line matter, plenty of folks from the Republican side of the aisle have yet to study the issues carefully enough to hit it completely out of the park once and for all (hit it out of the park means eliminate it). Some Democrat senators have done so and are prepared to take whatever heat comes with the job to stand firm against the nonsense that is written into this "energy" legislation.

It is still a scam; it will always be a scam. The scam comes from the mixture of corrupt politics and bad data. This is a potentially deadly mix, especially for our ailing economy.

The Most Unreliable Data in the World

The first thing you need to understand is that the "data" is very substantially compromised. Let me qualify that. The *temperature* data is substantially compromised.

Here are the top 5 reasons:

1. "Stevenson Screens," which should represent the standard temperature measuring apparatus, should be located at a minimum offset of at least a hundred feet from any structure, wherever temperature measurements are taken around the globe. Unfortunately, the "worst-case scenario" has been repeated thousands of times, and it matters. We have thermometers under

heat vents, on asphalt, on concrete, behind jet engine exhausts, all kinds of places where they don't belong, etc, etc, etc. I wish it was only one, etc. It's not; it's thousands, including one less than twenty miles from where I live, in El Dorado, KS.

2. The *dismemberment of thousands of temperature measurement stations* in primarily colder climates. This is important because "global" temperatures are measured in summary fashion across the globe. If a northern climate station is eliminated—and thousands have been—then the "daily" summary of "global" temperatures is materially altered, upward.

3. The "hockey stick," made so famous in *An Inconvenient Truth*, has been taken completely out of service by the IPCC, in spite of the fraudulent delivery of a Nobel Prize to the recipient who very well knew that the data had been manipulated by Michael Mann and nonetheless presented it in his "crocumentary" and had no place whatsoever in a scientific context. He has happily accepted the prize, but I suggest he has other unintended "prizes" awaiting him. How are you going to feel, Mr. Gore, when millions of people suddenly wake up to your fraud? Your time is gonna come, as Led Zeppelin would say.

4. The *IPCC* has major problems. Their current leader, Rajendra Pachauri, I predict, will be removed from office. He has no place in the global community of credible science. He has proven to be subject to bribery and other improprieties. Let him go out to pasture or feed him to the wolves; it's your choice, IPCC. You have access to all the data, and you know all about items 1-3 above, yet you refuse to take the actions necessary to clean up the data.

4. *Climategate*. You thought this would go away? No way; this is just beginning, from a lowly geophysicist in Kansas and thousands of others who just cannot accept that manipulation of data, suppression of data, and all machinations thereafter are *okay* for the global scientific community. You, Mr. Jones, also know all about

the incredible shortcomings of the fundamental data related to the global temperature measuring network. Yet you and your East Anglican colleagues, as well as others you regularly communicate with around the globe, have so far avoided taking the actions necessary to bring the system into compliance, such that we can actually begin to measure truly meaningful temperatures.

That's the broad-brush outline related to global temperature data issues. But it is necessary to more fully develop the context of the current fallacious temperature measuring system.

The Stevenson Screen was designed to capture "protected" weather information at such a location that would be in an open area, preferably grassy, well removed from buildings, and capable of withstanding high winds and other weather extremes.

Unfortunately, more than 25 percent of the world's weather stations are in anything but ideal, protected environments. The reality of these misplaced stations is that they materially misrepresent actual temperature and almost always misrepresent it upward.

This would not be a significant issue if it were simply a scientific experiment, poor though it were. What makes it significant is the unfortunate fact that organizations such as the IPCC, NOAA, NASA, and many others take this data without adjustment and incorporate it into the summary that is used to track global temperatures.

The errors are significant. In fact, the errors are as significant in many cases as the temperature variance they are attempting to measure, or in some cases, extrapolate.

Let's talk about weather stations with respect to geographic location. Globally. It is important to understand that it is not just a matter of location with respect to surrounding culture. Cultural effects, (aside from those demonstrated above), such as what is known as the "Urban Heat Island Effect" are readily identifiable on records that are near large urban centers across the globe. Discrepancies as high as 3 degrees Fahrenheit are easily detectable on records in urban centers, when juxtaposed or compared to rural settings within a hundred miles of such urban concentrations.

However, even beyond the issues cited above, it is also a matter of significant concern when we examine the relative weighting of weather stations in the less densely populated regions, as compared to those where densities are highest. To date, there is no effective weighting of this condition. In other words, the "cells" from which we draw weather data should be far more carefully regulated and weighted as to area. The higher population density areas overwhelm the averaging.

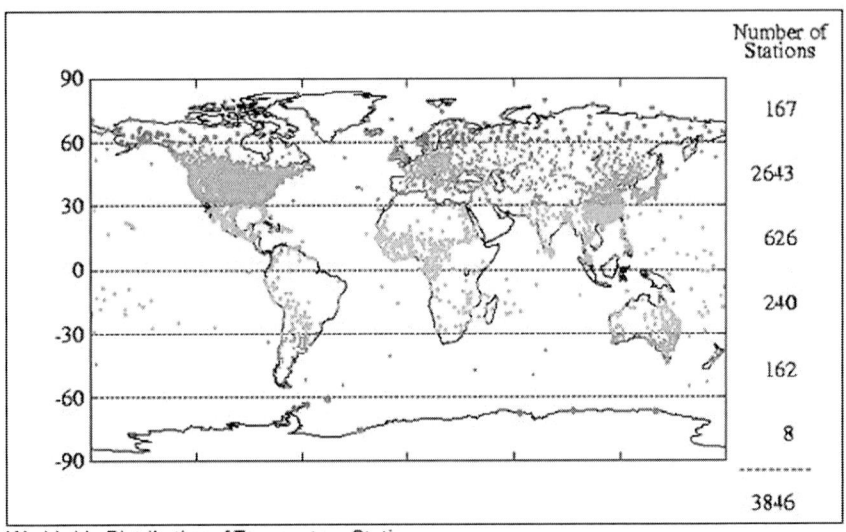

Worldwide Distribution of Temperature Stations

Latitude range	Number of Stations
60 to 90	167
30 to 60	2643
0 to 30	626
-30 to 0	240
-60 to -30	162
-90 to -60	8
Total	3846

Figure 12: Global Temperature Measuring Stations [2]

(For a more detailed look, view the colorized version of this image within the color section, page 151.)

With respect to the above figure, notice that the United States and Europe are particularly well covered and that Russia, China, India and Australia also demonstrate fairly high-density coverage. This image can be found at:

http://www.appinsys.com

What I really want you to understand is the very light weighting and coverage over the Polar Regions and high latitudes. Furthermore, *the high latitude regions in Canada and Russia have been materially altered in that thousands of stations have been taken out of service, commencing in 1990.*

This reality is exemplified below, with figures depicting the number of stations versus temperature.

Neither Russia nor Canada provides any explanation for the sudden reduction in measuring stations. However, one can surmise that there are probably two factors at play:

1. Government funding in support of "global warming"

2. Lack of government funding for a particular site, due to other priorities

In either case, the obvious skewing of temperature data is very substantial and most certainly impacts the global summation related to temperature averaging, on whatever cycle the data is plotted.

This is completely unacceptable scientifically, and you will not see any treatment of this systemic malfunction anywhere in IPCC Reports.

None.

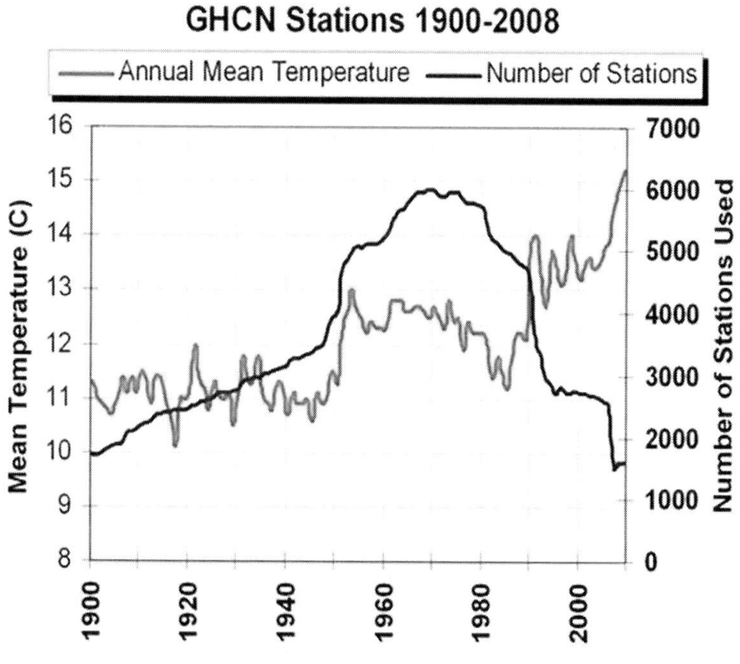

GHCN Stations 1900-2008

Figure 13: Global Historical Climate Network stations 1900-2010 [3]

This figure begs a couple of questions. Firstly, did the temperature really rise nearly 3 degrees Celsius (~5.0 degrees F) during the period of 1986-1991? Secondly, did the temperature actually rise nearly 2.5 degrees Celsius (~4.0 degrees F) from 1946-1953? In the case of the first question, the answer is absolutely not. In the case of the second, the answer is very likely not, but for different reasons.

In the first case, the apparent temperature rise was virtually solely due to the taking out of service those high latitude stations. In the second case, the "rise" in temperature was very likely due to the placement into service of a number of stations in "urban" areas subject to the heat island effect alluded to earlier.

The figure above comes from an IPCC Scientist, Joe D'Aleo (also has website icecap.com), who presented the graphic at the annual meeting of the International Conference on Climate Change, held in May 2010 in Chicago. What, you never heard of it? That's not surprising, since only one news organization was present to hear some of the scientific proceedings.

Please allow me to add this quote from a reporter (Marc Sheppard, American Thinker, June 26, 2010), who was there to observe.

> "And further investigation uncovered by a team lead by ICCC-4 presenter Joe D'Aleo revealed that the two primary U.S. sources of global temperature have also been manipulating land-based instrumental readings. NOAA has been strategically deleting cherry-picked, cooler-reporting weather observation stations from the temperature data and NASA has intentionally replaced the dropped NOAA readings with those of stations located in much warmer locales."
>
> Sheppard

In my professional opinion, I find it totally unacceptable that not one, but two, institutions that are profusely spending your and my tax dollars are fundamentally altering crucial decision-making data. This material manipulation must be stopped, and those in managerial positions accommodating this manipulation need to be taken to task. If I were in a position to do so, these "managers" would be terminated, immediately.

(In fact, as of this moment, I am not convinced that this sort of manipulation is not criminal, given the consequences this data has already had on misguided policy.)

The preponderance of the evidence, especially that connected to the dominating factor in our solar system, the sun, points to some serious reversals of temperature on the global scale. That has to do with sunspots, which have been carefully monitored for hundreds of years.

Let's take a look at one depiction of the sunspot record over the past 11,000 years:

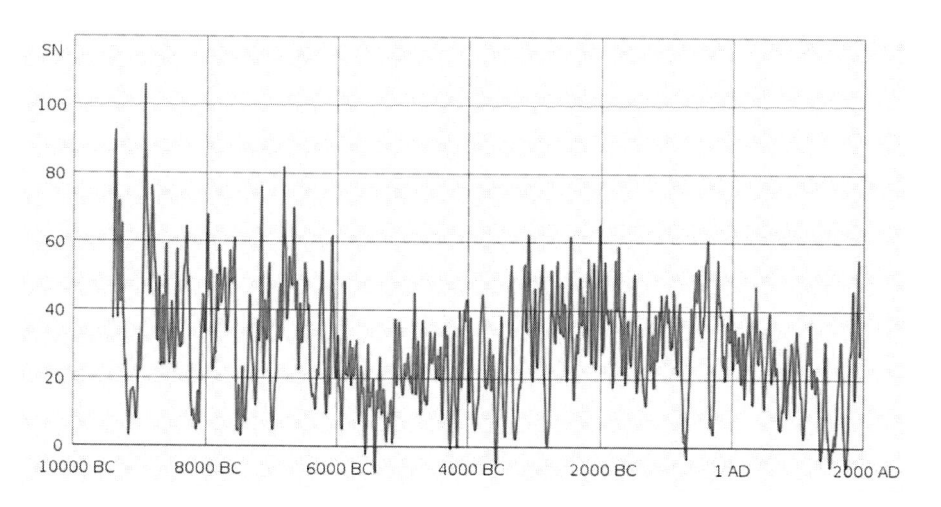

Figure 14: Sunspot Record over 11,000 Years [4]

The above reconstruction is "based on dendrochronologically dated radiocarbon concentrations," according to Solanski, et al's source paper:

> Unusual activity of the Sun during recent decades compared to the previous 11,000 years Nature, Vol. 431, No. 7012, pp. 1084 - 1087, 28 October 2004.

170 — *Global Environmental Survival — The New Green Earth*

While this is an example of a "proxy" relating to actual data, it is very interesting to note that the "Little Ice Age" coincides very nicely with the minimum occurring around 1600-1800 AD and that the current conditions imply that we are currently approaching higher trends actually experienced by real human beings from about 2000-3000 BC.

Focusing on a more recent trend from the period of 1870-2005 provides very useful data and insight as to the relationship between solar irradiance, temperature, and global hydrocarbon use. (Solar irradiance incorporates sunspot cycle amplitude, sunspot cycle length, solar equatorial rotation rate, fraction of penumbral spots and decay rate of the 11-year sunspot cycle, as researched by Soon, and Hoyt, et al). [5]

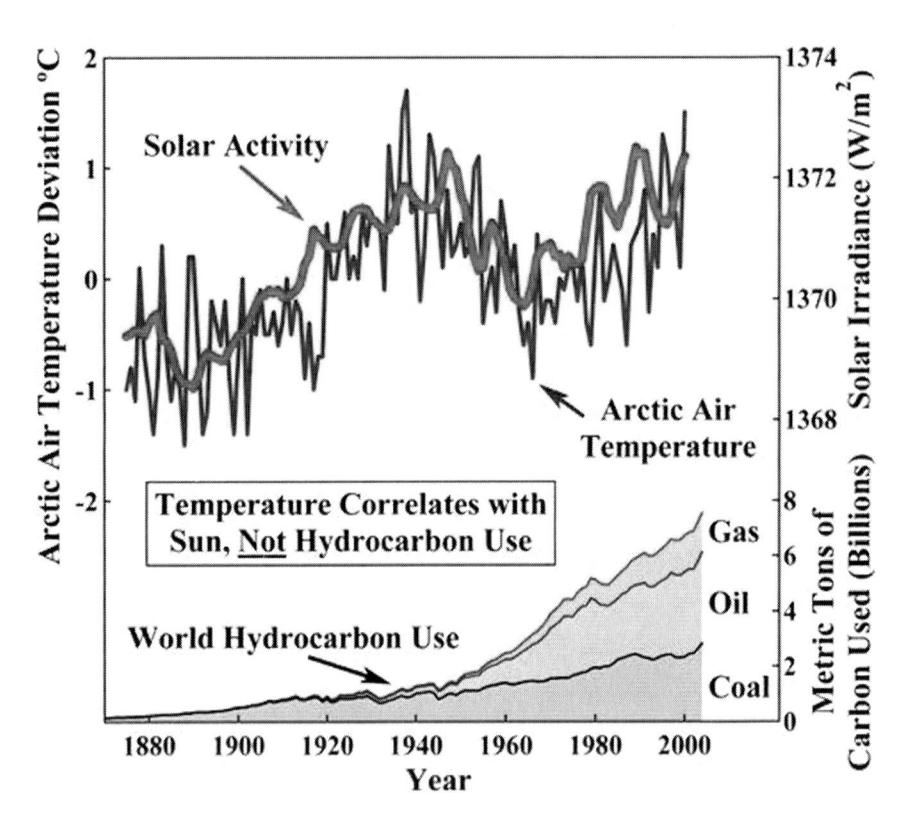

Figure 15: Solar Activity, Temperature, Hydrocarbon use, 1870-2006. [5]

(For a more detailed look, view the colorized version of this image within the color section, page 150.)

I have only one question to ask you, the reader, about the content of the above graphic summary:

What is it about the complete and total disconnect between temperature, supposedly correlated to CO_2 concentration, and hydrocarbon use, that is so difficult to understand?

I want to encourage you, the "green" protectors of society, in the strongest possible terms, to come to grips with reality, accept the data for what it simply describes, and allow mankind to continue to prosper by virtue of further refinement of the energy density opportunities man has been exploring for many centuries.

I want to further encourage you to allow the poverty-stricken peoples of the African continent, Indonesia, India, and others, to fully explore their natural resource domains, in order that they might enjoy the benefits of moving from the intensely polluting conditions of wood burning in tents, and the like, to the far less dangerous hydrocarbon chains the rest of the world enjoys.

Where is your compassion?

I submit that you "greens" lack the understanding required to provide your fellow men the freedom that hundreds of millions of people have been enjoying for more many centuries.

I will further state the following, that *this country faces virtually zero risk from the introduction of CO_2 into our atmosphere due to hydrocarbon combustion. This country, in fact the entire global economy, is facing a very grave risk related to misguided policy that is based on fallacious data, misinterpretation of that data, and outright fraudulent misrepresentation of that data.*

I could stop right here with the data side of this argument. In fact, most of you green adherents probably dropped out of this discussion on page one. However, for those of you who have chosen to stay with the data, and the real facts that relate to the real data, i.e. *not* the models, there is more to come.

Gate City

I'm just wondering how many "gates" we're going to have to go through with this mis-administration before the vast majority of the American public will finally say, "Enough is Enough!

Actually, there is a light at the end of the "Global Warming" tunnel. The U.S. Senate just acquiesced, at least temporarily, with respect to attempting to jam down the American throat yet another incomprehensible piece of very expensive legislation. We will see just how long they can hold back the likes of Al Gore and Obama as they salivate over the previously discussed CCX.

It's time to discuss Gates, EPA Gate and Climate Gate / IPCC Gate

Unless you have had an extended trip to incommunicado islands somewhere outside the bubble of global communication, you have heard of Climate Gate. But what about "EPA Gate"? What about "IPCC Gate"? I thought so. You may have heard a couple of phrases implying some minor misgivings at the EPA with respect to some minor data issues. And, you might have seen a couple of stories pertaining to the current man in charge at IPCC, Chairman Rajendra Pachauri, but probably not much more. I hope to provide you some additional context on all these subjects.

EPA Gate

This was the first in the series chronologically, so we'll revisit it first. Just so you know, the EPA budget for 2010 was $10.4 billion, and had at that moment around 18,000 employees. Here's a summary of their "offices":

- Office of Administration and Resources
- Office of Air and Radiation
- Office of Enforcement and Compliance Assurance
- Office of Environmental Information

- Office of Environmental Justice
- Office of the Chief Financial Officer
- Office of General Counsel
- Office of Inspector General
- Office of International Affairs
- Office of Prevention, Pesticides, and Toxic Substances
- Office of Research and Development
- Office of Solid Waste and Emergency Response
- Office of Water
- Office of Chemical Safety and Pollution Prevention

In addition to these "offices," they also have ten regional "offices." My home state is in Region 7, whose headquarters is located in Kansas City, KS. I hope I never really need to deal in any way, shape, or form with that facility. I did visit one of their offices in Arlington, Va. Quite a place, first class digs all the way, all paid for by you.

As I mentioned earlier, on May 19, 2009, I offered testimony at a public EPA hearing at the Potomac Yard. The hearing was one of two being held that week, the other being in Seattle, Wash., to take in testimonies of citizens in response to the EPA's then recently proposed *"Endangerment and Cause or Contribute Findings for Greenhouse Gases under Section 202(a) of the Clean Air Act"*.

Their "findings" were released on April 19, and they gave citizens a month's notice to participate in their public hearing process. I was not pleased to see most of the content inside their technical supplement; in fact, I am still not pleased with most of what is in that document. What was then a proposal is now a whole new set of regulations, thanks to BO. *It's now official; CO_2 is a major threat to your life, according to the EPA.* You need to be protected from too much of it, by them of course. That is, according to those 18,000 or so employees whose salary you pay *if* you are a taxpayer month in and month out. They are watching out for your best interest, and don't you forget it.

Here is what I had to say at their hearing:

> *Good afternoon.*
>
> *I'm a Consulting Geophysicist from Wichita, Kansas. I represent no interest group, although I will say that virtually my entire career has been spent in two industries: Energy and Environmental.*
>
> *I am also one of 34,000 American scientists, and counting, who have signed a Petition, that urges our government in the strongest possible terms to detach this country from any commitment to the Kyoto Protocol, or from anything that might resemble it in the future. I realize we are not here today to talk about Kyoto, per se, however, it does relate, as you are well aware.*
>
> *I have reviewed every page of your "Endangerment... Findings...," and I must say I have very strong disagreements with a number of your conclusions. Apparently, you have chosen to ignore large bodies of evidence. As a scientist, I am appalled, by many of your "findings."*
>
> *For example, the document issued the following statement:* "There is strong evidence that global sea level gradually rose in the 20th century and is currently rising at an increased rate." *However, the University of Colorado reports that the average sea level rise over the past 10,000 years was 4 feet/century, and that current sea-level rise is little more than 1 ft/century. In fact, the most recent evidence actually suggests that virtually zero increase has occurred since 2005.*
>
> *And we have the following:* "Ocean CO_2 uptake has lowered the average ocean pH (increased acidity) level by approximately 0.1 since 1750. Consequences for marine ecosystems may include reduced calcification by shell-forming organisms..." *However, data cited in a report (January 2009) by the Center for the Study of Carbon Dioxide and Global Change clearly shows that* "The 20th century has witnessed the second highest period of above average calcification in the past 237 years."
>
> *Administrator Jackson, you took a serious grilling last Tuesday at the Senate Environment and Public Works Committee hearing,*

where rightly so, Wyoming Senator John Barrasso repeatedly cited a White House memo.

That memo points to some very telling and problematic circumstances which are essential in attempting to quantify the character of earth's atmospheric conditions.

For example, the memo states, "Some issues to cover that would address costs, benefits, and risks include the following:

Quality and homogeneity of temperature data from surface networks that may affect estimates of past temperature trends, and calibration and verification of models.

With respect to this point, you should be aware, and I would be very surprised if you are not, that from 1989-1991 an abrupt change occurred in the number of weather stations that had been recording temperature data in Canada and Siberia.

The number of stations recording data went from approximately 12,000 to approximately 6,000. And guess what, the average global temperature suddenly soared from about 10 degrees C to about 11.5 degrees C, in the span of one year, continuing throughout the 1990's—the "hottest decade ever"!

Entirely due to the elimination of 6,000 COLD weather stations!

I could go on for hours, but I'm going to leave you with this:

The American people are going to find out more and more every day about these very sorts of improper handling of fundamentally important data relevant to this discussion.

Each and every one of you has the deep responsibility to deliver the truth to the American people. I sincerely hope you can find the courage to override the prevailing "consensus."

Thank you for your time.

Not one of the five EPA panelists seated in my line of sight was smiling at any time during the reading of the message, and the audience of about a hundred, which was virtually full of Green Peace, Sierra Club, etc., was generally appalled that anyone would have the gall to speak up in opposition to the EPA's proposed "findings."

As I left to go back to Capitol Hill for various meetings, a reporter from SNL Energy, Charlottesville, VA, home to one of my alma maters, the University of Virginia, approached me, and we had a conversation for about a half hour in the hallway outside the hearing room. Her story appeared a couple of days later in a local print journal, and I was impressed with the accuracy and the sense that I may have swayed her opinion during my delivery and the ensuing discussion. That's one down, and about 250 million to go, although the momentum is shifting with each opening gate.

EPA Gate opened up a few weeks later when the courageous Alan Carlin "leaked" an internal EPA document, from within the National Center for Environmental Economics, a subgroup within the Office of Policy, Economics, and Innovation. Their internal report was titled, "Proposed NCEE Comments on Draft Technical Support Document for Endangerment Analysis for Greenhouse Gas Emissions under the Clean Air Act." [6]

This draft was produced sometime in late March 2009, just after the EPA released its "Proposed Endangerment...Findings." The EPA ignored the cautions submitted on many levels related to these findings, and ended up releasing the proposed findings on April 17, 2009.

Picking up in the preliminary comments by Carlin:

"I have become increasingly concerned that EPA has itself paid too little attention to the science of Global Warming. EPA and others have tended to accept the findings reached by outside groups, particularly the IPCC and the CCSP*, as being correct without a careful and critical examination of their conclusions and documentation."...

> (*CCSP = Climate Change Science Program, the program responsible for coordinating and integrating research on Climate Change by U.S. government agencies from February 2002 to June 2009)

"As of the best information I currently have, the GHG*/ CO_2 hypothesis as to the cause of Global Warming, which this Draft TSD** supports, is currently an invalid hypothesis from a scientific viewpoint because it fails a number of critical comparisons with available observable data."...

*GHG = Greenhouse gas
**TSD = Technical Support Document

"A new 2009 paper finds that the crucial assumption in the GCM* models used by the IPCC concerning strongly positive feedback from water vapor is not supported by empirical evidence and that the feedback is actually negative…"

*GCM = General Circulation Model

"These inconsistencies between the TSD analysis and scientific observations are so important and sufficiently abstruse that in my view EPA needs to make an independent analysis of the science of Global Warming rather than adopting the conclusions of the IPCC and CCSP without much more careful and independent EPA staff review than is evidenced by the Draft TSD.....

"If their conclusions should be incorrect and EPA acts on them, it is EPA that will be blamed for inadequate research and understanding and reaching a possibly inaccurate determination of endangerment. Given the downward trend in temperatures since 1998 (which some think will continue until about 2030 given the 60 year cycle described in Section 2) there is no particular reason to rush into decisions based on a scientific hypothesis that does not appear to explain much of the available data…

Carlin, pg. 10

The figure on the following page is excerpted from page 38 of the Carlin report:

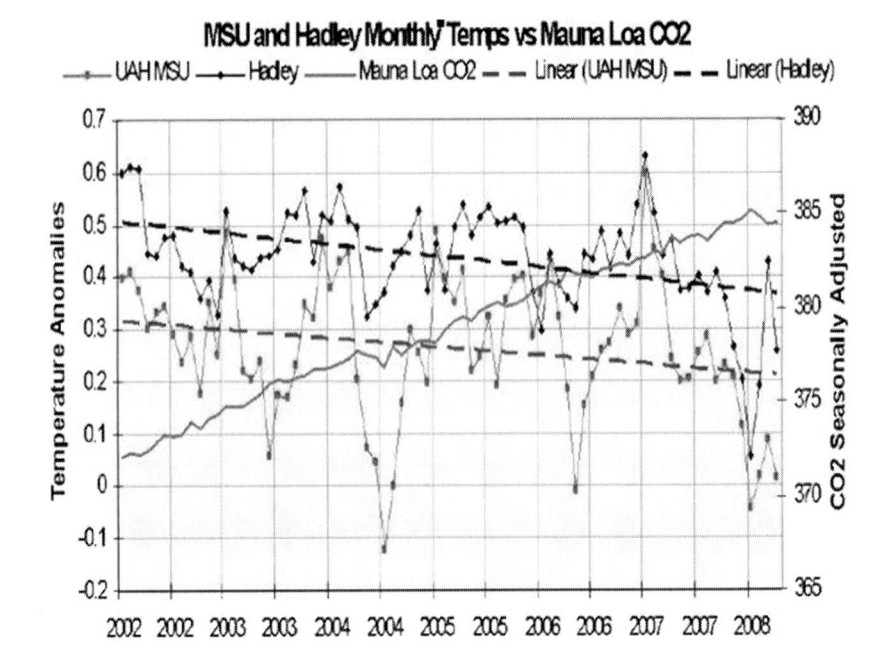

178 — *Global Environmental Survival — The New Green Earth*

MSU and Hadley Monthly Temps vs Mauna Loa CO2

Figure 16: Monthly Global Temperature Records vs CO_2 at Mauna Loa Volcano. [6]

(For a more detailed look, view the colorized version of this image within the color section, page 151.)

Some explanation is necessary to appreciate the full measure of this figure.

UAH houses one of our country's finest climate research centers and is directed by Dr. John Christy. One of his staff members is Dr. Roy Spencer, author of *The Great Global Warming Blunder* (2010). These men represent the finest America has to offer in attempting to gain a clearer understanding of what goes on in our atmosphere. They stand in very stark contrast to the Michael Mann's of this world, who have fed the "opposite" side of this crucial argument. I am very grateful for the likes of John Christy and Roy Spencer.

Hadley Centre in Great Britain is a counterpart to UAH, albeit far more focused on modeling and on the lookout for "Climate Change." (If only Margaret Thatcher knew what she was starting in 1990.) Nonetheless, they do provide some of the data that is presented above.

As to the graphic itself, firstly, and fundamentally, look at the continuous green line, upward increasing from left to right, and relating to the rightmost scale ranging from 370 to 385, seasonally adjusted CO_2 concentration as measured at Mauna Loa volcano.

Next, look at the dashed line trends, both down to the right, related to actual temperatures measured by two different sources, UAH/MSU and Hadley. We will revisit Hadley later. The essence is that the temperature is down materially from 2002 to nearly 2009.

The temperature trend is down.

The CO_2 trend is up.

I'm not one to emphasize short-term trends, but this one is just too compelling to set aside without noting. We will certainly keep an eye on this clearly opposing relationship. I'm willing to bet it will change materially within the next twenty years. Don't get too hooked on short-term trends, as tempting as they may be.

Carlin's paper also included this graphic (his Figure 2-5), which was excerpted from an outside research paper, with the following citation: Joel M. Kauffman, "Climate Change Reexamined," *Journal of Scientific Exploration*, Vol. 21, No. 4, pp. 723–749, 2007.

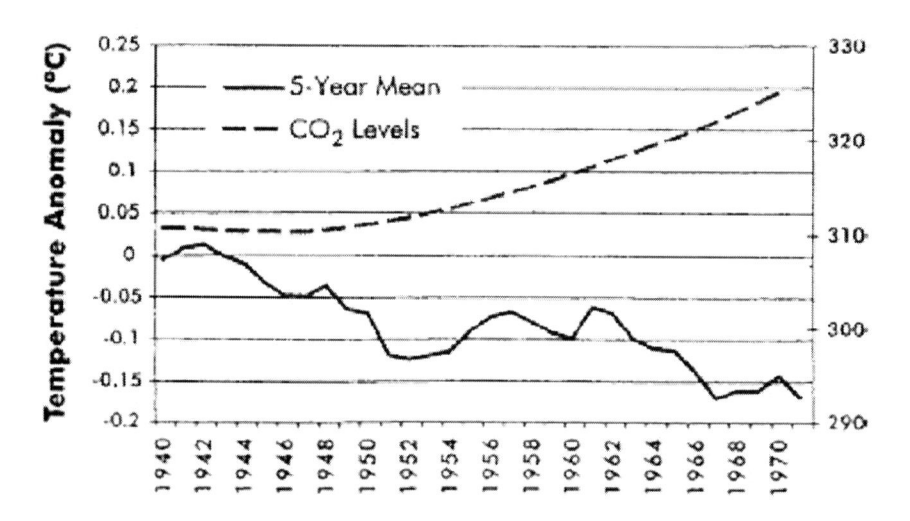

Figure 17: Global Surface Temperature, 1940-1971

Notice that this is a longer thirty-year trend, showing absolute divergence of CO_2 moving significantly up, while temperature moves significantly down during the same period. As a matter of fact, the "consensus" of opinion being developed by alarmists at that moment was that we were most certainly heading for another Ice Age.

It is also worth noting that by the end of the war (1945), America entered what might be arguably the most intense economic growth and peacetime prosperity in her history. Just look at how global temperatures responded to all that fresh, new CO_2 being introduced to earth's atmosphere.

I could go on at length as to the very substantial challenges raised by Carlin in this report. He even made an appearance on Glenn Beck one evening, providing direct testimony on his internal report. However, I will close this segment with a pull quote from Wikipedia:

> Carlin, was discouraged by his superior at EPA, Al McGartland, "from filing comments on the proposed finding and told ... that whatever he submitted was not likely to affect the final report, implying that the decision had already been made by early March 2009. After receiving Carlin's comments, McGartland told him that he would not forward them to the office preparing the final report. 'The time for such discussion of fundamental issues has passed for this round,' he wrote on March 17. 'The administrator and the administration has decided to move forward on endangerment, and your comments do not help the legal or policy case for this decision.' A few minutes later, he instructed Carlin to 'move on to other issues and subjects.' He also told Carlin not to discuss Climate Change with anyone outside his immediate office.
>
> Wikipedia, http://en.wikipedia.org/wiki/Alan_Carlin

Climate Gate / IPCC Gate

On Monday, November 19, 2009, the story started breaking that a "hacker" managed to leak thousands of emails from multiple scientists engaged in the University of East Anglia Climate Research Unit (CRU), one of the world's supposedly esteemed climate science institutions.

There are now multiple websites dedicated to nothing but Climate Gate, and I am very grateful for their efforts to keep this issue very much alive. One of the best I've seen is www.climate-gate.org.

In addition, I am very grateful that entities such as www.Heartland.org, and the Science and Public Policy Institute, www.scienceandpublicpolicy.org, are vigilant and consistently conducting actual research and reviews of credible scientific work related to earth's climate.

Phil Jones, the man running the show at East Anglia, should have resigned under no uncertain terms once it was revealed that he had a direct role in suppressing scientific evidence that substantially refutes the notion of human-induced, or anthropogenic, Climate Change. The scientific community is loathe in its lack of responsible policing of these affairs. Considering that Jones and Michael Mann, made oh so famous by his fraudulent "hockey stick," have regular communication, it is simply fitting that both should resign. Neither one of them should be allowed to publish again in any scientific journal or derivative thereof.

This is very serious stuff, the suppression of scientific evidence, the control of scientific information that theoretically could become available to the general public, or specifically the scientific world, that has not been able to see the light of day. I have written peer-reviewed work in the past, and I cannot imagine how absolutely, pathetically bad things have gotten inside the "green" science domain. This is something that must change.

So exactly why would "scientists" stoop so low as to block credible data from publication? Why would "scientists" manipulate existing data to steer attention into corners that should not exist?

Fraud, pure and simple. Just follow the money.

Chasing billions of fraud-filling coffers that should not exist. The "Climate Change" industry is growing faster than NASA did at the height of our race into outer space.

The Obama administration has proposed $2.6 billion for the 2011 Global Change Research Program, a 21 percent increase over 2010.

This level of funding exceeds that of any administration, dating back to 1989, the first year the U.S. funded "Global Warming" research. According to Fox News reporter Gene Koprowski, from February 10, 2010, many experts find it appalling that the Obama administration has boosted funding to these levels, for example:

> Professor Don Easterbrook at Western Washington University's department of geology, said the federal money "ought to be spent carrying out real research on the climate."
>
> Easterbrook said most of the federal funds so far have been spent on what he terms "political science," which aims to find a manmade cause of Global Warming when there are any number of ways to investigate the causes of temperature change. These are political motivations rather than purely scientific reasons, he said.
>
> What, exactly, will the American taxpayer get for its Global Warming research dollars? The EPA is spending $43 million to implement the greenhouse-gas reporting rule, to perform regulatory work for the largest stationary sources of greenhouse gases, and to develop new standards for cars and trucks.
>
> Research being funded at the National Science Foundation seeks to promote "discoveries needed to inspire societal actions leading to environmental and economic *sustainability (emphasis added by author)*," according to an agency statement. The NSF's portfolio for Global Warming will reach $766 million.
>
> Last year's budget provided $2.0 billion for the climate science program, a figure that doesn't include the half a billion dollars in stimulus money that the White House directed to Global Warming, as Obama's science adviser recently told Congress.
>
> For a more thorough read, please go to:
>
> http://www.foxnews.com/scitech/2010/02/11/obama-spending-increase-global-warming-research/

My point in all of this is to focus on Professor Easterbrook's comments about doing "real research." There certainly is a need to do real, credible, non-political, scientific research on our climate. Give us a few extra hours to prepare for and understand Atlantic hurricanes. Give us a few extra minutes to prepare for potentially damaging tornadoes. That is something worth paying real money to accomplish.

Speaking of those pesky Atlantic hurricanes, there's something I think you'll be interested to learn about their supposed increasing intensity with "Anthropogenic Global Warming," you know, all that extra energy that's being absorbed by the ocean, due to human-induced CO_2. Here's a quick look at a graphic that speaks very directly to that "fact." It is taken from a 2007 research paper by Harvard astrophysicist Willie Soon and co-authors A.B. Robinson and N.E. Robinson (*Environmental Effects of Increased Atmospheric Carbon Dioxide*). The data supporting the graphic can be found at these locations:

Landsea, C. W., Nicholls, N., Gray, W. M., and Avila, L. A. (1996) *Geophysical Research Letters* 23, 1697-1700.

Goldenberg, S. B., Landsea, C. W., Mesta-Nuñez, A. M., and Gray, W. M. (2001) *Science* 293, 474-479.

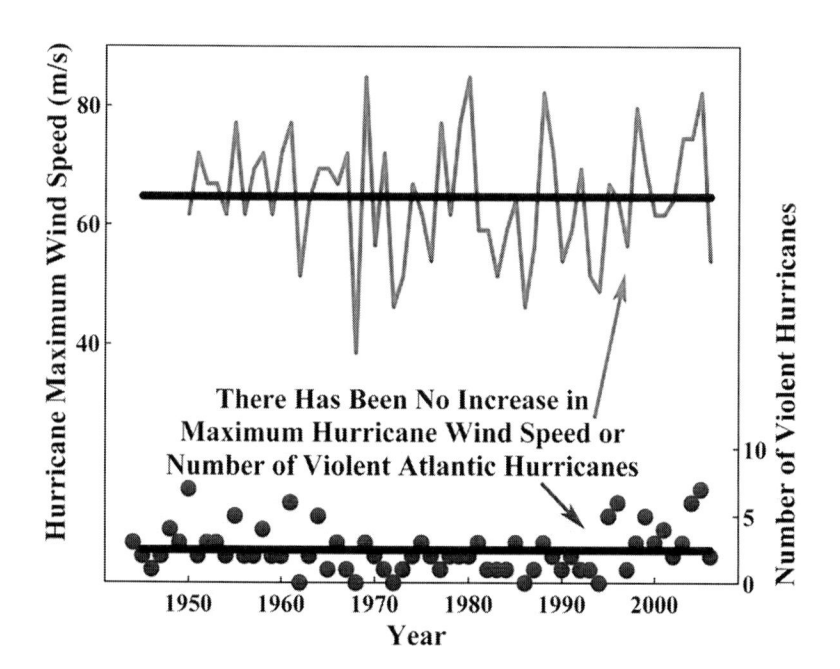

Figure 18: Hurricane Wind Speed and Number of Violent Hurricanes, 1940-2008

This flat-line trend continues back at least as far as 1900.

Does this data compilation match up with what you have heard from Al Gore and the vast majority of media outlets, including especially the Weather Channel?

As to Climate Gate, and the ensuing difficulties that have been had at the IPCC, the reality is that unless they encounter real "push back" from the populations of the world, they will continue unabated with their fraud, their sucking of billions, if not trillions, of dollars out of the global economy to satisfy their thirst for funding of their monstrosity.

As to the IPCC, the *Wall Street Journal* ran a story on February 19, 2010 (co-authors *Jeffrey Ball, Keith Johnson, Guy Chazan and Ian Talley*) with the following headline:

"Climate Group Admits Mistakes," with the subtitle, "*Some IPCC Officials Say the U.N.-Sponsored Group Must Improve Procedures for Reviewing Reports.*"

I have a better idea. How about halting the "reports" altogether?

On August 30, 2010, a news story flashed the results of a "review" of the IPCC, with the headline, "Panel Calls for 'Fundamental Reform' of IPCC." I have absolutely zero confidence in that body's ability to police anything in the way of its internal machinery. The group has been biased from its inception, and I see no evidence of that changing with the "fundamental reform" they are suggesting.

Here is an excerpt from the news flash:

> "The report says that the increasingly varied, complex, and numerous literature on climate has taxed the limited resources of IPCC's staff members and its hundreds of volunteer reviewers, just as climate science has come under greater public scrutiny. To help the authors deal with the onslaught, the report suggests that review editors, who oversee each chapter's multistep review process, be given more authority to force chapter authors to respond to public comments. At the same time, the report suggests that it would be easier to process the thousands of comments that flood into IPCC for each chapter

if authors responded to "the most significant ones" as decided by the review editors."

Kintisch, Science Insider, 30 August 2010

Source (Eli Kintisch, *Science Insider*): http://news.sciencemag.org/science insider/2010/08/panel-calls-for-fundamental-reform.html?sms_ss=email

I hope you can begin to understand my skepticism.

The world will get along just fine if they never utter another single sound from the podium at our beloved United Nations, with regard to the IPCC.

~~~

Just after the election, a renewed boldness has surfaced, from the entrenched adherents to Anthropogenic Global Warming. The victories countrywide that brought forth a Republican conservative majority in the House of Representatives have struck a nerve among the warmists, and they are now out to get the deniers, like me. So now, the American Geophysical Union, of which I am not a member, claims that seven hundred climate scientists have agreed to speak out as experts. (I am a member of the Society of Exploration Geophysicists, which has refrained from taking a public position on the matter.) According to releases through the media, a gentleman named "John Abraham of St. Thomas University in Minnesota… is organizing a 'Climate Rapid Response Team,' which so far has more than three dozen leading scientists to defend the 'consensus' on Global Warming in the scientific community." (Neela Banjerlee, Tribune Washington Bureau, appearing in the *Wichita Eagle*, November 8, 2010).

Now, I'm guessing that the following leading scientists that I am aware of on the other side of this issue will not be signing their petition:

John Christy, the University of Alabama, Huntsville, director of the Earth Science Systems Center; Roy Spencer, same organization, former NASA Senior Scientist; Richard Lindzen, Alfred P. Sloan Professor of Atmospheric Science, MIT; Patrick Michaels, former state climatologist of Virginia, currently fellow at the CATO Institute, to name a few.

That would not include the more than 33,000 scientists, engineers, and other credible individuals, including myself, who have signed an alternate petition stating our absolute disagreement with any suggestion that man's activities are primarily responsible for the climate conditions prevailing upon the planet today.

I would venture to guess that any one of the men mentioned above would be most happy to debate the matter in any forum in America or elsewhere, if necessary, provided the ground rules were fair and well organized.

Bottom line, bring it on. We will be happy to accommodate the debate. I volunteer right here and now to be the moderator, if not a willing participant in the debate itself. It is certainly high time the debate became fully involved so that the American people and the world can see what it means to lay the science on the line.

I have some additional examples of IPCC modeling, as compared to real world data. The first comes from relatively recent research conducted by Syun-Ichi Akasofu at the International Arctic Research Center, University of Alaska, Fairbanks. This research demonstrates an interesting cyclic indication of global temperature, termed the Multi-decadal oscillation. The graphic below demonstrates the suggested oscillatory correlation, as compared to IPCC projections beyond year 2000. We now have ten years of empirical data to see how each methodology plays out against real world data.

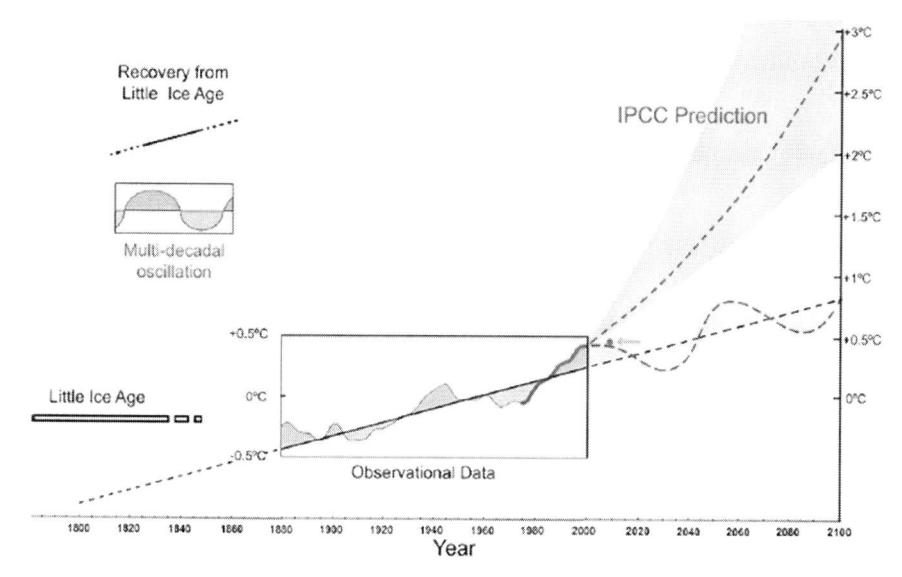

Figure 19: Multi-decadal Oscillation, 1880-2100 [7]

(For a more detailed look, view the colorized version
of this image within the color section, page 152.)

The dot at around 2009 shows the relative goodness of fit of either method. I will go with Akasofu and emphasize that the trend has a very good fit going back to around 1800, the beginning of our global pullout from the "Little Ice Age."

I will put a wrap on the inherently inaccurate IPCC predictions coming out of their 2007 report. I do wish to emphasize that much of what they have contrived relates to those individuals at East Anglia, who yet insist, in the face of Climate Gate email revelations, that they are standing by their "science."

Let's take a look first at the IPCC model versus the real world for the period 1981- 2010, to establish a baseline for a follow-up IPCC prediction. This graphic comes courtesy of the Science and Public Policy Institute, based just outside Washington, DC.

(As an aside, I was recently asked to make a presentation with a group of panelists on a college campus. When similar data was presented, one of the panelists, a student at the college, commented that the SPPI is supported by Koch Industries, one of America's most successful private companies, with interests in agriculture, energy, and materials processing. My comment to her was and is, "I do not care where the data comes from, provided it is accurate and stands the test of pure scientific review. Furthermore, I am very glad that Koch Industries supports SPPI". So, here you go, as I proudly display results compiled by SPPI.)

IPCC predicts rapid, exponential CO_2 growth that is not occurring

www.scienceandpublicpolicy.org

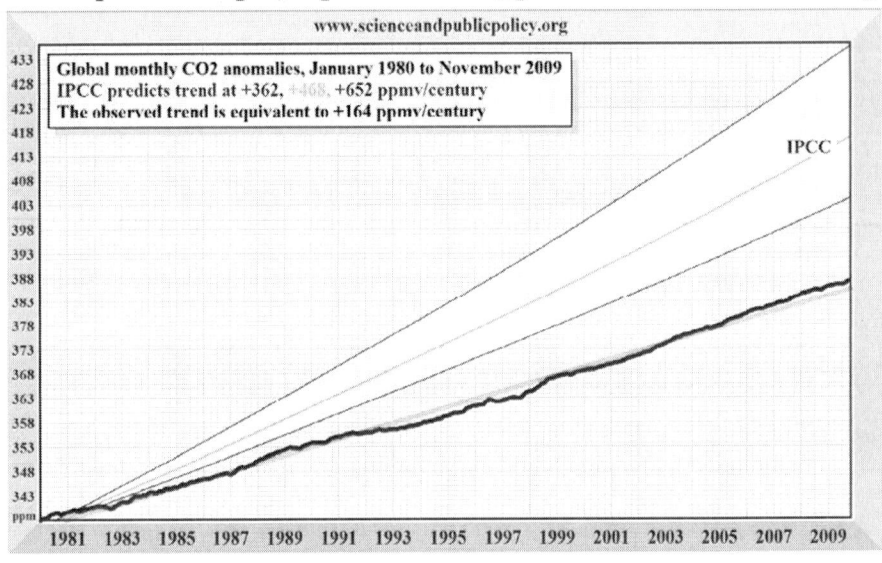

Global monthly CO2 anomalies, January 1980 to November 2009
IPCC predicts trend at +362, +468, +652 ppmv/century
The observed trend is equivalent to +164 ppmv/century

Figure 20: IPCC Predicted CO_2 Exponential Growth, 1982-2009 [8]

(For a more detailed look, view the colorized version of this image within the color section, page 152.)

The point made via this figure is that the data from 1981 to the present is very clearly indicating a linear relationship in CO_2 growth, not "exponential," as suggested by IPCC modeling. This makes a very significant difference in any attempt to accurately predict a future trend. The data for the next graphic below begins at year 2000, carrying forward to year 2100 with the linear trend established above.

Projecting the past decade's CO2 trend to 2100 halves IPCC forecasts

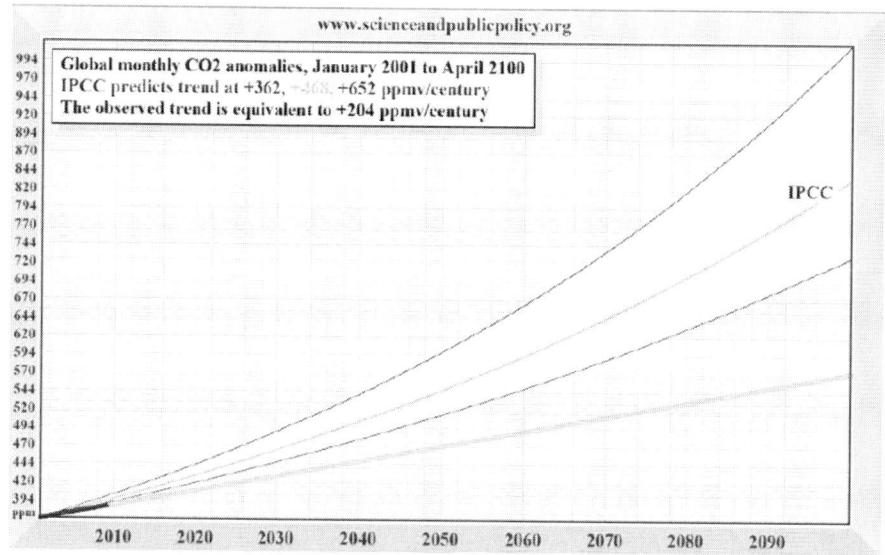

Figure 21: IPCC Predicted CO_2 Growth 2009-2100 [9]

As is very evident, the IPCC model, based on an exponential projection, is very likely to be in serious error by 2100. The average IPCC prediction for CO_2 concentration is present day + 468 ppmv, or about 853 ppmv. The SPPI prediction, on the other hand reaches present day + 204 ppmv, or about 589 ppmv.

I will leave you with this to ponder. (In the first place, I will reiterate that *any* attempt to contain, control, or otherwise influence the content of CO_2 in earth's atmosphere will be futile. The logic behind that statement is demonstrated later in Chapter 5, dedicated exclusively to CO_2.)

Guess what the "acceptable" concentration of CO_2 in U.S. submarines happens to be?

8,000 ppmv. [10]

This data was provided by William Happer, professor at Princeton University. On February 25, 2009, he testified before a U.S. Senate Committee on Environment and Public Works. I'm sure Professor

Happer made Barbara Boxer's day. She doesn't do well with facts like these.

If it's *okay* for our sailors to be exposed to this concentration, I submit we have very little to worry about at 385 ppmv, which is less than 5 percent of the amount in those subs.

But please, don't tell Mrs. Boxer (yes, I am referring to you as Mrs.), or Mr. Kerry (used to be Lieberman-Warner) that you, a lowly peon citizen, have seen any of these reports. If you did that, you might hurt their feelings and cause them to revisit their beloved scheme related to not only "cap and trade," but the whole, comprehensive, behemoth range of new regulations and mandates that they feel we Americans must have in order to preserve our environment.

The chart below speaks volumes about just how far off-scale the federal government has overreached in its belief that in every respect it knows better how to handle our affairs than we poor, peon citizens. If they get their way, this is what you and I will pay for and be legally subject to. I can assure you, BO is all over this one, too. I've never heard him utter one word against this unbelievable maze of agencies and regulations.

The Audacity of Freedom — *191*

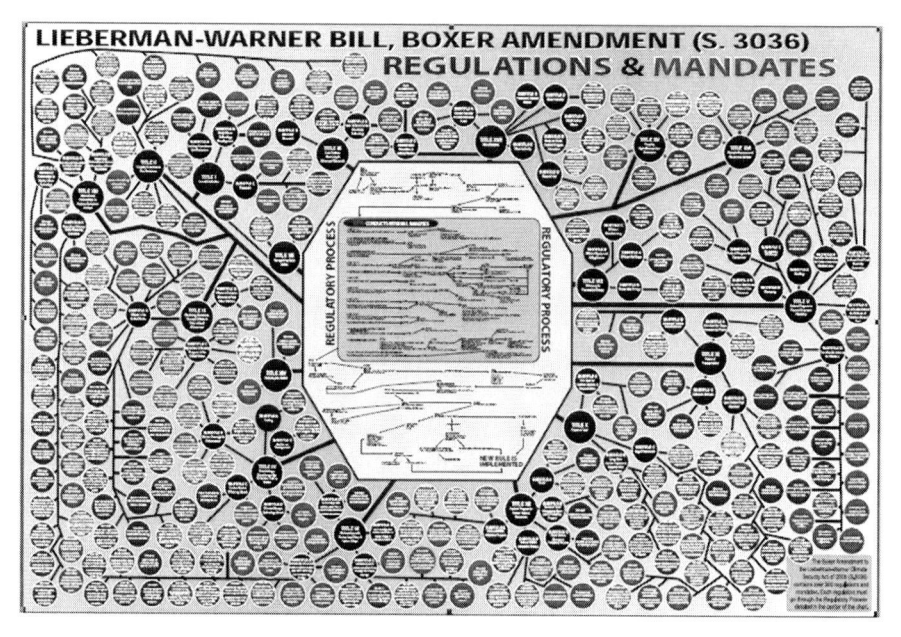

Figure 22: Lieberman, Warner, Boxer Regulation-Mandate Chart, Small Scale [11]

(For a more detailed look, view the colorized version
of this image within the color section, page 153.)

The chart above was produced by the U.S. Chamber of Commerce, which as you might imagine, has studied what has now become known as HB 2454 (Waxman-Markey) in great detail.

The summary of proposed regulations, mandates, and regulatory processes are buried within what used to be Senate Bill 3036, the precursor to the current Senate bill complementing the already passed House legislation known as the "American Clean Energy and Security Act of 2009" (HB2454).

The interior content of the chart in the stretched-out hexagon—that's the purview of the EPA. That stays in play even if 'cap and trade' is struck down. They will continue to manipulate mankind as we know it by virtue of their onerous processes of rule writing, regulations, and every other manner of disruption they can fashion up on businesses and individuals alike. So, in certain respects, it is dangerous not to produce legislation that serves to better define exactly what it is we should do to produce a viable "Clean Energy and Security Act." Let's see exactly what the incoming Congress does to offset or restrain the long arm of the EPA, if that is even possible, due to the maze of existing laws and regulations. To date, the newly revamped House of Representatives is taking a significant look at defunding multiple EPA programs, but it remains to be seen whether they will, in the final vote tally dealing with Appropriations, actually follow through on restraining this agency that may inflict untold economic damage on our country.

Exactly how are they going to "track" greenhouse gas emissions? Are they going to hook up a meter to your air conditioning unit, your water heater, your kitchen stove, your washer, your dryer, your car's tailpipe, your boat's engine, your bodily functions, your animal's bodily functions, your fireplaces, and your barbeques, with a similar set of devices to track all your business's activities?

Are you ready for them to deeply impose and embed themselves into virtually every aspect of your life, to track what amounts to a colorless, odorless, tasteless, essential, and naturally functioning significant component of the earth's entire biosphere?

This is absolutely insane, and hopefully, we will not take it lying down.

In the event you still question the validity of the baseless attack being made on CO_2 and those awful fossil fuels that are supposedly almost wholly responsible for the creation of it, according to Al Gore and the whole host of environmental protectors, I have some additional data for you to ponder. While we have periodically touched upon CO_2 in previous discussions, this special "pollutant," as the esteemed EPA has now deemed it to be, deserves it's very own chapter.

Carbon Dioxide (CO_2)

What an incredible chemical compound. Two oxygen atoms covalently bonded to a single carbon atom. Linear, very symmetric, very stable. Courtesy of Wikipedia.

Figure 23: CO_2 Molecule

Carbon Dioxide (CO$_2$)

Here's another image that you are all too familiar with:

Photo 4: Coal-Fired Power Plant

(For a more detailed look, view the colorized version of this image within the color section, page 149.)

Jeffrey Energy Center, near St. Mary's, KS. Photo by author, February 1, 2011. Temperature at time of photograph: ~4 degrees F..

I mean, can't you just feel the weight of all that CO$_2$ coming out of those smokestacks? The problem is that the one thing you are *not* seeing in this image is CO$_2$. Just so you know, CO$_2$ is colorless, odorless, tasteless, and for all intents and purposes, harmless.

Other than primarily steam, there may actually be some sulfur dioxide (SO$_2$), and other potentially damaging concentrations of other actual potentially polluting compounds that do need to be monitored, but I submit to you in the most honest and forthright manner possible, CO_2 is not one of them. There is *no* reason whatsoever to monitor CO_2 as anything remotely close to a harmful substance.

There are a few additional stats relating to this essential component of our atmosphere that you need to know. But first, you need to know just how much CO_2 is out there in the first place. Here are the approximate numbers as to the fundamental contributions to today's earth's atmosphere:

ELEMENTS AND COMPOUNDS IN EARTH'S ATMOSPHERE

Element / Compound	Chemical formula	Percentage
Nitrogen	N_2	78.090%
Oxygen	O_2	20.950%
Water Vapor	H_2O	~1.000%
Argon	Ar	0.930%
Carbon Dioxide	CO_2	0.039%

Table 3: Elements and Compounds in Earth's Atmosphere

Carbon dioxide's contribution has actually been rounded up, given that it's actual globally averaged concentration is most recently estimated to be 0.0390 percent, or as some like to term it, 390 parts per million (ppm).

That's less than four one hundredths of one percent.

Now, some would say that that number understates the importance of CO_2 as a greenhouse gas, which is really what this is all about, right?

Let's look at those "greenhouse gases" and their respective contributions to the "greenhouse."

Greenhouse Gas Components

Element/Compound	Chemical formula	Percentage
Water vapor	H_2O	95.00%
Carbon Dioxide	CO_2	3.50%
Methane	CH_4	~0.50%
Others (Chlorofluorocarbons, etc)		~1.00%

Table 4: Greenhouse Gas Components

CO_2 is 3.5 percent of the "greenhouse gases".

The best available data indicates that the contribution of CO_2 coming from *human activity* is about 3.5 percent of the 3.5 percent.

Get out your calculators, as that comes to 0.1225 *percent* of the greenhouse.

That works out to less than 0.5 ppmv of all those atmospheric gases coming from your comprehensive, combined, overwhelming human activities.

So, the apparent contribution of humans is far less than 1 percent of the total currently measured CO_2 concentration (if the estimates are anywhere close to correct, and given the IPCC, NOAA, and other estimators, I do wonder about that number).

And this .8 percent CO_2 concentration (of the overall greenhouse) coming from humans is driving up the temperature such that all the glaciers are melting, all the polar bears are going to die, and Miami will be under water by the close of the 21st century?

I beg to disagree.

The glaciers are melting, but it has absolutely nothing whatsoever to do with CO_2.

It has everything in the world to do with the planet pulling away from the "Little Ice Age," commencing around 1850.

The Audacity of Freedom — *197*

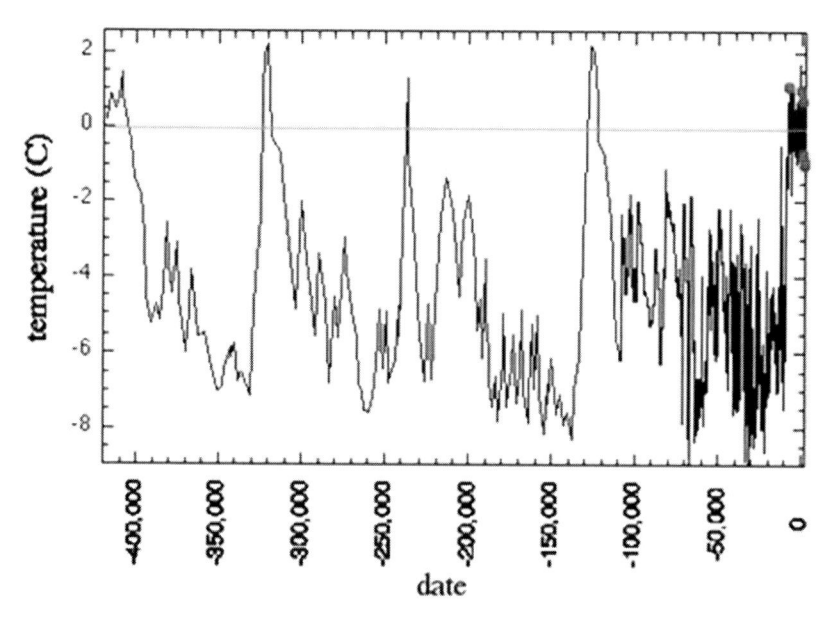

Figure 24: 400,000 Year Global Temperatures via Ice Cores [1]

(For a more detailed look, view the colorized version
of this image within the color section, page 153.)

This graphic represents the global temperature estimated from ice cores dating back by some estimates approximately 400,000 years. The last segment, incorporating red dots with actual temperature data since about 1724, provides reference as to how we compare to conditions dating back apparently more than four hundred millennia.

The end of the "Little Ice Age" was at about 1850 AD, less than -2 degrees Celsius below the zero line in blue. Around thirty thousand years before present, it was apparently -8 degrees Celsius (about 16 degrees Fahrenheit) colder than today.

You cannot calculate the hydrocarbons required to maintain planet "comfort" during the winter months with that sort of temperature departure from today.

It is highly improbable that mankind can somehow manipulate this trend by extricating CO_2 from earth's atmosphere.

Since the thermometer was introduced in 1724 by Daniel Gabriel Fahrenheit and followed up with a different scale by Anders Celsius in 1742, man has been very interested in temperature.

Where I live, temperatures range from about 0 degrees F (-18 degrees C) to about 100 degrees F (+38 degrees C). When it gets to either of these extremes, I get uncomfortable. When it gets to the lower extreme, I get *real* uncomfortable, which I assume is consistent with about 99 percent of earth's population.

My favorite temperature is about 70 degrees F (21 degrees C), but who am I to judge the ideal?

And, just for curiosity, who is to judge the "right" concentration of CO_2, if it has any relevance to temperature whatsoever?

I posed that very question to the immediate past Kansas Secretary of Health and Environment, Mr. Roderick Bremby, at a seminar he presented at Wichita State University in the spring 2009.

He could not (would not) answer the question.

Just so you know, I would love to see Al Gore behind bars, for fraud. Then I would prosecute George Soros, then Andy Stern, then Valerie Jarrett, then…

The problem is that it would get really expensive and clog up the courts for such a long time. I am out for the truth, the ability for man to accurately gauge his condition, his needs, and his ability to respond to his circumstances.

Where are you in this deal?

This is as challenging a condition as we have ever faced as a country and as a human race. And the challenge has absolutely nothing to do with the concentration of CO_2 in earth's atmosphere. The challenge has everything to do with the scourge of insensitivity to the rampant fraud in government programs, the lack of discernment in dealing with fundamentals of economics, and the intense corruption we know exists in our own government in America.

Are you going to simply sit back and continue to tolerate this nonsense?

If you choose to do nothing, and I truly hope some of this material and data has struck a nerve, I can only wish you the best as the rest of us who do understand the magnitude of this problem make the preparations to act in accordance with our innate sensitivities. I would really like to have you with us, as opposed to either sitting on the sidelines or in opposition to the fundamental facts.

Where you do not want to go is "green."

This "green" movement has distorted the word *green*. In actuality, higher CO_2 concentrations promote more true greening of the plant world. Are you aware that greenhouses materially and very intentionally enhance their CO_2 concentrations to stimulate plant growth?

So, what else do we know about CO_2? And why is it essential to set out the facts, as opposed to allowing the fraud to continue unabated? I'll tell you why: Your life depends on it. If we fail to get a proper grip on this subject, and the current "powers that be" have their way, you can kiss this republic good-bye, and ready yourself to be "policed" into a controlled nation of unfounded regulations and very expensive mandates. If they get their way, they will maim the economic system in this country, and the consequences will spread across the globe like relative wildfire.

A *Wall Street Journal* poll released June 24, 2010, showed that at least 63 percent of Americans listed control of emissions as a top concern, as opposed to 31 percent who did not, with 6 percent undecided. A 2-to-1 margin concerned about CO_2? All due to a highly organized, very well-funded, sophisticated propaganda machine, led by Al Gore and George Soros.

Somehow, we must get the good people of this country to have an opportunity to see the incredible range of facts that absolutely dispute any notion that CO_2 and human-induced global warming warrant one more second of our attention, much less trillions of tax dollars that could and should go for truly worthy projects.

While I foresee significant energy supply disruptions in the relatively near future *if* we do not get off this strangulation strategy, I am not one of the proponents of Boone Pickens' plan, which seeks to deploy very expensive energy sources such as massive wind and solar farms across America.

Our fundamental access to fossil fuels should be greatly expanded, without any apology to anyone. If we do go on that very practical, far more energy efficient, higher energy density pathway, we will materially soften the possible impacts of future likely supply shortcomings.

I have friends (by now, perhaps had) employed in the "wind energy" business, some as well in the business of CO_2 sequestration. Upon seeing the mountains of evidence, I can see no justification whatsoever for expending tax dollars in support of subsidizing either of these endeavors. If you and your supporting entities want to compete in the global energy marketplace on a level playing field, then we welcome you to the competition. But I will forever resist the notion of paying more, far more, for fundamental energy needs than I must. I will forever resist the notion of *anyone* paying far more for their energy than is necessary in the free market.

It is important to contrast the actual subsidies that are directed toward these 'renewable' energy sources, as opposed to the supposed 'subsidies' that are claimed to be directed toward the fossil fuel industry, specifically the oil and gas sector. Providing tax incentives for such items as intangible drilling costs related to the capital intensive activity associated with a highly risky and complex operation is in no way correlative to constructing a wind tower, or a solar panel in the desert. These facilities have virtually zero risk associated with construction. The risk associated with them comes from natural forces that are predictable with a high degree of certainty.

There is a huge difference between these scenarios. Furthermore, in most states and counties within those states where oil and gas production occur, significant revenues are captured at the wellhead and delivered to state treasuries via severance taxes, and county treasuries via ad valorem property taxes. The combined draw from these taxes amounts to anywhere from a minimum of about 12% to a maximum of perhaps 18%. In addition, royalties paid to mineral owners range from an additional 12.5% to as much as 25%. The net profit margin for the typical independent oil and gas company in the United States (which provides approximately 75% of the crude oil and natural gas supply produced in this country) is approximately 7.5%. For comparative purposes, the highest profit margin industry in this country in the recent past is the shipping industry, netting margins above 50% in many cases. [2]

While current global conditions portend high oil and gas prices, the reader needs to understand that current policies are, if anything, worsening the pressure on the supply side of products available to the marketplace. This is largely due to limitations placed on the industry, especially in the United States, in favor of 'green' energy.

⁓⁓

I'm sure you have heard that the glaciers are melting, that the polar bears are running out of places to live due to Arctic ice receding beyond belief. Well, they got the beyond belief part right. Don't believe it.

Here's what we *know* about the extent of Antarctic sea ice extent:

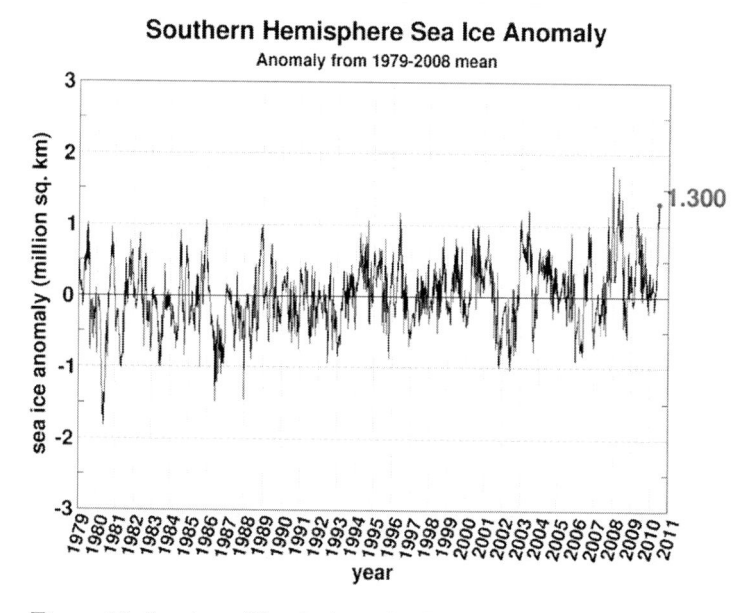

Figure 25: Southern Hemisphere Sea Ice Anomaly, 1979-2010 [3]

202 — *Carbon Dioxide (CO$_2$)*

What the graph clearly shows is that in the period from 1979, when we first started using satellite data to monitor ice conditions, until the present, there has been virtually no material change in Southern Hemisphere sea ice extent, save the minimum recorded in the spring of 1980 and the *maximum* you see for late 2007.

Antarctic sea ice extent has been virtually constant over the past thirty years.

Let's look at some bird's eye views of the top of the world in the opposite hemisphere:

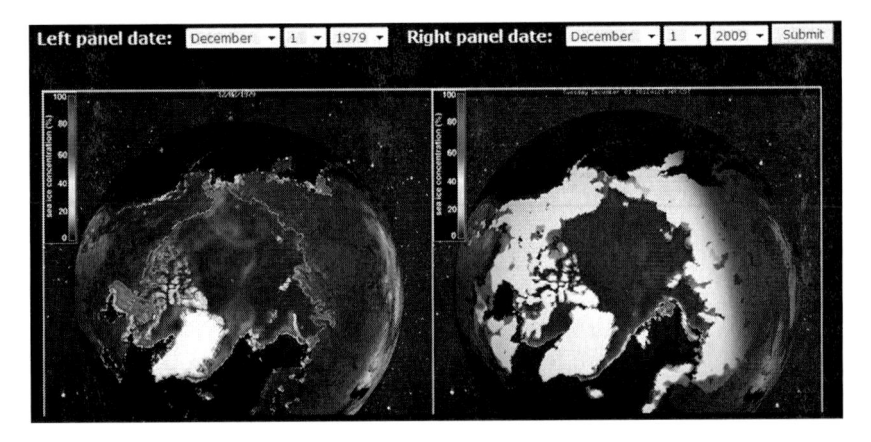

Figure 26: Arctic Sea Ice Extent, 1980-2009 [4]

(For a more detailed look, view the colorized version of this image within the color section, page 154.)

The area in purple is the focus of this display. The photo from 2009 leaves the snow cover in the rest of the northern hemisphere, while that from 1980 has that component removed. Again, this data is provided by research at the University of Illinois.

Let's look at actual temperatures in the Arctic:

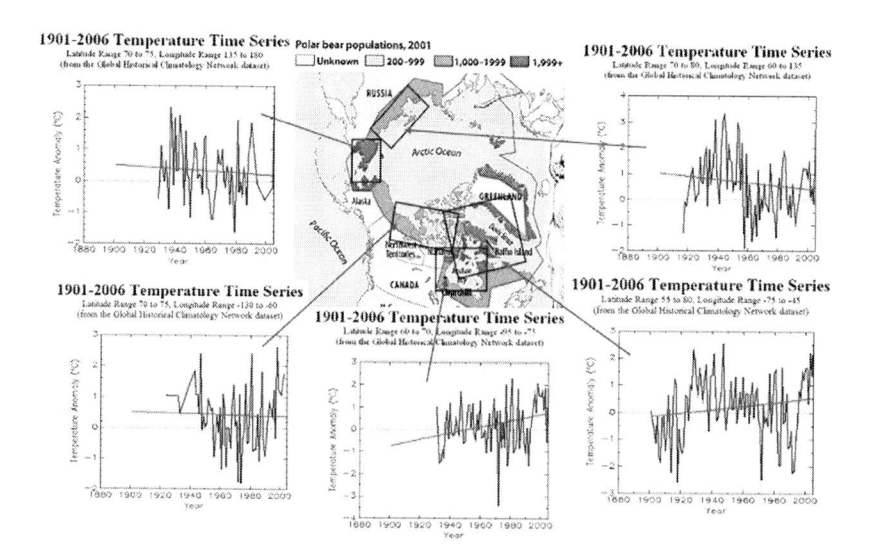

Figure 27: Arctic Temperatures 1901-2006 [5]

(For a more detailed look, view the colorized version of this image within the color section, page 154.)

The montage above covers the period from 1901-2006, the latest for which data was available at the time this data was compiled. It depicts the departure from the mean, with the average baseline being that at 1901.

This provides a sense of temperature departure from the mean over that period, across a broad spectrum of Arctic sites. One can see that some regions experienced upward temperature trends during the period, while others experienced downward trends. It would be incorrect to conclude that Arctic temperatures have anything approaching a fixed temperature trending regime.

But what about the temperature trend, and the relationship to CO_2, if any?

204 — Carbon Dioxide (CO_2)

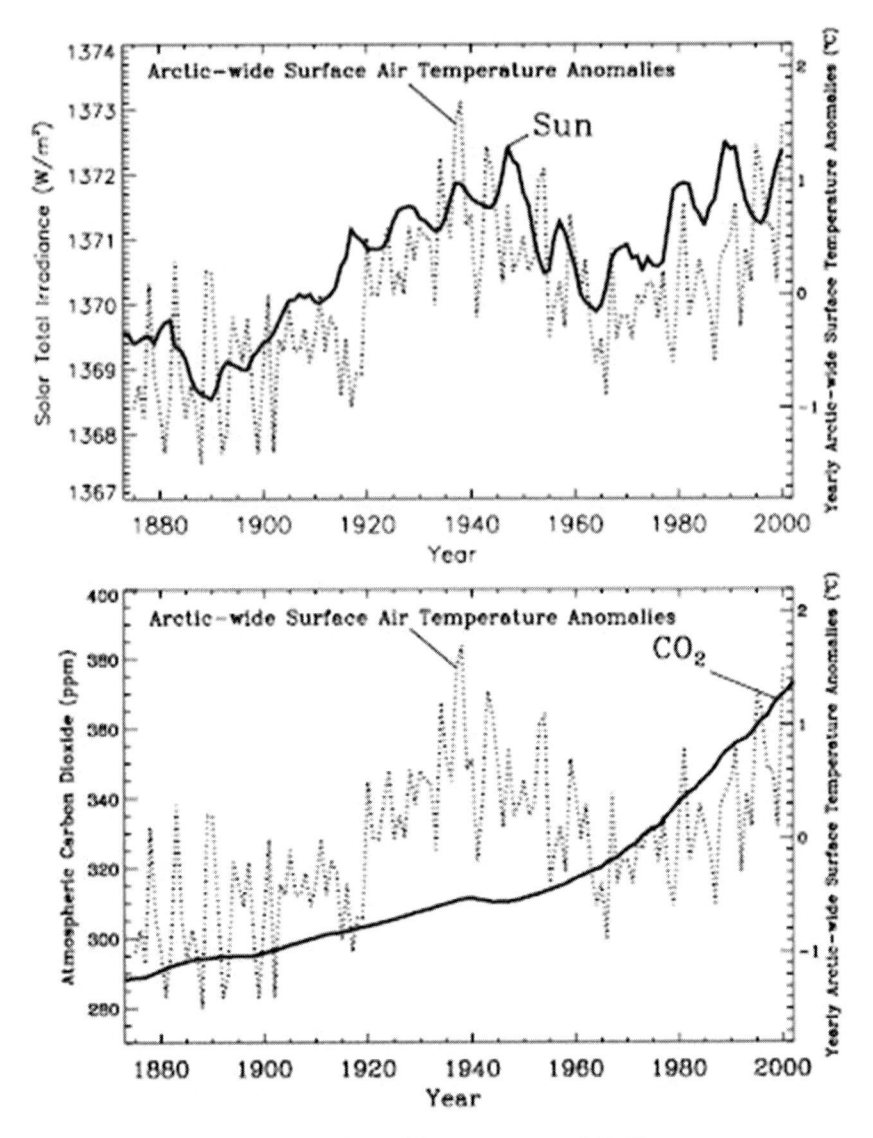

Figure 28: Arctic Temperature vs CO_2 [6]

The upper image was embedded in an earlier graphic in the previous chapter, where the correlation to hydrocarbon consumption (lack thereof) was illustrated. In the lower image now, we have the correlation (lack thereof) of Arctic temperature to CO_2 concentration.

Now, do you suppose that Dr. Soon, of the Harvard-Smithsonian Center for Astrophysics, somehow stays up very late at night "doctoring" data just so he can make the rest of the scientific community look foolish when they attempt to correlate CO_2 to either temperature or human-induced Climate Change?

Dr. Soon testified before the United States Senate Committee on Environment and Public Works, (July 29, 2003) in an effort to straighten out the distortions in the record with respect to human-induced Global Warming. Do they have eyes that can see or ears that can hear? You'll have to ask them, especially now that BO has them back hot on the trail of "energy policy."

I do want to note that the generally upward trend of temperature in these graphs relates to the very clear and simple correlation to earth's finally leaving the devastating conditions (humanly speaking) associated with the "Little Ice Age," you know, that minor event discrepancy that caught the fraud of Michael Mann's famous "hockey stick." Yes, it was a very real global phenomenon but only one in a long line of proxy-measureable temperature events throughout earth's history. Let's look at more data:

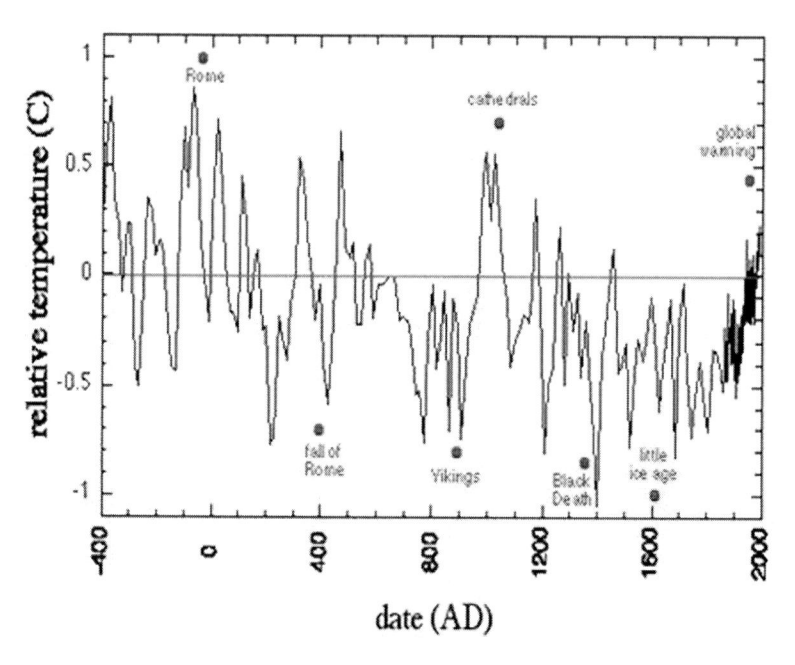

Figure 29: Global Temperatures, 400 BC to 2000 AD [7]

206 — *Carbon Dioxide (CO₂)*

In the above image, oxygen isotopes yield an estimate of ancient temperatures combined with total global ice volume, to provide a proxy correlation to the previous images of more recent earth history. The gray shaded and darker highlight near the end of the time frame represent actual temperature data, as opposed to the proxy. Needless to say, real people occupied the globe throughout this entire time frame. I do not recall any historical evidence whatsoever from the Romans as to how unbearably "hot" it was, as they were out conquering the then known world. What we do know about the "Little Ice Age" is that living conditions were very difficult, with the Thames River freezing for many months each winter. No fun. Greenland was occupied first by the Vikings around 900 AD, but the island was largely vacated due to the Little Ice Age low point at around 1400 AD.

This section just wouldn't be complete without your seeing the comparison of CO_2 fraud-laden temperature manipulation, as measured against real history or proxies thereof.

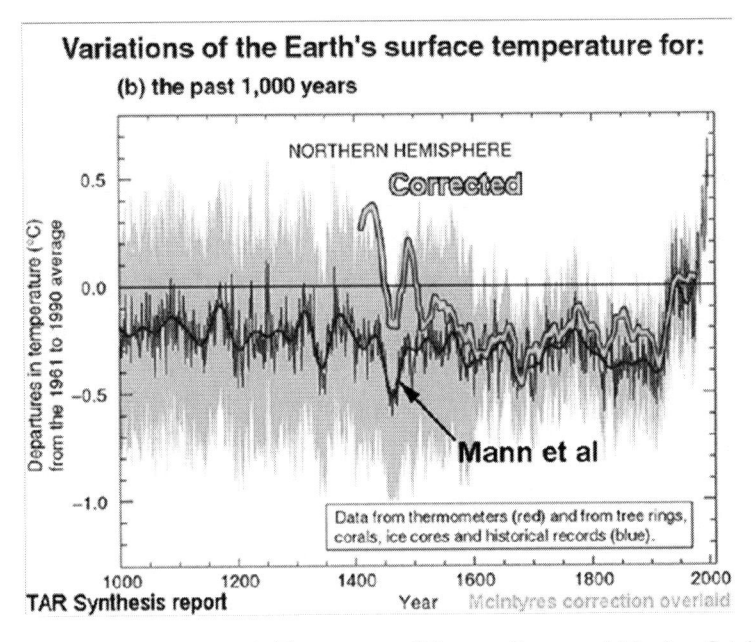

Figure 30: 1,000 Year Earth Temperature History: Corrected Hockey Stick [8]

(For a more detailed look, view the colorized version of this image within the color section, page 155.)

This graphic vividly portrays the degree to which bad science can produce policy directives wholly unsupported by the real data. In this case, Michael Mann's background hockey stick portrayal (gray, blue, black, and red curves) is overlaid by the corrected data provided by Stephen McIntyre (green curve). Forget about Mann's prediction as to the "red" curve indications—they didn't happen.

Just so you know, the corrected data was available well in advance of the release of *An Inconvenient Truth*, yet Al Gore refused to acknowledge even the existence of the corrected data. His Oscar-winning performance was *substantially* enhanced by this fraudulent data.

Let's take a look at some more of the data related to those pesky hurricanes. You know, those beastly CO_2-related weather events that are just getting worse and worse and worse.

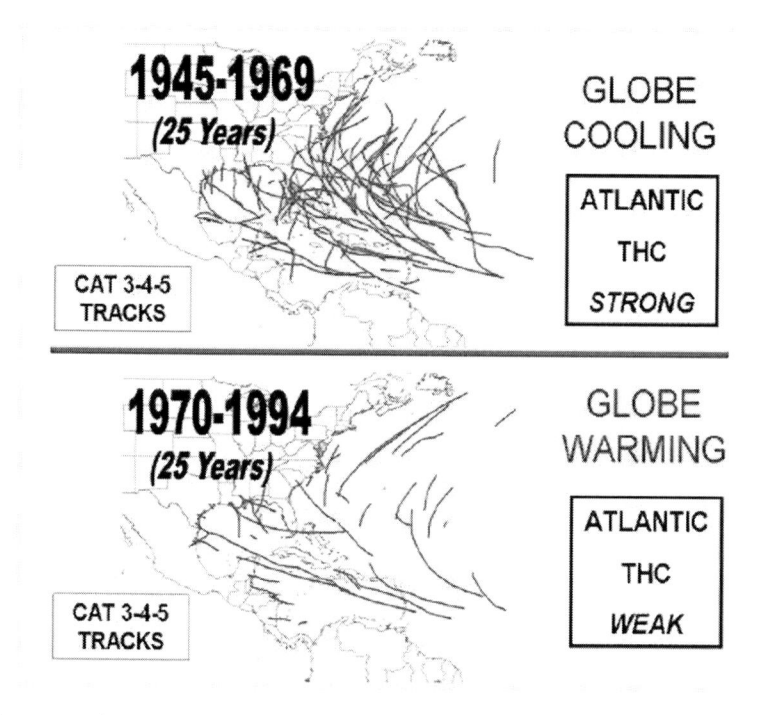

Figure 31: Atlantic Hurricane Tracks: Globe Cooling vs Globe Warming [9]

(For a more detailed look, view the colorized version
of this image within the color section, page 156.)

Notice that the hurricane tracks for the "warming" period are substantially lower density than those when the globe was cooling. How does that fit any "science-settled" models?

What a bunch of charlatans.

CO_2 and Ocean Acidification

Here's another in a long line of fraudulent claims that have no actual basis in fact. The theory proffered by multiple scientists says that because we humans are pumping all this new CO_2 into the oceans due to our emissions into the atmosphere, we are decreasing the pH of the oceans, thereby killing the corals by way of weakening the "calcification" process, generally devastating the sensitive oceanic environment.

The data does not support the hypothesis in the least; in fact, the data again goes in the opposite direction from the conjecture. Thank God for people like Craig Idso, and the "Center for the Study of Carbon Dioxide and Global Change."

Let's look first at what we have observed at one of the earth's most extensive reef systems, the Great Barrier Reef (GBR) off Australia's northeast coast. One would think that if "Global Warming" and the supposed companion effect of acidification was real, this would be one of the first places to obtain confirmation of the hypothesis.

Please forgive me for having to break the news:

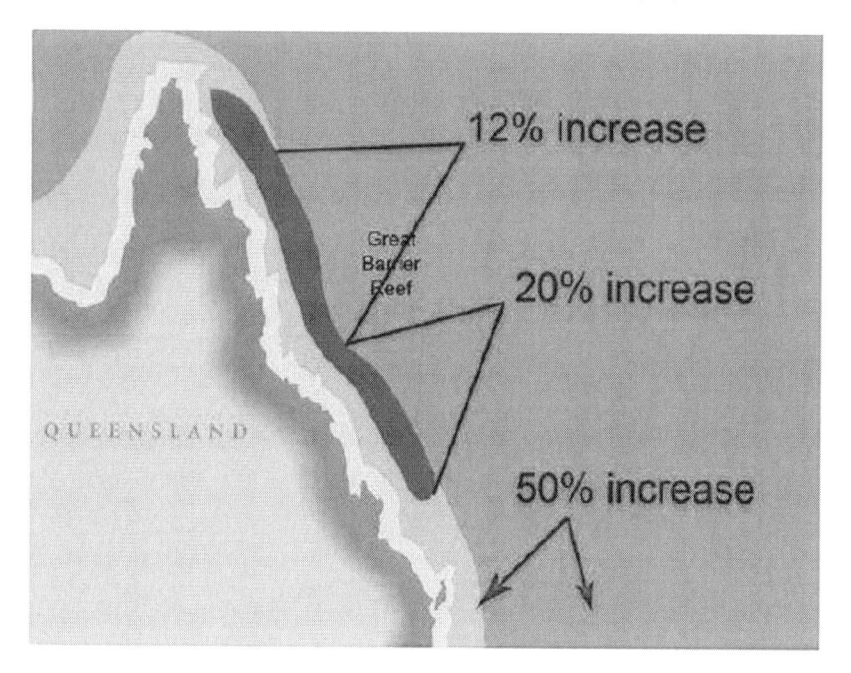

Figure 32: Great Barrier Reef Calcification Observations [10]

We do happen to have real data, as opposed to IPCC models, to draw from. I consider it quite significant that real data from 1903-1998, which is somewhat likely to fall in the window of influence of fossil fuels on CO_2, presents a significant and absolute contradiction to the suggestion of coral degradation. What the graphic shows is that the northern reaches of the GBR increased in substance by about 12 percent during the period 1979-1998, when all that bad CO_2 was accumulating, and the southern reaches of the reef experienced about 20 percent growth over the same period. In the southernmost region studied, calcification increased by 50 percent. This is just more evidence absolutely refuting the claims that CO_2 is somehow detrimentally impacting the ocean environment.

It is not happening.

The graphic above, as well as the one below, are sourced from an eighty-three-page research paper,[10] including voluminous references and commentary for policymakers. Just how much attention do you think they paid to this actual, factual data, as opposed to the infamous IPCC's wondrous models?

Let's take a closer look at a non-coral organism, the phytoplankton *Emiliania huxleyi*, just one more in a long line of calcareous (calcified) organisms showing sensitivity to CO_2:

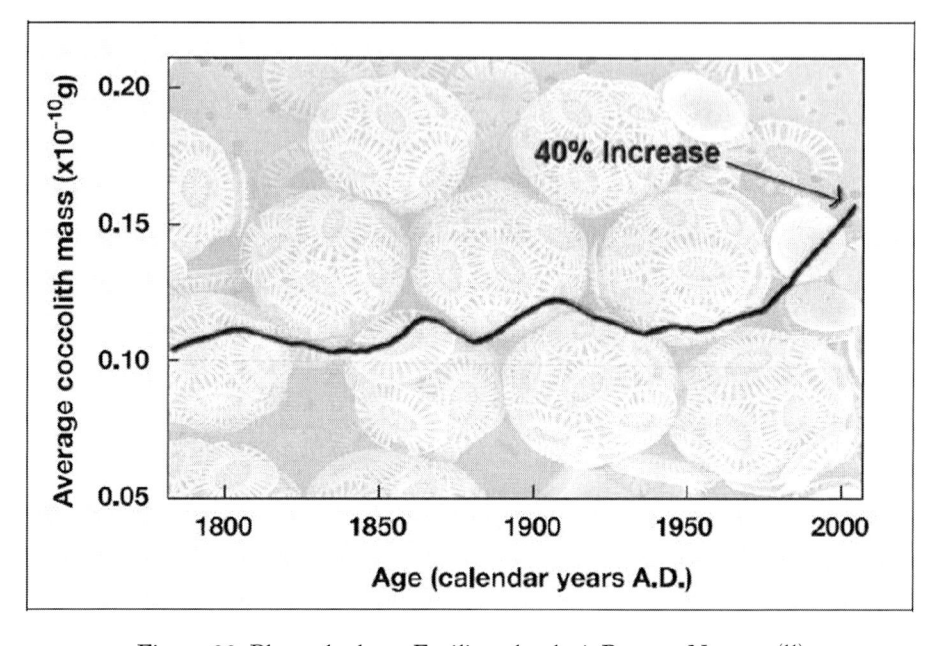

Figure 33: Phytoplankton Emiliana huxleyi, Bergen, Norway [11]

U. Riesebell issued a research paper in 2004 that dealt with CO_2 experiments conducted south of Bergen, Norway, where nine enclosures moored to a floating raft were aerated in triplicate with CO_2-depleted, CO_2-normal, and CO_2-enriched air of 190, 370 and 710 ppm CO_2, respectively, in order to simulate glacial, present-day, and predicted end-of-the-century atmospheric CO_2 conditions, respectively. [3]

Here's what the data shows as to its reaction to increasing CO_2 concentration:

To quote Idso:

"Riebesell finds even more reason to believe that "coccolithophores may benefit from the present increase in atmospheric CO_2 and related changes in seawater carbonate chemistry," in contrast to the many negative predictions that have been made about rising atmospheric CO_2 concentrations in this regard."

Idso

Again I ask you, do you think Idso and Riebesell are working overtime to fool you with some manufactured, inconsequential data?

The magnitude of freedom we are about to give up in support of outrageous legislation causes me to work overtime to fight the legislative nonsense prevailing in Washington, DC, and other similarly loaded capitals.

One leader who did stand up against Climate Change hysteria, Prime Minister Kevin Rudd of none other than Australia, is now on the outside, after elections in June 2010. He has been replaced by a former ally, Julia Gillard, who has apparently seen a new light for her future political path.

A news headline from Bloomberg, June 27, 2010, read as follows: "Australia's Gillard May Slow Population Growth to Focus on Sustainability"

Oh, how sweet it is. The Aussies have also bought into the fraud, like lemmings to the sea.

Here's more from the Bloomberg article:

"The change of direction is to put front and center the *sustainability* issues," Gillard said in an interview with the Nine television network today "There are environmental issues about water and about soil. But there are also *sustainability* issues about planning, about services."

Gillard has distanced herself from some of Rudd's policies since gaining the role unopposed in a Labor party-room ballot on June 24. The 48-year-old Wales-born lawyer already revisited two of Rudd's most unpopular decisions by reconsidering a carbon-trading system shelved in April and agreeing to negotiate with the mining industry on a proposed tax increase.

Bloomberg

Oh, thank God, she is looking out for Australia's interests as to those bad, bad mining interests, those horrific capitalists. You know, those folks that are currently experiencing double-digit unemployment in many regions. I'm sure a tax increase on the mining industry will be just what the doctor ordered. She will fit right in with BO and Harry Reid.

That's all I have on CO_2 and corals, except to say that in my view, the corals will be just fine, just as they have been during the many changes they have experienced over the previous millennia.

CO_2, Temperature and Sea Level

This really has to do only with temperature and sea level, but given the fetish for CO_2 and temperature linkage, I'll leave the subtitle as is.

I recently visited the Pacific Northwest United States, as well as a piece of extreme Southwest Alberta, Canada.

While on a whaling expedition, I asked the guide, who has lived in the area for about forty years, if he had any evidence to support sea level change.

None.

According to the experts, he should have noticed a variation of a few inches, but no go.

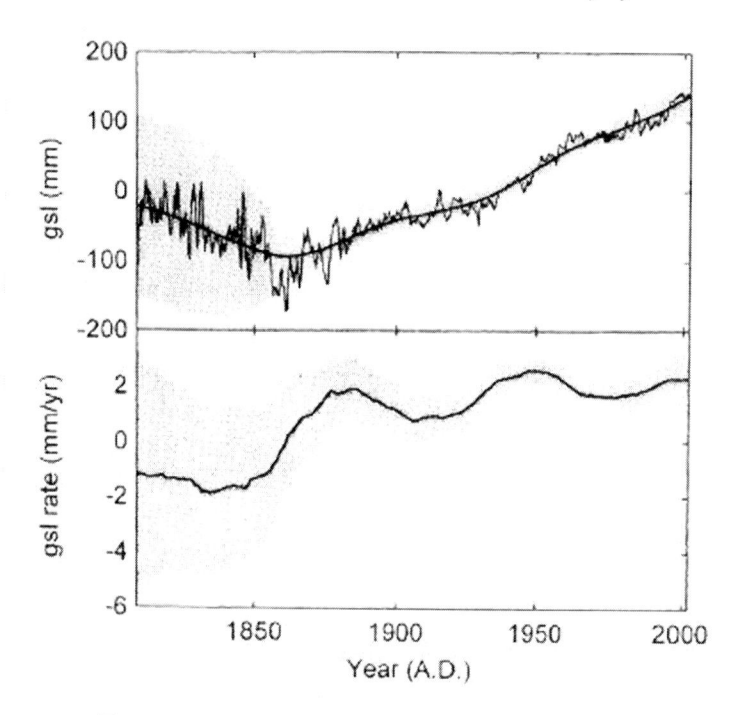

Figure 34: Global Sea Level Change 1800-2000 [12]

What one can easily glean from this image is that global sea level change, in millimeters, has been generally on the rise since around 1850, once again bringing up that pesky "Little Ice Age" (LIA). What's more, we can see that the rate of change has been largely stable, close to around 2 mm per year since 1950.

In 2008, Jevrejeva, et al, released an updated study which allowed for backing the record to 1700, with somewhat similar, but slightly more elaborate error calculations. Virtually all time from 1800 back to 1700 was within the LIA. Minimum sea level seems to have occurred just after 1800 in the context of this graph. [12]

214 — *Carbon Dioxide (CO$_2$)*

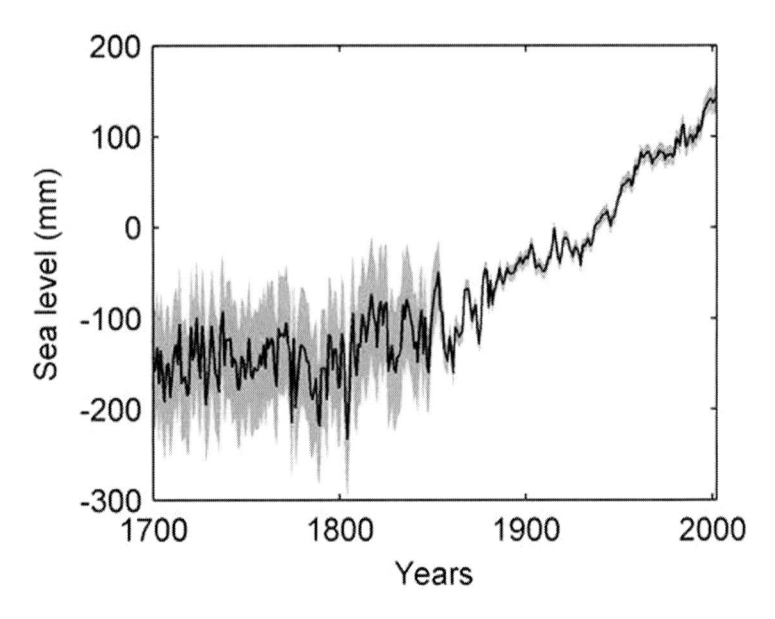

Figure 35: Global Sea Level Change 1700-2000 [12]

Let's take a closer look at more recent data from research underway at the University of Colorado, bringing us up to 2010. What we can glean from the image below is that the average rate of sea level rise since 1992 appears to have been about 3.2 mm/year, about 50 percent higher than the rate calculated above. Bear in mind that the measurements at the University of Colorado are satellite based and cover a much shorter time window.

Before we look at the details, it's interesting to note that the average sea level rise over the past ten thousand years appears to have been approximately 4 feet per century, which is equivalent to about 12 mm/year. However, during the entire twentieth century, sea level appears to have risen just 8 inches, or about 2mm/year, as was demonstrated on page 213.

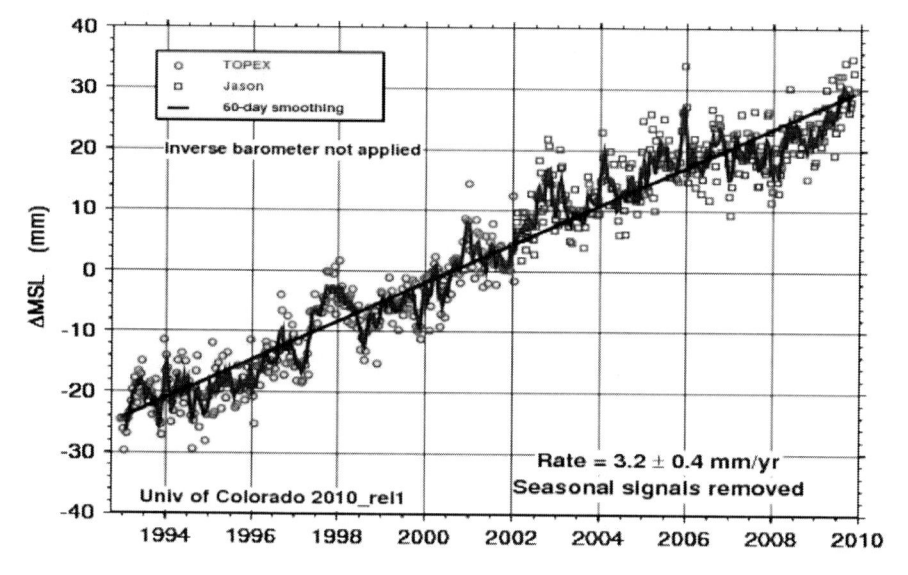

Figure 36: Global Sea Level Change 1992-2010 [13]
(For a more detailed look, view the colorized version
of this image within the color section, page 156.)

Now, let's consider the IPCC's latest predictions, along with some others you may have heard about. As recently as 2001, the IPCC predicted that sea level would rise as much as 3 feet during the twenty-first century. By 2007, they had trimmed that back to about 2 feet per 100 years.

As I look at the data above, I note a fairly significant change in slope (departing from the average trend line) commencing late 2002-early 2003. I'm guessing that is what prompted the IPCC to modify to about 2 feet/year. I think that is still too high, and others agree, including Nils-Axel Morner, retired former Head of the Paleogeophysics and Geodynamics department at Stockholm University, and formerly chairman of the International Union for Quaternary Research (INQUA) International Commission on Sea Level Change:

Despite fluctuations down as well as up, "the sea is not rising," he says. "It hasn't risen in fifty years." If there is any rise this century, it will "not be more than 10cm (four inches), with an uncertainty of plus or minus 10cm."

James Hansen's (NASA) prediction: 16 feet by 2095 [14]

Here's an excerpt from an interview from the Australian Broadcasting Company [ABC] with Hansen on March 13, 2007 (referring to levels of CO_2 in earth's atmosphere) [15]

KERRY O'BRIEN: After your 20 years as a scientist of trying to raise awareness of the dangers of Global Warming, are you ultimately optimistic or pessimistic about the future?

JAMES HANSEN: I think that we're likely to pass the 450 parts per million, which is probably the dangerous level. However, I think there is a lot of encouraging evidence in the last year or two that people are starting to get it, and so - if we can keep it close to that level, and take some additional actions. You know, there are other climate forces besides carbon dioxide, and some of those-it would be very useful to reduce those. And so if we begin to address carbon dioxide and methane and black carbon and tropospheric ozone then I think we can avoid the dangerous Climate Change but we'll have to get going very soon.

Not only is his purported alarm at CO_2 concentration of 450 ppm ridiculous, I am not happy that I am paying part of his federal salary at NASA. This guy needs to be fired. And he wants to regulate methane…

But is the sea actually level? Let's look at the data. The first image below is satellite captured data mapped to the global environment, with "No IB" (inverted barometer) correction applied. The data clearly shows a significant variation of sea level rise of +/- 15 mm/year. This is the best data available to the global scientific community.

The red/magenta areas are indicating upwards of 12 mm/year rise, while limited darker blue regions indicate downward to about 12 mm/year decreases. The lower image in the pair indicates the relative possible error in the measurements. The areas with the highest variance also contain the highest error potential.

Variance occurs due to thermal expansion, continental/sea floor movement and other minor factors. The bottom line is that we have significant uncertainty in these measurements.

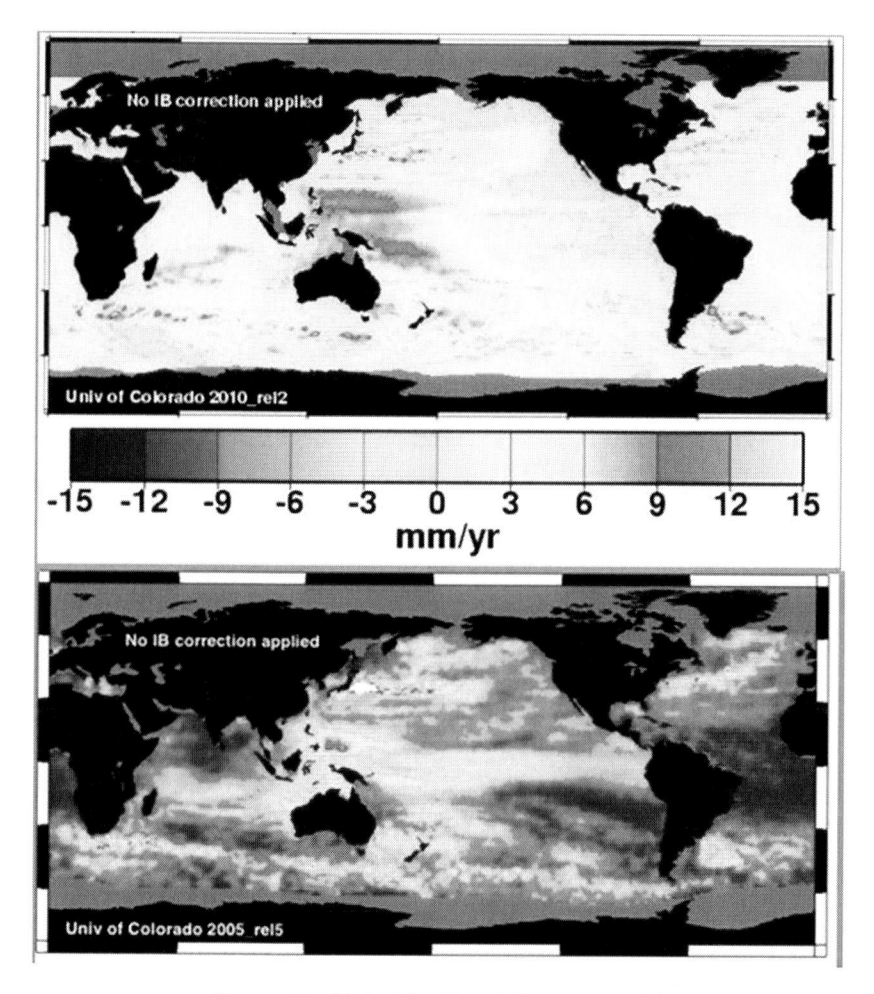

Figure 37: Global Sea Level Corrections [16]

(For a more detailed look, view the colorized version of this image within the color section, page 157.)

I will go out on another limb and suggest that the "apparent" rise in sea level in the vicinity of the Maldives may be due as much to uncertainty or other global movement as anything else. In the upper image, the Maldives are located in the lightest blue-green shaded area, off the southwest coast of India, in a region where apparent sea level may be rising at a rate of up to 3mm/year.

Ask any of the natives about seal level rise in the past hundred years, and they will tell you the change has been indetectable, just as was the case of the sea captain from Washington earlier in this section.

Isostatic adjustments of continental masses, as well as floating sea masses over the past hundred years, have generally compensated for any melting that has occurred due to our leaving the LIA behind for the time being.

My goal in all of this, the past few chapters in dealing with energy and environmental issues and policy, has been to bring you data and insight that perhaps you had not been exposed to in the past.

The decisions we contemplate going forward in each of these areas could not be more important, and so while I have scattered bits of sarcasm into the dialogue, please understand that I am dead serious in attempting to bring a very strong measure of reality and reliability as to the data and projections we scientists attempt to make within a very complex, beautiful system.

I will conclude this chapter with one more graphic summary. In engineering analysis, we frequently conduct *cost-benefit analyses*. The base concept should be taught in every household in America, certainly in every schoolhouse. It attempts to answer the question of exactly what cost will be required to achieve a certain benefit. If the cost to achieve a given outcome on a project is too great, the project simply does not go forward. CO_2 emissions "control" can be analyzed in this manner, and, in fact, it has been done. Have you heard about it? Probably not, so here it is, all encapsulated in a couple of 3x5 graphs:

The Waxman/Markey Climate Bill will scarcely affect sea level

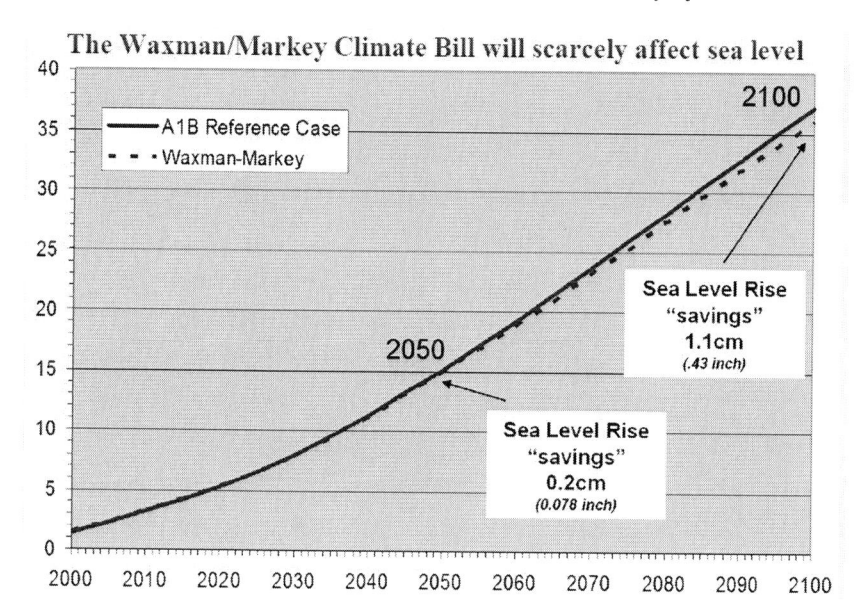

Figure 38: UN Predicted Sea Level Rise "Savings" Due to Waxman-Markey [17]

All you have heard about sea level so far is that its rise must be arrested. Well, the result above is what you get from 'cap and trade', right on out to 2100. If the image has not sunk in, I want you to think long and hard about the "saved" 0.43-inch rise in sea level that will be accomplished by the UN's own calculations. The cost to achieve that sea level rise "saving" will be a mere $18 trillion. That's trillion, with a *T*.

How many starving African children could *you* feed with $18 trillion? Let me have a crack at it, Messrs. Waxman and Markey. If you didn't have your couchy, tenured positions in Congress, I'd lock you both up and throw away the key. I can assure each of you this: You are doing the American people no favors whatsoever by stealing $18 trillion hard earned dollars from tax-paying citizens.

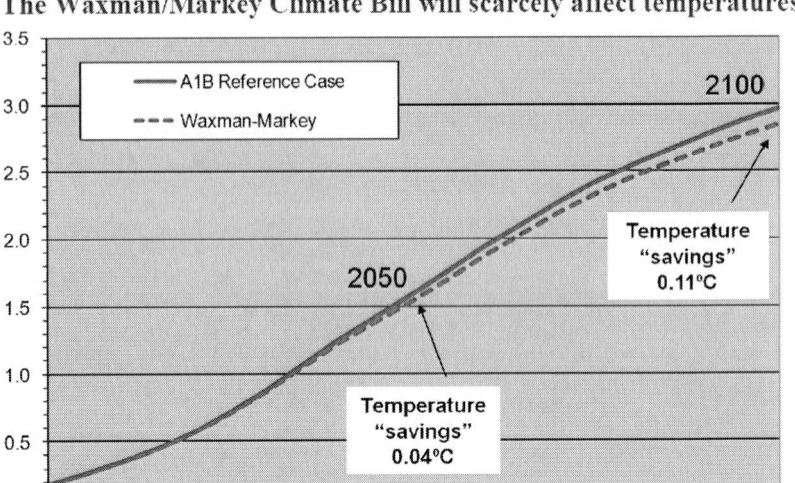

The Waxman/Markey Climate Bill will scarcely affect temperatures

Figure 39: UN Predicted Temperature "Savings" Due to Waxman-Markey [18]

Finally, here's a look above at the incredible impact cap and trade is predicted to achieve with respect to temperature reduction, again out to 2100. These estimates are again provided by the UN itself. Same dollars allotted, same time frame.

Let me put that into a frame of reference you might better understand. The temperature savings, at either the 2050 moment, or the 2100 moment, will be so small as not to be measurable. For those of you who don't understand the Celsius scale, the 0.11 degrees Celsius cited above is about equivalent to 0.25 degrees Fahrenheit. Indetectable.

That's your hard-working government servants at work.

If you are one of those people who just can't wait to spend $18 trillion to arrest 0.2 degrees Fahrenheit, I want to meet you for a personal interview and provide you the evidence that a moderate temperature increase of this magnitude would actually be very beneficial for virtually all living things on planet earth. I would also point out to you that a considerable amount of data demonstrates that the Medieval Warm Period was probably about as warm as that indicated by the upper temperature ranges in the IPCC model.

Now, it's time to switch gears from hard science to softer but equally as crucial political science.

Economics: The Fed, Frank, Dodd, & Obamanomics

Here we go into seemingly unconnected territory. But I submit it is very connected, and many of the head honchos from the environmental world, who, trust me, want to control as much of your life as they possibly can, are at the top of this world as well. They don't just want to control your life; these people want your money more than you could ever imagine.

Ludwig von Mises, and F.A. (Friedrick) Hayak, they got "it."

In this case, "it," (as opposed to what "is" is, on another case involving a former president of the United States), refers to understanding money and economics. Hayak, who worked for von Mises for a time and who wrote the timeless *The Road to Serfdom*, provides firsthand accounting of the profound differences between capitalism and socialism (Marxism). Von Mises was an Austrian economist and a classical liberal who had a profound effect on free-market thinking. In 1920, he wrote *Socialism: An Economic and Sociological Analysis*, from which I quote:

> "The only certain fact about Russian affairs under the Soviet regime with regard to which all people agree is: that the standard of living of the Russian masses is much lower than that of the masses in the country which is universally considered as the paragon of capitalism, the United States of America. If we were to regard the Soviet regime as an experiment, we would have to say that the experiment has clearly demonstrated the superiority of capitalism and the inferiority of socialism.
>
> Von Mises

It will take nearly every ounce of wherewithal we commoners have to stave off the forces that want to take us down the very dark road to socialism. They have a *lot* of momentum, dating back frankly to about 1913 in America, back further than that in Europe. The election of 2010 will not purge this influence, though it will awaken some of the masses to reconsider some of our past mistakes.

Here's the biggest picture I can paint for you. They run this "thing" like a monarchy, where they of course rule, and we serve. That is not so obvious today, but I can assure you that if we don't take the necessary action soon, our servanthood to them will be more obvious than you could ever imagine.

(Thankfully, we have some very bright people who have been on the lookout for us. They actually understand what is going on inside the Federal Reserve, at least as much as can be understood about an extremely secretive, non-transparent, non-forthcoming, independent-from-Congress group can be. They also understand what is happening inside the European Central Bank and the International Monetary Fund, to name a few.)

As President Obama has already alluded to in the past, he's ready to "fundamentally transform" this country. He's about two steps away from getting all his wishes to come true. As soon as he and Timmy Geithner, Benny Bernanke, Larry Summers, and Georgie Soros get their way, we will see hyperinflation to match any the world has ever seen. And that will only be the beginning. While Timmy, Benny and Larry are not yet billionaires, their friend George has already carved out his preeminent position, and he will happily provide his understudies all the help they need to withstand the storm.

They will have plenty of company, like Bill and Hillary, the Rockefellers, the Rothschilds, the Kissingers, King Saud, the list just goes on and on, until you get to we mere serfs. Don't you dare try to break into their party; it may be very costly.

Fractional Reserve Banking

You banking types can create money from nowhere, and our Fed is only too happy to accommodate, and while the rest of our country is suffering from residential foreclosures due to insane congressional legislation, you are literally laughing all the way to the bank. I hate to have to come down so hard on you all at Citibank, Bank of America, Chase, and the like, but you leave me little choice. I know, you don't actually print the money; you leave that up to the Fed to direct at our various mints throughout America. But, you do know exactly what I mean.

According to wordIQ, Fractional Reserve Banking is described as follows:

> In economics, particularly in financial economics, fractional-reserve banking is the near-universal practice of banks of retaining only a fraction of their deposits to satisfy demands for withdrawals, lending the remainder at interest to obtain income that can be used to pay interest to depositors and provide profits for the banks' owners. Fractional-reserve banking allows for the possibility of a bank run in which the depositors collectively

attempt to withdraw more money than is in the possession of the bank, leading to bankruptcy. This is possible because both the borrower and the depositor have a claim to withdraw money deposited at the bank. It also increases the money supply through a mechanism called the deposit creation multiplier, explained below, which leads to inflation by definition. Most governments impose strictly-enforced reserve requirements on banks, with the exact fraction of deposits that must be kept in reserve generally set by a central bank.

Some political libertarians and some supporters of a gold standard use the term *fractional-reserve banking* for the practice of only partially backing a nation's currency with gold or other accepted stores of value, as occurred in various countries before the adoption of unbacked fiat money in most developed countries in 1971 with the collapse of the Bretton Woods Agreement. This usage is superficially similar to the standard usage in economics, in that the ability of a country to redeem only part of its currency in gold can be seen as analogous to the ability of a bank to redeem only part of its deposits in cash, but referring to partially-backed currencies as a form of fractional-reserve banking may create more confusion than it alleviates. Mainstream economists do not generally make this analogy. [1]

Our country's Central Bank is of course the Federal Reserve, which was created by an Act of Congress in 1913, during the Wilson administration. I have no intention of ragging on the fed, except to say that I agree wholeheartedly that it operates under far too much secrecy and that must change. It does contain/control virtually every single dollar of the "fractional reserves" that banks are required to maintain, which are, of course, derived largely from American citizens.

One other thing; they print money at will, without any permission from you, the Congress, or any other entity on the face of the earth. They can print it really fast if they so choose. In case you were not aware, when they print more money than they destroy, or take out of circulation, they create inflationary conditions. It can lead to a slow, bleeding death, or it can lead to a guillotine effect, if they believe it necessary. That's another way of saying *hyperinflation*, or that condition where they print the money so fast that the value of every single dollar in circulation becomes significantly devalued. What used to cost $1 a month ago now costs $100. You think it can't happen here?

I am certainly not alone in my skeptical view of the Fed. Notwithstanding Congressman Ron Paul, there are others who have an opinion of the way our money is processed, including economist Thomas E. Woods, Jr.:

> "The Fed's policy of intervening in the economy to push interest rates lower than the market would have set them was the single greatest contributor to the crisis that continues to unfold before us. Making cheap credit available for the asking does encourage excessive leverage, speculation, and indebtedness. Manipulating interest rates and thereby misleading investors about real economic conditions does in fact misdirect capital into unsustainable lines of production and discombobulate the market." [2]
>
> Woods, pages 8-9

The graphic below depicts a quick look summary of Fed money printing activity since about 1998. Note the significant events such as Y2K, 9/11, and then those benchmarks known as QE-1 and QE-2. Quantitative easing, or "monetization of our debt," is the latest twist to the fed's attempts to somehow ease the access to capital? Aside from Alan Blinder's attempt to provide cover to Ben Bernanke (WSJ editorial, November 15, 2010), I think Mr. Bernanke is going in for rougher and rougher sailing on the seas ahead. By the time this book reaches the populace, we may well be seeing the first vestiges of serious inflation coming out of the closet. [3]

228 — *Economics: The Fed, Frank, Dodd & Obamanomics*

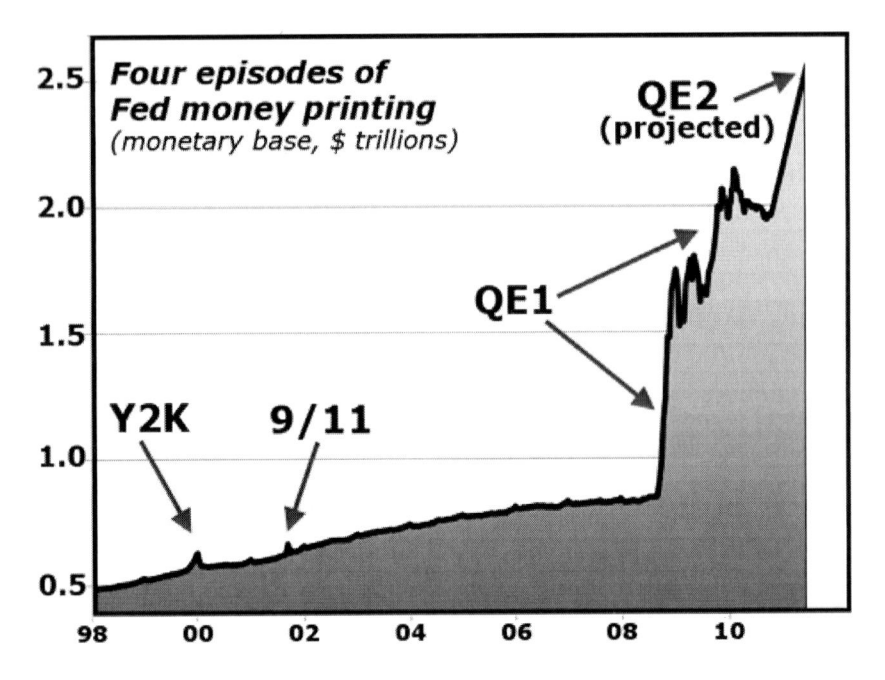

Figure 40: Fed Monetary Policy Headed into Steeply Uncharted Territory: Quantitative Easing (Courtesy of Martin Weiss, PhD.) (3)

The Fed system was the brainchild of Alexander Hamilton, our first secretary of the treasury. Does that raise any red flags? How about Timothy Geithner's sliding over from the presidency of the New York Fed (by far the largest of the twelve regional Fed banks scattered across the U.S.), to the Secretary of the Treasury of the United States? The president of the Federal Reserve Bank of New York was not obligated to pay his share of income taxes just prior to taking over our Treasury? A true Obama first-teamer.

There are forces at work here that are, frankly, much, much bigger than the Federal Reserve of New York or of the entire U.S. banking system. These forces are largely European, and I'm not certain today that we will be able to survive the onslaught. The onslaught will include not just Europe, but China, Japan, the Oil Rich Muslim Middle East, all that Latin America has to offer, and last, but not least, Russia.

Let me simply state my agreement with the bulk of the current world leaders, as well as the majority of U.S. economists who find the current U.S. strategy of buying $600 billion worth of bonds over the course of six months through May 2011 to be extremely risky and counterproductive as to any attempt to balance foreign currencies. Given the U.S.'s current debt exposure to China, it seems wholly inappropriate to attempt to dictate any aspect of Chinese monetary policy.

Barack Obama is finally finding out what it means to listen. He tried to float his deficit-laden, stimulus reenactment to the G20 during June 2010, and he now knows just how serious a deficit-laden economy can become. I do not count on him or Tim G. to bring us out of our deficit problem, and although I do have a strategy for that, no one is going to like it. Especially not the unions, and a host of entitlement programs.

I'll save that for last.

For the moment, let's look at the stated assets of the Federal Reserve, as of 12/31/2009. According to that stalwart Wiki, all Fed banks assets totaled $2.238 Trillion. For comparison, let's look at the Forbes 400, which, for 2009, tallied about $1.57 trillion.

Quick math yields that four hundred people have assets equivalent to about 70 percent of the Federal Reserve.

The projected deficit for the U.S. budget for this year, according to the Congressional Budget Office, is somewhere near $1.6 trillion.

Mr. Obama, let's quit pussy-footing around here. Here's your solution staring you right in the face. Just round up that $1.57 trillion to $1.6, put those four hundred industrialists in San Quentin, expropriate their bank accounts, better still, reopen Alcatraz for efficiency to deploy more federal employees, and your problem for 2010 is solved. I mean, that's the communist way; remember Mikhail Khordokovsky. There's your precedent.

We understand that you would prefer to move on us in a slightly more delicate fashion, what with Mr. Soros's strategy not including his own imprisonment, but you are the president, after all. Go ahead, play George's bluff.

Unfortunately, there will probably be the "inconvenient year" known as 2012, then 2013…

Just so you know, that second tier after the first four hundred will cut pretty deep. It'll probably reach the White House.

This is getting to the true *cost* of freedom.
Eventually, it gets to the fraud, the deceit, and the misrepresentation.

This is a whole lot bigger than Barack Obama. It is way bigger than the Deepwater Horizon and BP's Macondo discovery. This is a real, very big deal. You might even say it's "global."

Comprende?

Is there a way out?

I believe so, but it will not be clean, easy, or without significant pain. The question is, are *you*, the America we thought we had and knew, ready to take the steps to take it back?

It will be entirely up to you.

As to Frank n' Dodd, I am so grateful for their dedication to "protecting" me from those evildoers on Wall Street and the banks they so carefully regulated before the residential real estate meltdown they themselves produced through their "creative legislation." Mr. Dodd, apparently you saw the writing on the wall and decided to get out while you could still take down nearly the same pay as before in your active Senate role, without so much as lifting a finger. By my math, according to standards associated with the Civil Service Retirement System (the precursor to the current Federal Employees Retirement System), you will be taking out a minimum of $115,000 per year, worst case. I recognize that is only a drop in the bucket compared to all the perks and side issue support you are accustomed to receiving, but it will put bread on your table, will it not?

The point of all of the above is that the current controllers of the currency, today's economic wizards, have a very different view of the world than those who appreciated free markets and the capitalistic model that has seen the test of time and has won out so handily that America's prosperity is the absolute best testimony one could imagine, as was aptly put by von Mises. But that evidence is not good enough for the socialists. They despise the free market fruits of capitalism, and they are hell-bent on taking it out of America at their earliest opportunity.

What has been the case is that U.S. policy has been gradually shifting away from the best economic model known to man, to one where a slow Socialistic mantra has been gaining so much momentum, through ill-conceived legislation (like FDR's New Deal, and LBJ's Great Society), that we were not able to see through the fog what was being created. I believe that is finally changing, now that BO has come out of the closet and made it very clear exactly where he and his cadre of comrades are headed.

One other point here.

The SEC. You now, that entity that protects us from all that could go wrong on Wall Street, that capitalistic bastion that must be regulated in order to operate efficiently and "fairly." As of August 26, 2010, it just got a whole lot more "fair" for the labor unions. I mean, I'm sure it's got to be a good thing for representatives of labor unions to sit on the boards of directors of public companies. Mary Shapiro brought that dream to reality, along with the assistance of two other members of the board of the SEC. Mary Shapiro got to this place because of Frank 'n Dodd.

I need to be fair here and emphasize that this condition we are now contending with was not only propagated by liberal Democrats but was ably assisted by plenty of Progressive Republicans, many of whom are still in office. Will we clear them out? (It did not happen in 2010.) I don't know, but they need to be identified, played out, and exposed for exactly who they are, and then we need to let the people decide. One thing has become only too obvious in the past couple decades—we are getting precisely the government we deserve.

It's time to take a closer look at some of their handiwork and where it will take us very soon—*if* we stand by and let it happen.

As for me, I have no intention of standing idly by. How about you?

Killer Apps

Medicare and Social Security Face Large Deficits

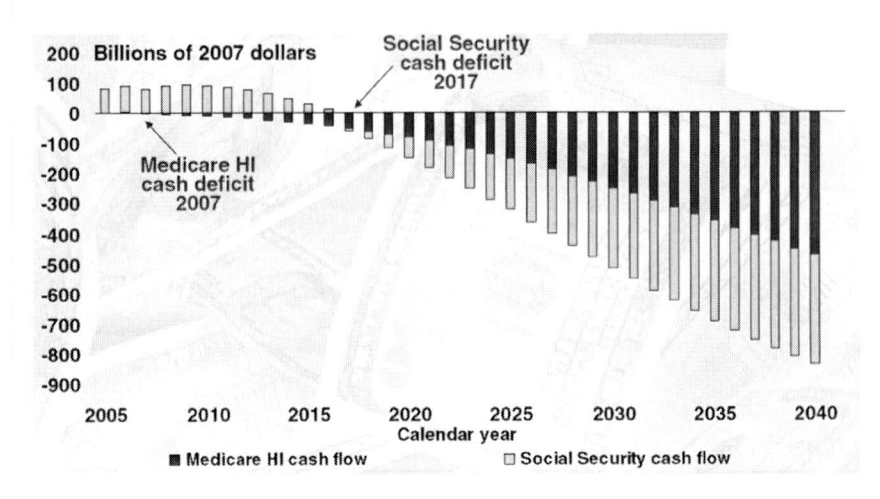

Figure 41: Medicare and Social Security Deficits through 2040 [4]

I call these "Killer Apps" because these really are the clinchers, or should I say the "cinchers," due to the fact that the bleeding cash flow headed our way in the very near future will cause every "taxpayer" to cinch his/her belt in a way that is almost unimaginable.

The source of this data is the Governmental Accounting Office, which is as current as it gets. The GAO appears to be mostly trustworthy for at least the time being. Notice that these projections are based on "the intermediate assumptions of the 2007 Trustees' Reports," whoever they are. Furthermore, the consumer price index was used to adjust from current to constant dollars.

The Medicare system already hit the wall in 2007 in terms of "cash flow." That simply means that in 2007, we started paying more into Medicare than we had the money to cover the transaction. Hello to another source of inflation.

The best projections available today from the GAO (FY 2008), tell us that both Social Security and Medicare will hit a major cash wall around 2017, the point at which *both* these programs will be, for all practical purposes, in default. That simply means that "we," the people, will have to pay more and more dollars into an abject, poverty-laden system.

Perhaps the above graphic and discussion didn't grab your attention or elevate your sensitivity as to "entitlements,' which is what every red-blooded American is entitled to, right?

I have one more financial summary graph, again courtesy of the GAO. One has to take for granted that the data they have compiled for this graph is based on sound modeling. I am uncertain as to just how far I am willing to go with their data, data that you and I paid for, but this is the best we have for the moment:

The Risks of Growing Entitlement Spending

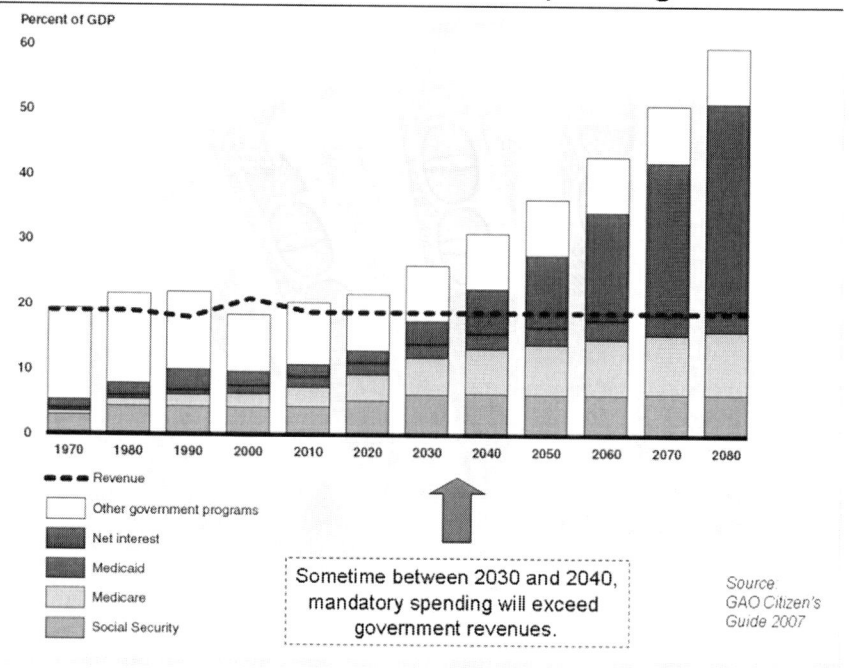

Figure 42: Risks of Growing Entitlement Spending [5]
(For a more detailed look, view the colorized version of this image within the color section, page 158.)

The above graphic was generated on the basis of data as indicated from the GAO Citizen's guide 2007. They are projecting flat revenue over the next seventy years? I'm guessing the white part of each vertical bar relates to something like "federal pensions."

According to the U.S. Debt clock (www.usdebtclock.org) on the afternoon of May 1, 2011, the calculated national debt was about $14.34 trillion, increasing at a rate of about $42,000 per second. At about the same time, the U.S. GDP was estimated to be about $14.69 trillion, yielding a debt/GDP ratio of about 97.6 percent.

On November 1, the day before the election of 2010, the debt stood at $13.67 trillion and the GDP was $14.52, yielding a debt/GDP ratio of 93.7 percent. At this rate, our debt/GDP ratio will hit the Geithner milestone of 100 percent by about September 30, 2012. Just in time for the 2012 election…What an accomplishment he and BO will have achieved. But don't leave George Soros out of this; let's give credit where credit is due. His guidance has been impeccable.

That bothers me, a lot. How about you?

Finally, I feel compelled to share one other bit of financially relevant data with you. As of this same date, it is estimated that we have "unfunded liabilities" just down the road around 2017, related to Social Security ($14.7 trillion), prescription drugs ($19.4 trillion), and Medicare ($77 trillion), for a rounded total of about $111 trillion. That number is just way too easy to remember.

Your 'share' of that unfunded liability: $358,064

For clarification, that's the share per capita. Unfortunately, a whole bunch of those "capitas" don't work, or don't pay taxes, or somehow do not relate at all to the number (illegal aliens, who happily draw from Medicare, for example). So, quite honestly, I do not know exactly what your share of that load happens to be. What I do know is it's way too much.

That's about all the good news I can come up with on the financial side.

But I do wish to comment ever so briefly on my elation with the recently passed "financial overhaul," thanks to Frank 'n Dodd. Now, you see, they'll be able to track all my financial transactions over $600. Furthermore, they have now made it law that representatives of labor unions will automatically have representation on the boards of U.S. corporations. That should make for some very interesting negotiations between corporations and unions. If only I could get my competitors into the same room with me as I bid on new contracts in our firm's search for energy.

I think I might just move to Massachusetts, inside the Fourth Congressional District. Just for the chance to give Barney a run for his money, I guess I should say my money, since a slice of his paycheck comes right out of my back pocket.

To be fair to Barney, he only passed it off to Christopher Dodd, who then received sweeping support from that Tea Party favorite Scott Brown and the two lovely RINO's from Maine, Collins and Snowe. They missed a golden opportunity to begin to restore some sense of fiscal sanity to the American financial system. Now, this becomes another in a long list of repealable acts, happily signed by America's greatest socialist of all time, BO.

According to Michael Medved (August 12, 2010, *Wall Street Journal*), we conservatives have a great uphill battle on our hands if we are to beat Obama. The demographics are nowhere near in our favor at this moment.

We can change that picture, and we can take back the White House in 2012 with the right candidate.

A New America—
Ex-Obama

It didn't have to be this way. It really could have been "change" we could have believed in. But, of course, it didn't happen. Instead, we got warmed over socialism, Marxism, and communism as temporary administration preferences. BO apparently forgot we fought wars to avoid that infringement in our country and a few others just to keep the rest of the world honest. The first one, with George Washington at the helm, is what truly made this a great country, because we were a good country while becoming great. We did concern ourselves with the common man, with his beliefs in a Creator, not an impostor who came out of the woodwork around 600 AD and spoke to a despotic, deranged "prophet" named Muhammad, but a real Creator, whose handiwork is still every bit as evident today as it was from the beginning, which He ordained.

America, this is no time for soft-pedaling. If there has ever been a time to kick it up a notch since World War II, this is it. That is, unless you really don't care that much about your God-given freedoms of life, liberty and the pursuit of happiness (property, as the original wording would have read).

An Alternate Proposal to Restore America

1. Reduce the federal government "footprint" to *75 percent* of what it is today. It starts with a freeze of all programs budgeted for fiscal year 2012, and is followed by 2.5 percent cuts every year until the 25 percent cutback level is reached. If the currently projected level of spending for FY 2012 is adhered to, we will have spent approximately $3.73 trillion by year's end. So let's start with that number. Whittling it back at 2.5 percent per year will get us to about $2.79 trillion by the end of FY 2024. Currently, US Gross Domestic Product (GDP) is above $14.68 trillion, so quick math shows that *if* we cut back to $2.79 trillion (today's dollars), it would be roughly equivalent to in excess of 19% of GDP. My belief is that 19% is a stiff management fee. We can do better. It will require resolve that has heretofore not been achieved by any prior administration. It will require a significant change in mentality as to just exactly how we intend to manage our public affairs.

    There are *way* too many people working for the federal government today. So, what are we going to do with those who will be displaced by these cutbacks that can certainly be trimmed? (The private sector cutbacks are far greater than 2.5 percent per year since the Great Recession began, yet federal government continues to expand.) We take responsible action that will reduce the onerous federal burden on businesses in the way of ineffective environmental strategies, wholly uncalled for tax increases, consistent policies that stabilize, not distort free markets, and other means available to do those things that actually create jobs, not eliminate them.

Here are some additional facts and figures related to our federal employment system, taken from the commerce Department's Bureau of Economic Analysis, as of August 2010:

The average federal employee is earning $123,049 per year in salary and benefits, as compared to the average private sector employee, who makes $61,051. Take away the benefits and the numbers are $81,258 federal and $50,462 private. Talk about some incredible benefits packages, Obama can't hire them fast enough, and now you know why.

While the rest of America is in the deepest "recession" since the Great Depression, the federal government is adding new jobs at a rate of 10,000 per month. As of this writing, private sector jobs continue to contract and diminish.

According to the federal government's Office of Personnel Management, we have the following: [1]

- 382,758 federal workers earn $100,000 or more, a 46 percent increase from December 2007 to June 2009;

- 66,538 federal workers earn $150,000 or more, a 119 percent increase from December 2007 to June 2009;

- 22,157 federal workers earn $170,000 or more, a 93 percent increase from December 2007 to June 2009.

According to their website, the OPM is dedicated to "Recruiting, Retaining and Honoring a World-Class Workforce to Serve the American People."

2. Bell, California, please hold open your files.

Enact the Energy Plan in chapter 3, and act accordingly to do everything possible to test it for a minimum of five years. This is about energy security, moving toward lower dependence on imported products. I am not going to belabor this, given the earlier treatment that provides plenty of specifics.

3. Substantially modify the departments of energy and education. Neither one of them even remotely approach a pass on fundamental cost/benefit analysis. In fact, the Department of Education has probably set us back at least one decade since its inception in 1980. Yes, I said a decade. I have yet to meet a single teacher who has said that he or she is in favor of any elements of the No Child Left Behind Act. Contrary to what union leaders in education will tell you, teachers are very receptive to the notion of "merit pay," or whatever equitable incentive programs might be instituted. Bring the free market into the classroom, and you will see competition do its magic. On the other hand, continue with class warfare and the inestimable damage of tenure, and you will continue to see the results we now experience across the American public school system.

Why is it so difficult to understand that freedom to compete works incredibly well? It is not difficult to understand; in fact, the Progressives understand it very well—they can't stand it; it takes the power out of their hands and into the principals and the teachers, exactly where it belongs. The teachers have been largely brainwashed into believing that only a strong union will get them what they demand: entitlements, pensions, and other long-term destructive characteristics that undermine teaching and learning.

As to the Department of Energy, the department has proposed a $28.4 billion budget request for DOE for FY 2011[2], an approximate 6.7 percent increase from 2010. The largest individual category by far, if approved, would be "science," with approximately $5.12 billion requested. Next, most significantly, we see approximately $2.35 billion directed toward energy efficiency and renewable energy. I note with great interest the line item for "Clean Coal Technology," -$0-, just as it has been for FY 2009 and 2010.

But, lest you forget, the stimulus plan provided DOE with $38.3 billion, so they have more than a minor amount of your hard-earned tax dollars to "play with," as they work to tweak our system into a more efficient, purring energy machine.

As was pointed out earlier, the DOE was created in 1977 during the Carter administration, specifically to wean us of our dependence on foreign oil.

The more I study its budget, its architecture, and its current goals, I am more convinced than ever that this department would fit very well within the above proposed cutbacks out to year 2025. It should retain certain vital functions, which I will not elaborate here, but which do serve the public interest. One such function is that related to nuclear energy research, a national interest that needs to be materially advanced.

4. Eliminate future pensions (defined benefit plans) for all federal employees, and replace them with defined *contribution* plans, in stages those currently in place, such that by 2025, the defined benefits reach zero. That includes the military. Devise some other incentive program so that when they leave, the obligation to them is zero. *[The only exception will be for wounded veterans, who shall have support for life.]* An incentive for active military would be to provide an equivalent of matching funds for a 401-k type plan while they are in the service. They manage their personal plan and sink or swim with the rest of us. They also benefit by wisely investing their own "profits (savings)".

The sooner America gets completely away from the current "entitlements" mentality, the sooner we can restore this republic and return to the vision of the founders of this great nation. I will not accept the notion that pensions are a fundamental right of any employee in any organization, public or private. My "pension" plan is completely self-funded, and every working American should have the ability to define his or her own private plan that will be portable if and when they change employment domains.

The days of "double-dipping" at the expense of the American taxpayer need to be made a part of history, or the United States of America will cease to exist as anything other than a nanny state. Ask Greece how it's working out for them.

No more double-dipping for police officers, firemen, not anybody. Work for a living, pay your fair share of taxes, budget to save, and you will be amazed at how well the system can work.

5. Convert labor union pension plans into work incentive plans, similar to the plan suggested above for federal employees. (Of course, millions of federal employees are union members already.) Provide bonuses for exceptional performance, knowledge building, and free market ideas. The only beneficiaries of union dues are the union leaders who live the lavish lifestyles that union dues provide for their exclusive benefit. Unions brought Detroit down, and they will bring down anything around them, *if* we let them. Being a member of a labor union will never bring you the success you deserve if you work hard. The fruit of your honest labor will be duly appreciated by the free market. You do not need a huge, overstuffed set of middle men to watch out for your profitability.

6. Develop a plan to extinguish Social Security by 2025. Replace it with "private employee owned" retirement plans that are managed by shareholders (citizens) themselves. Perhaps you are glancing back at that graph in chapter 6, and you cannot imagine how to fight this battle. We can, and we *must* find a way to do exactly that. As I indicated above, we gradually wind this thing down from an "entitlement" to a personal strategy, whereby the money that has been captured over many decades from millions of employees becomes an asset that is personally managed and becomes detached from any government intervention. Individuals in the system today begin to incrementally transfer their assets into these accounts, and new, incoming working individuals simply initiate their private accounts at the startup of the new system, foregoing any interaction with the federal system.

I can only imagine the weeping and gnashing of teeth as the feds see their loss of control of those billions of dollars coming into their coffers. Worse still, they will actually have to come up with real money, called "funded liabilities" that satisfy the obligations they have been stacking up over decades. Before you know it, it will be over with, never to be visited again.

7. Enact a balanced budget amendment that forces the federal bureaucracy to balance spending with revenue, no exceptions. There has never been a more opportune time to bring this idea to the front burner. Provide the president with a line-item veto authority to eliminate unworthy programs. He can live with the consequences, and he will simply have to sleep on every such decision. That's why we pay him the big bucks.

   For the first time in the history of budgetary planning in this republic, the Congress failed to produce a budget of any kind for the prior fiscal year. That's yet another piece of evidence relating to the incompetence of the headmaster of this administration. If ever there was a time for an administrator to be fired…

8. Enforce our border and immigration laws. Take appropriate action to extradite foreign nationals who have broken our laws—there is no reason for us to pay for their ongoing incarceration expenses. Create very heavy penalties for recidivism.

   A lawyer I am not, but I will state unequivocally that I find it unconscionable that our Justice Department is wasting taxpayer dollars on the prosecution of a case against the State of Arizona and now against one of the most forward-looking sheriffs in America. The DOJ has crossed a line that they will come to regret, much sooner than they imagine. I applaud the governor of Arizona and would support any move Jan Brewer makes to stand up to the DOJ, as well as any other states that join in this crucial battle for freedom and justice.

President Obama must believe that if he can simply bring in the illegal votes, he will be a shoo-in for 2012. I say he is dead wrong, that this strategy will backfire more sharply than he ever imagined. He has struck a raw nerve in this country, and there will be no winners in the war ahead over this issue, if it comes to that. That decision rests in Washington, DC.

This nation was founded upon a rule of law, and it appears to me that this administration is trampling all over not just that rule, but the entire Constitution in this process. This will make its way to the Supreme Court, and if Obama makes yet another appointment before the case makes it there, I shudder to think of the consequences of a wrong decision. Wrong means a vote in favor of illegal immigration, without any material consequences.

9. Restore America's health care system such that it is doctor-patient focused, rather than government-control focused, and driven by the free market. Improve transparency, and drive the system to greater efficiency and accuracy.

    This is a lot easier said than done, and I claim no expertise in the field of health care, but it seems only too obvious to me that the moment you bring government between the doctor and the patient, which is absolutely the case with the legislatively-approved model we now begin to extract, major problems arise. That is only one simple example of how problematic this system will become, *if* we allow it to happen. *The law needs to be repealed, and now.*

    If we continue to unpack this debacle, it will be a disaster, and you really can thank President Obama for singlehandedly forcing this down the throat of America. The people repeatedly polled against it by wide margins. The legislature gave up on the "public option" and, in effect, the entire morass, but President Obama and his socialist regime managed to manhandle ineffective legislators into a very bad decision. While the claim was repeatedly made that this would "save" Americans money if only they gave this a chance, we now already know the increased costs associated with this monstrosity will result in the virtual extinguishment of the private-sector health system we have historically enjoyed in this country. Cases have already been logged in where corporations have seen their Blue Cross/Blue Shield insurance costs increase more than 30 percent in the first year of implementation of this plan. This is progress? Absolutely, if you are in a federal administrative role on the other end of this scheme.[3]

10. Substantially modify "tenure" in American educational institutions. Yes, it can be done, and it will lead to constructive competition in the teaching ranks, unlike anything we have seen since the 1950s. Tenure, as structured today, destroys creativity and creates a welfare state inside schoolhouses and universities. Tenure *does not* improve education. If, for some reason, you do not believe that incentives work, take a look at the public education system in our nation's capital, formerly operated by Chancellor Michelle Rhee. That woman is incredible, accomplishing what no other educational manager has for decades—she took on the American Federation of Teachers and won. She has now stepped away from that system, but I am confident she will continue to be a force for positive education reform in this country.

11. *Eliminate, not increase the Inheritance Tax.* This is fundamentally egregious, absolutely counterproductive, "recidivist," and it truncates future job growth potential that propagates from the continuation of estates. The only reason this tax exists in the first place is to provide the "government" more resources with which to "operate." I submit to you that it is not the government's responsibility to "operate" anything, but rather to conduct services that cannot otherwise be provided by individual states. That range of services must be constrained, not expanded. The "constraining order" needs to be applied and executed by the American people immediately. If the American people fail to

apply this constraining order, America will decline significantly within twenty years, in fact within five years.

Parting Thoughts

I hope and pray this does not fall on deaf ears. If it does, then I will have failed miserably and substantially miscalculated the belief I have that there is still an America out there that cherishes freedom above collectivism, fascism, socialism and communism.

From day one of this project, I have bet on the fact that Americans still love freedom of speech, freedom of religion, and freedom from exorbitant taxation. If I find enough of you out there who agree with my thesis, and who therefore spread the word, it will give me great, renewed hope in our republic. If the message does not manage to penetrate, for whatever reasons, then so be it.

My insertion of foreign policy at the outset, specifically as it relates to Israel, was anything but accidental. Most ordinary Americans have no clue as to the importance of that tiny, little country that occupies less than 1 percent of the landmass in the vicinity of the dominantly Arab world surrounding it. The neighbors across the Mediterranean are far more moderate and friendly toward this enigmatic entity, but few of them would extend an open arm of support to Israel if she needed it at a moment's notice.

Saudi Arabia is one of Israel's closest neighbors—you can see Saudi Arabia from the port city of Eilat on the Gulf of Aqaba. You are probably not aware that recently the Saudis granted Israel permission to pass through their air space in the event it becomes necessary to deal with Iran. Saudi Arabia does not feel the least bit comfortable that Iran will have the capacity to deliver a nuclear warhead to targets in the region.

Has the implication of a fully loaded, nuclear Iran settled any questions you may have as to the importance of Israel? If not, and if you still think it unimportant, please take a closer look at what has recently taken place in Korea, and reconsider your answer to that question.

Are you ready for a new world order where China is now consuming more energy than the USA? That day seems to have already come, as of July 2010. For the moment, China denies this apparent status. Some evidence supports China's contention at this particular moment, but it is only a matter of time before they substantially overtake the U.S. in energy consumption, therefore the demand for energy on the world marketplace.

Do you now have a clearer understanding of energy density (thank Robert Bryce if you do), and do you understand the implications of attempting to trim less than 0.25 degrees Fahrenheit off apparent global temperature or perhaps a few tenths of an inch of sea level rise, due to the "containment strategy" against a colorless, odorless, tasteless, harmless gas, affectionately known as CO_2?

Do you now have a different understanding of the meaning of "green"?

I want you to understand that I have been a card-carrying member of the Division of Environmental Sciences of the American Association of Petroleum Geologists since the inception of that entity in 1989. I pay very close attention to the environment, as it relates to petroleum exploration or any other globally significant commodity. I care deeply about our planet and the protection thereof. She is incredibly resilient and capable of dealing with just about anything man throws at her.

So far, that has included real nuclear detonations, oil spills of colossal magnitude, temporary pollution of some of her rivers, temporary pollution of her airspace, and so on.

Nonetheless, she has repeatedly bounced back with astounding dexterity, at a pace that defied all the experts and the absolute ability to demonstrate exactly who's boss, as in recent volcanic eruptions, earthquakes, tsunamis, hurricanes, tornados, floods, etc.

We are merely temporary occupants, some of us a bit longer than others, occupants nonetheless. Nobody *here* actually owns the place, but I suggest to you that it *is* owned.

The Laws *of* the Land

As was alluded to in the Foreword, on January 24, 2011 I was sworn in as the 125th representative in the 2011-2012 Kansas legislature. This is an incredible time, and I feel privileged to serve the citizens of Kansas, specifically those constituents of the 99th District. Making laws is unlike anything else I have ever done, and I hope to contribute in a way that would make my parents, grandparents, siblings, and all family members proud.

It is a fair question to ask just where our laws came from. Many of us can quickly cite the Bible as the fundamental guiding document, from which our Judeo-Christian value system has developed. Others, many others, challenge this simple notion ferociously, and that is the crux of the matter. This tension will very likely persist until the end of mankind. Although it does not have to be that way, the probability is quite high, as you can imagine, that the forces of good and evil will contend for souls until the final judgment moment arrives. Arrive, it will. I'm not making some bold prediction. I'm simply restating the obvious that has been a part of the background since Creation. Sorry to have to raise another bone of contention, but your view of even that 'term' will produce contrast beyond the walls of your home, possibly within the walls of your home.

The United States of America needs to stand with Israel every step of the way, without hesitation, and without wavering. The status quo will not cut it. The wolves are gathering around her from all sides, hungrier than they have ever been. Only this time nuclear weapons are involved, and destruction unlike mankind has ever seen will come with incredible fury—unless we take the necessary steps NOW to reverse the current tide.

Who and what is the primary enemy of Israel? It is Islam, pure and simple. Israel is the Little Satan, and the United States is the Big Satan. You who are not Muslim are the Infidels, and it is the primary task of adherents of Islam to take out the Infidels the world over, but especially Israel and the United States.

Islam seeks to take out our Judeo-Christian based Rule of Law, and replace it with their version, Sharia law. This is no secret, although we will likely find that fewer than 5% of Americans have any concept of the seriousness of this matter. This is changing, but ever so slowly. Perhaps this book and others like it will assist to change that picture.

America, we are at a crossroads. There are at least two primary paths ahead:

The first path, the one that appears to be the easy one, includes continuing fiscal irresponsibility, non-adherence to the rule of law—including, perhaps especially immigration law, social and philosophical malfeasance (welfare on steroids, unsustainable entitlements, green everything), etc.

The second path, certain to be far more difficult, will involve trillions of dollars of cutbacks at the federal level, billions at multiple states, and belt-tightening at every governing level below. It will also involve considerable legal overhaul, returning to the Founding

Fathers' principles that provided guidance to the effect that 'he who governs least governs best'.

Will we ever get back to those wonderful ideals? That is up to each of us to decide, as this will not work in the context of 'blanket conversion'. The collective wisdom can only emerge from the mass of individuals each making up his / her mind that we want to see a different set of results.

The United States of America did not come about by accident—far from it. Tyrannical authorities of various sorts drove common men to accomplish uncommon tasks, including a Revolutionary War, and the establishment of a more perfect union that has yet to be surpassed by any civilization on the face of the earth. Freedom was the overarching goal: Freedom of Speech, Freedom of Religion, Freedom to Prosper, Freedom to own property, and the Freedom to live life to the fullest.

Our Declaration and our Constitution stand alone as guiding documents for a free, highly productive people that have no reason whatsoever to apologize for becoming the leaders of the world in oh, so many categories. This 'Land of the Free and Home of the Brave' does have the wherewithal to withstand any human-based pressure brought upon it. The pressures of the day are material, but certainly not insurmountable. The pressures of the day can be reduced to a vapor if we choose once again to differentiate ourselves by our Rule of Law, insisting that its basis is well beyond being fundamentally sound. Its basis is provided by He who guides anyone who will allow himself, of his own free will, to be guided with purpose, with honesty, with forbearance, and with Liberty and Justice for All.

That is a path well worth the taking for the long haul ahead.

Bibliography & Recommended Reading

Alinsky, Saul D., *Rules for Radicals: A Pragmatic Primer for Realistic Radicals*, New York, Vintage Books: 1971.

Bryce, Robert, *Power Hungry: The Myths of Green Energy and the Real Fuels of the Future*, New York, NY, Public Affairs: 2010.

———, *Gusher of Lies: The Dangerous Delusions of Energy Independence*, New York, NY, Public Affairs: 2008.

Coulter, Ann, *Godless: The Church of Liberalism*, New York, NY, Random House: 2006.

Economides, Michael J., and D'Aleo, Donna Marie, *From Soviet to Putin and Back: The Dominance of Energy in Today's Russia*, Houston, TX, Energy Tribune Publishing, Inc.: 2008.

Gabriel, Brigitte, *Because They Hate: A Survivor of Islamic Terror Warns America*, New York, NY, St. Martin's Press: 2006.

Gaubatz, P. David, and Sperry, Paul, *Muslim Mafia: Inside the Secret Underworld That's Conspiring to Islamize America*, Los Angeles, CA, WorldNetDaily: 2009.

Goldberg, Jonah, *Liberal Fascism*: *The Secret History of the American Left from Mussolini to the Politics of Meaning*, New York, NY, Random House: 2008.

Gotto, John Taylor, *The Underground History of American Education*, New York, NY, The Odysseus Group: 2001.

Hayek, Friedrick A., *Road to Serfdom*, Chicago, IL, University of Chicago Press: 1944.

Horner, Christopher C., *Red Hot Lies: How global warming Alarmists Use Threats, Fraud, and Deception to Keep You Misinformed*, Washington, D.C., Regnery: 2008.

_____., *The Politically Incorrect Guide to Global Warming and Environmentalism*, Washington, D.C., Regnery: 2007.

Horowitz, David, *The Professors: The 101 Most Dangerous Academics in America*, Washington, D.C., Regnery: 2006.

Koch, Charles G., *The Science of Success: How Market-Based Management Built the World's Largest Private Company*, Hoboken, N.J., John Wiley and Sons: 2007.

Krupp, Fred, and Horn, Miriam, *Earth, the Sequel: The Race to Reinvent Energy and Stop Global Warming*, New York, NY, W.W. Norton: 2009.

Michaels, Patrick M., and Balling, Robert C. Jr., *Climate of Extremes: Global Warming Science They Don't Want You to Know*, Washington, D.C., CATO Institute: 2009.

von Mises, Ludwig, *Socialism: An Economic and Sociological Analysis*, Weimar Germany, Gustav Fisher Verlag: 1922.

Rosenberg, Joel. C., *Inside the Revolution: How the Followers of Jihad, Jefferson and Jesus Are Battling To Dominate the Middle East and Transform the World*, Carol Stream, IL, Tyndale House: 2009.

_____, Epicenter: *Why the Current Rumblings in the Middle East Will Change Your Future*, Carol Stream, IL, Tyndale House: 2006.

Singer, S. Fred, and Avery, Dennis T., *Unstoppable Global Warming: Every 1,500 Years*, Lanham, MD, Rowman and Littlefield: 2008.

Skousen, W. Cleon, *The 5,000 Year Leap: A Miracle that Changed the World*, National Center for Constitutional Studies, www.nccs.net: 2006.

Sowell, Thomas, *Applied Economics: Thinking Beyond Stage One*, New York, Basic Books: 2009.

Spencer, Roy W., *The Great Global Warming Blunder: How Mother Nature Fooled the World's Top Climate Scientists*, New York, Encounter Books: 2010.

Undisclosed Authors (The Invisible Committee), *The Coming Insurrection*, 2009, Los Angeles, CA Semiotext: 2009.

Woods, Thomas E., *Meltdown: A Free-Market Look at Why the Stock Market Collapsed, the Economy Tanked, and Government Bailouts Will Make Things Worse*, Washington, D.C., Regnery: 2009.

End Notes

Preliminaries & Acknowledgements

(1) Gotto, John Taylor, *The Underground History of American Education*, New York, NY, The Odysseus Group: 2001.

(2) Horowitz, David, *The Professors: The 101 Most Dangerous Academics in America*, Washington, D.C., Regnery: 2006.

The Enemies Within vs The Friends of Freedom

(1) Undisclosed Authors (The Invisible Committee), *The Coming Insurrection*, 2009, Los Angeles, CA Semiotext: 2009.

(2) Coulter, Ann, *Godless: The Church of Liberalism*, New York, NY, Random House: 2006.

(3) Goldberg, Jonah, *Liberal Fascism: The Secret History of the American Left from Mussolini to the Politics of Meaning*, New York, NY, Random House: 2008.

(4) Sowell, Thomas, *Applied Economics: Thinking Beyond Stage One*, New York, Basic Books: 2009.

(5) Rosenberg, Joel. C., *Inside the Revolution: How the followers of Jihad, Jefferson & Jesus Are Battling To Dominate the Middle East and Transform the World*, Carol Stream, IL, Tyndale House: 2009.

(6) Rosenberg, Joel. C., *Epicenter: Why the Current Rumblings in the Middle East Will Change Your Future*, Carol Stream, IL, Tyndale House: 2006.

U.S. Foreign Policy

(1) http://investors.nobleenergyinc.com/releasedetail.cfm?ReleaseID=394724

(2) http://www.haaretz.com/print-edition/business/givot-olam-meged-has-1-5b-barrels-of-oil-1.308683

(3) Harrison, Edward, Credit Writedowns, 'Top Ten U.S. Foreign Aid Recipients', July 10, 2010. Online: http://www.creditwritedowns.com/2010/07/top-ten-us-foreign-aid-recipients.html?utm_campaign=Twitter&utm_medium=twitter&utm_source=twitter

(4) The 2005 Annual Megacensus of Religions. (2007). In Britannica Book of the Year, 2006. Retrieved January 6, 2007, from Encyclopædia Britannica Online: http://www.britannica.com/eb/article-9432655

(5) http://politics.usnews.com/news/religion/articles/2008/04/07/understanding-islam.html

(6) Miller, Tracy, ed (October 2009). *Mapping the Global Muslim Population: A Report on the Size and Distribution of the World's Muslim Population.* Pew Research Center. http://pewforum.org/newassets/images/reports/Muslimpopulation/Muslimpopulation.pdf

(7) Bagby, Ihsan, Perl, Paul M., Froehle, Bryan T. (2010-02-20). Council on American-Islamic Relations (Washington, D.C.)

(8) May, Clifford D., 'Understanding who our enemies are', NorthJersey.com, September 9, 2010; http://www.actforamerica.org/index.php/home/10-newsmaster/2095-understanding-who-our-enemies-are-.

(9) http://www.washingtonexaminer.com/opinion/blogs/beltway-confidential/obamas-new-mission-for-nasa-reach-out-to-muslim-world-97785979.html

(10) http://www.nydailynews.com/blogs/dailypolitics/2010/08/president-obamas-speech-on-ram.html

(11) Davis, Bob, 'Who's on the Hook for the IMF's Bailout?', The Wall Street Journal, Europe News, May 10, 2010; http://online.wsj.com/article/SB10001424052748704866204575224421086866944.html

(12) http://www.defense.gov/news/newsarticle.aspx?id=59004

(13) http://www.nti.org/e_research/cnwm/securing/warhead.asp

(14) http://www.state.gov/f/releases/iab/fy2009cbj/

U.S. Energy Policy

(1) http://www.eia.doe.gov/pub/oil_gas/petroleum/data_publications/company_level_imports/current/import.html

(2) Wikipedia, May 25, 2010

(3) http://blog.heritage.org/2010/10/21/morning-bell-renewable-electricity- standards-kill-jobs-too/

(4) Trebilcock, M., Speaking Truth to "Wind" Power, Science and Public Policy Institute Reprint Series, April 2009.

(5) Wikipedia, public domain.

(6) Krupp, Fred, and Horn, Miriam, *Earth, the Sequel: The Race to Reinvent Energy and Stop global Warming*, New York, NY, W.W. Norton: 2009.

(7) Bryce, Robert, *Power Hungry: The Myths of Green Energy and the Real Fuels of the Future*, New York, NY, Public Affairs: 2010.

(8) Elcock, D. Projected Corn-Based Ethanol Production Would Dominate Water Consumption for the Energy Sector1, Argonne National Laboratory, 1/29/2009; http://www.ead.anl.gov/new/dsp_news.cfm?id=94

(9) Pimentel, *Natural Resources Research* (Vol. 12, No. 2).

(10) Tans, Dr. Pieter, NOAA/ESRL (www.esrl.noaa.gov/gmd/ccgg/trends/)

(11) http://www.eia.doe.gov/oiaf/aeo/pdf/trend_2.pdf

(12) Trebilcock, M., Speaking Truth to "Wind" Power , Science and Public Policy Institute Reprint Series, April 2009.

(13) http://www.cbsnews.com/8301-503544_162-4962412-503544.html

(14) Bryce, Robert, *Power Hungry: The Myths of Green Energy and the Real Fuels of the Future*, New York, NY, Public Affairs: 2010, pg 114-115.

(15) http://www.pentaxforums.com/forums/post-your-photos/41648-you-dont-see-every-day-wind-generator-fire.html

(16) http://www.youtube.com/watch?v=kBYJul2ykZs

(17) Lefler, Dion, 'Renewable Energy Law Could Cost Consumers', Wichita Eagle, November 9, 2010.

(18) Bryce, Robert, *Power Hungry: The Myths of Green Energy and the Real Fuels of the Future,* New York, NY, Public Affairs: 2010, pg 133.

(19) _____, *Power Hungry: The Myths of Green Energy and the Real Fuels of the Future*, New York, NY, Public Affairs: 2010, pg 112.

(20) Science and Public Policy Institute, SPPI Monthly CO2 report, Sept 2009, pg 7.

(21) International Energy Agency, World Energy Outlook 2008, Table 16.2.

(22) Hurst, Timothy, U.S.' *Only National Carbon Market Shutting Down at the End of 2010*, Matter Network, November 11, 2010. http://www.matternetwork.com/2010/11/us-only-national-carbon-market.cfm.

(23) Bryce, Robert, *Power Hungry: The Myths of Green Energy and the Real Fuels of the Future*, New York, NY, Public Affairs: 2010, pg 175.

(24) _____, *Power Hungry: The Myths of Green Energy and the Real Fuels of the Future*, New York, NY, Public Affairs: 2010, pg 182.

(25) _____, *Power Hungry: The Myths of Green Energy and the Real Fuels of the Future*, New York, NY, Public Affairs: 2010, pg 192. Original source Howell, David, Progress Report for Energy Storage Research and Development, U.S. Department of Energy, Office of Vehicle Technologies, January 2009, http://www1.eere.energy.gov/vehiclesandfuels/pdfs/program/2008/_energy_storage.pdf,4.

(26) David Howell, "Progress Report for Energy Storage Research and Development," U.S. Department of Energy, Office of Vehicle Technologies, January 2009. http://www1.eere.energy.gov/vehiclesandfuels/pdfs/program/2008_energy_storage.pdf,4.

(27) http://www.eia.gov/dnav/pet/hist/LeafHandler.ashx?n=PET&s=MCRFPMT1&f=M

(28) http://www.eia.gov/dnav/pet/hist/LeafHandler.ashx?n=PET&s=RCRR10SND_1&f=A

(29) http://www.eia.gov/dnav/pet/hist/LeafHandler.ashx?n=PET&s=MCRFPUS1&f=M

(30) http://gregor.us/mexico/post-peak-mexico/

(31) U.S. Energy Information Administration, http://www.eia.doe.gov/cneaf/electricity/epa/epat1p2.html

(32) http://www.sunflower.net/facilities.aspx

(33) http://www.eia.doe.gov/oiaf/aeo/assumption/pdf/electricity.pdf#page=3

Global Environmental Survival—The New Green Earth

(1) Hollingsworth, Barbara, *Who's Who on Climate Fraud*, Washington Examiner, December 4, 2009. http://www.washingtonexaminer.com/opinion/columns/Who_s-who-onclimate-frad-8625428-78462462.html

(2) http://www.appinsys.com/GlobalWarming/GW_Part2_GlobalTempMeasure.htm#historic

(3) Courtesy of Joseph D'Aleo, International Conference on Climate Change, Chicago, May 2010.

(4) Solanski, S.K., et al. 2005, 11,000 Year Sunspot Number Reconstruction. IGBP PAGES/World Data Center for Paleoclimatology Data Contribution Series #2005-015. NOAA/NGDC Paleoclimatology Program, Boulder CO, USA.

(5) Soon, W. (2005) *Geophysical Research Letters* 32, 2005GL023429. Hoyt, D. V. and Schatten, K. H. (1993) J. Geophysical Res. 98, 18895-18906.

(6) Carlin, A., *Proposed NCEE Comments on Draft Technical Support Document for Endangerment Analysis for Greenhouse Gas Emissions under the Clean Air Act*, EPA internal document, March, 2009.

(7) Akasofu, Natural Components of Climate Change During the Last Few Hundred Years http://people.iarc.uaf.edu/~sakasofu/pdf/Natural_Components_of_Climate_Change.pdf

(8) SPPI, April 2010, Monthly CO2 Report, page 10.

(9) SPPI, April 2010, Monthly CO2 Report, page 11.

(10) Happer, William, Statement Before the U.S. Senate Committee on Environment and Public Works, February 25, 2009, http://scienceandpublicpolicy.org/reprint/happer_senate_testimony.html

(11) "Cap and Trade: Impact on Jobs in the West, and the Nation", The Senate Western Caucus and House Western Caucus, William L. Kovacs Senior Vice President, Environment, Technology and Regulatory Affairs U.S. Chamber of Commerce, July 30, 2009, page 8. http://www.uschamber.com/sites/default/files/testimony/090730_capandtrade_test imony.pdf

Carbon Dioxide (CO_2)

(1) http://www.muller.lbl.gov/pages/IceAgeBook/history_of_climate.html

(2) http://www.nasd100.com/2010/01/ranking-us-industrial-stocks-by-profitmargin-updated-182010.html

(3) http://arctic.atmos.uiuc.edu/cryosphere/IMAGES/seaice.anomaly.antarctic.png

(4) http://arctic.atmos.uiuc.edu/cryosphere/

(5) Global Historical Climatology Network (NOAA)

(6) Variable solar irradiance as a plausible agent for multidecadal variations in the Arctic-wide surface air temperature record of the past 130 years, Geophysical Research Letters, Vol. 32, L16712, doi:10.1029.2005GL023429, 2005.

(7) http://www.muller.lbl.gov/pages/IceAgeBook/history_of_climate.html

(8) McIntyre, Stephen, McKitrick, Ross, Corrections to the Mann, et al (1998) Proxy Base and Northern Hemispheric Average Temperature Series, Energy & Environment, Volume 14, No. 6, page 766.

(9) Philip J. Klotzbach, William M. Gray, Extended Range Forecast of Atlantic Seasonal Hurricane Activity and Landfall Strike Probability for 2009, Dept. of Atmospheric Science, Colorado State University, 2 June 2010, page 50. http://tropical.atmos.colostate.edu/forecasts/2010/june2010/jun2010.pdf

(10) Craig D. Idso, CO2, Global Warming and Coral Reefs: Prospects for the Future, Center for the Study of Carbon Dioxide and Global Change, and the Science and Public Policy Institute, 12 January 2009, page 45. http://co2science.org/education/reports/corals/coralreefs.pdf

(11) _____, page 55.

(12) Jevrejeva, S., J. C. Moore, A. Grinsted, and P. L. Woodworth (2008), Recent global sea level acceleration started over 200 years ago?, *Geophys. Res. Lett.*, 35, L08715, doi:10.1029/2008GL033611.

(13) University of Colorado, 2010 Report, release 1, image updated to Q2 2011: http://sealevel.colorado.edu/content/global-mean-sea-level-time-seriesseasonal-signals-removed

(14) http://www.newscientist.com/article/mg19526141.600-huge-sea-levelrises-are-coming--unless-we-act-now.html

(15) http://www.abc.net.au/7.30/content/2007/s1870955.htm

(16) Leuliette, E.W., R.S. Nerem, and G.T. Mitchum, 2004: Calibration of TOPEX/Poseidon and Jason altimeter data to construct continuous record of mean sea level change, Marine Geodesy, Vol. 27 (1-2), pgs 79-94. http://sealevel.colorado.edu

(17) SPPI Monthly CO2 Report, June 2009, Vol. 1, No.6, page 18 http://scienceandpublicpolicy.org/images/stories/papers/originals/june_co2_report.pdf

(18) _____, page 17.

Economics: The Fed, Frank, Dodd, & Obamanomics

(1) http://www.wordiq.com/definition/Fractional-reserve_banking

(2) Woods, Thomas E., *Meltdown: A Free-Market Look at Why the Stock Market Collapsed, the Economy Tanked, and Government Bailouts Will Make Things Worse*, Washington, D.C., Regnery: 2009, pgs 8-9.

(3) http://www.moneyandmarkets.com/fed-money-printing-getting-evenwilder-40784?FIELD9=3. Graphic courtesy of Weiss Capital Management, 7111 Fairway Drive, Suite 102, Palm Beach Gardens, FL 33418.

(4) Government Accounting Office (GAO) Analysis of data from the Office of the Chief Actuary, Centers for Medicare and Medicaid Services. Projections based on the intermediate assumptions of the 2007 Trustees' Reports. The Consumer Price Index (CPI) is used to adjust from current to constant dollars.

(5) GAO Citizen Guide 2007.

A New America: Ex-Obama

(1) Whistleblower, World Net Daily, October 1010, pg 21.

(2) Department of Energy, FY 2011 Congressional Budget Request, February 2010. http://www.mbe.doe.gov/budget/11budget/Content/FY2011Highlights.pdf

(3) HR 3200, 111th Congress, 1st Session, *To provide affordable, quality health care for all Americans and reduce the growth in health care spending, and for other purposes*, July 14, 2009.